Writing in Psychology

This book helps readers become better writers of psychology and better writers in general. After reading thousands of course papers, theses, and dissertations, Dr. Miller knows and addresses the issues that students find most challenging when writing about psychology. Written with the utmost flexibility in mind, the chapters can be read in any order. More comprehensive than similar texts, this book provides detailed coverage of how to write empirical reports, research proposals, and literature reviews and how to read meta-analyses. Readers will also find invaluable strategies for improving one's writing, including how to adopt an engaging yet accurate style, thorough coverage of grammatical and word-use rules that govern writing in general, and the APA (American Psychological Association) rules that govern the expression of that content.

Readers will appreciate these helpful learning tools:

- Descriptions of the most common APA style rules encountered and references to the *Manual* when more detailed knowledge is required.
- Numerous examples from journal articles that help readers gain a clearer understanding of content they will encounter in writing psychological reports.
- Chapter exercises that provide an opportunity to apply the points conveyed in each chapter.
- Examples of the most common mistakes made by students and how to avoid them and *best practices* for improving one's writing.
- Tables that help readers gain a clearer understanding of the new standards in the *Publication Manual of the American Psychological Association, 6th ed.* (Appendix A).
- Errors in APA style exemplified via an improperly formatted paper and another version noting corrections pertaining to APA style and grammar, to highlight the most common pitfalls encountered by students (Appendix B).

Ideal for courses on writing in psychology or as a supplement for graduate or advanced undergraduate courses in research design or research methods, this book also serves as a resource for anyone looking for guidance on how to write about psychological content.

Scott A. Miller is Professor Emeritus at the University of Florida.

Writing in Psychology

Scott A. Miller

University of Florida

Routledge
Taylor & Francis Group

NEW YORK AND LONDON

First published 2014
by Routledge
711 Third Avenue, New York, NY 10017

and by Routledge
2 Park Square, Milton Park, Abingdon, Oxon OX14 4RN

Routledge is an imprint of the Taylor & Francis Group, an informa business

Library of Congress Cataloging-in-Publication Data
Miller, Scott A., 1944–
Writing in psychology / Scott A. Miller.
    pages cm
  1. Psychology—Authorship. 2. Report writing. I. Title.
  BF76.7.M55   2014
  808.06'615—dc23   2013025359

ISBN: 978-0-415-85451-1 (hbk)
ISBN: 978-0-415-85452-8 (pbk)
ISBN: 978-1-315-86984-1 (ebk)

Typeset in New Caledonia
by Apex CoVantage, LLC

Contents

About the Author

Scott A. Miller is Professor Emeritus in the Department of Psychology at the University of Florida. He was a faculty member in Psychology at the University of Michigan prior to joining the University of Florida's Psychology Department in 1977. Dr. Miller is a member of the Cognitive Development Society, the Jean Piaget Society, and the Society for Research in Child Development and a Fellow of the American Psychological Association and the Association for Psychological Science. He is the author of *Developmental Research Methods*, *Child Psychology* (with Robin Harwood and Ross Vasta), *Cognitive Development* (with John Flavell and Patricia Miller), and *Theory of Mind: Beyond the Preschool Years*. His research has examined various aspects of cognitive development in young children, and his current research focus is on the development of theory of mind during the preschool and grade-school years.

Preface and Acknowledgments

The goal of this book is to help its readers become better writers—better writers of psychology, in particular, but also better writers in general. I also hope to help them become more informed readers of the psychology content they encounter.

This book is for anyone who wants to learn how to do writing in psychology. Its main audience will undoubtedly be students enrolled in courses such as Writing in Psychology or Research Methods in Psychology. I hope, however, that the book may also be a helpful resource beyond the bounds of course requirements—for example, for students writing a thesis or dissertation.

Several aspects of the book are meant to distinguish it from other books devoted to the task of writing in psychology. Most generally, the book is informed by my 30-plus years of teaching courses in research methods, in the course of which I have read several thousand papers by Psychology students. Directing or serving on committees for honors theses, master's theses, and dissertations has provided further experience with psychology writing of a variety of forms and a variety of levels. When I look at how-to-write books, I see space devoted to issues that in my experience seldom if ever occur in student papers; conversely, I see little or no space devoted to topics that students struggle with. A partial list of the latter includes when to quote, how to paraphrase when not quoting, which statistics to include in a Results section, when to use tables or figures, and how to express numbers in APA style. I hope that this book benefits from its grounding in a thorough knowledge of its primary target audience.

As the preceding indicates, my experience with student papers ranges from the first attempts at such writing in response to some course requirement to dissertations or articles submitted for publication. This book is designed to be helpful for tasks at both ends of this spectrum. Various aspects of the presentation are intended to make the content accessible to those for whom this sort of writing is new, including frequent use of examples as well as end-of-the chapter exercises that allow application of the points being taught. Even students with a fair amount of writing experience, however, typically have room for improvement (a point, indeed, that applies to most of us throughout our careers), and my discussions are intended to be at a high enough level to allow such students to build upon existing skills.

One of the ways in which this book is designed to speak to the more advanced student is its frequent citation of further sources that offer more detailed and often more advanced treatments of particular topics. Another way is through the offer of choices rather than mandates for aspects of writing that are matters more of personal preference than of clear-cut right or wrong. Many books on writing consist mainly of do-it-this-way prescriptions. Such prescriptions are perfectly appropriate when rules of grammar or of APA (American Psychological Association) style are at issue, and I offer many such prescriptions myself. Much of writing, however, is a matter not simply of following rules but of finding one's own optimal approach, and my book is intended to help students in this quest.

In addition to the end-of the-chapter exercises, two further pedagogical features are worth noting here. Appendix A reproduces a table from an article on standards for empirical journal articles that APA commissioned at the time of the most recent revision of the *Publication Manual*. Appendix B presents two examples of a paper in psychology, one that contains numerous errors in APA style and a second in which the errors are marked and explained. Both appendixes are excellent resources for learning both what to do and what not to do.

There is no single best way to organize material on writing in psychology. The organization adopted here is my preferred way; after the introductory Chapter 1, however, the chapters can be read in whatever order an instructor or student prefers.

As will be seen, the coverage is divided into the two main topics in writing in psychology: what to say and how to say it. In contrast to some how-to-write texts, the coverage of the first topic is not limited to one sort of writing but rather encompasses four important forms: empirical reports of research, research proposals, literature reviews, and term papers. The coverage of the how-to-say-it question includes a chapter on strategies for improving one's writing, another chapter devoted to general principles of English composition (with a fuller coverage of such principles than is found in most such books), and a chapter that summarizes the APA rules that govern all writing in psychology.

The last of these topics deserves a bit of comment. If you are a student and are doing your writing as a course requirement, you may be expected to follow APA style fully (as students in my courses do), partially, or not at all, and you may or may not be expected to have the APA *Publication Manual* next to you as you write. Whatever the instructor's requirements, they obviously take precedence, and this book should be usable for any of the situations just described. I will add, however, that if you continue in Psychology, the coverage of APA style provided here will definitely be helpful. Whatever your current needs, if you become a psychologist you will need APA style. Writing in psychology *is* APA-style writing.

I am grateful to various people for help in the preparation of this book. I would like to thank the following colleagues who reviewed the manuscript: Marie T. Balaban, Eastern Oregon University; Elaine S. Barry, Penn State Fayette, The Eberly Campus; Kenneth C. Elliot, University of Maine at Augusta; Nancy Davis Johnson, Queens University of Charlotte; Travis Langley, Henderson State University; Amy E. Lindsey, Utica College; Claudia J. Stanny, University of West Florida; and Lori Van Wallendael, University of North Carolina at Charlotte. I also want to express special thanks to Tony Onwuegbuzie for permission to reproduce the material in Appendix B and to APA Permissions for permission to quote from the APA *Publication Manual* on pages 7, 15, 16, 23, 44, 53, 60, 65, 67, 88, 113, 114, 125. Finally, I am grateful for the excellent support provided by the Routledge/Taylor and Francis editorial and production team: Debra Riegert, Miren Alberro, and Rebecca Willford.

1

The Importance of Writing

When I teach courses in research methods, the students do a lot of writing. For many, it is a new experience, and for many it is not an experience that they look forward to. I like to begin, therefore, with a pep talk about the importance of writing.

WHY WRITE?

The first point I make is the most basic one. Science is a matter of shared information, and a scientific finding is simply not a finding until it has been communicated to others. Some such communication is oral—for example, presentations at professional conferences. By far the most important way in which scientists communicate, however, is through writing—through publication of their work in books or professional journals. Communication is an intrinsic part of science, and writing is an intrinsic part of being a scientist.

One way to think about the importance of writing is to reflect on what you have learned from your study of psychology. Some things you have learned may have come from—or at least been reinforced by—personal experience. Most of what you know, however, you know because someone wrote it down. This is obviously true of learning through textbooks or journal articles. But it is equally true of learning from lectures. A lecture, after all, is simply an oral summary of information gleaned from the written records of the field.

The discussion to this point may suggest that writing is a kind of necessary evil—a service to the field certainly, but of no value to the researcher himself or herself. In fact, as anyone who has done much research knows, such is far from being the case. The need to communicate one's work to others—to explain the reasoning behind a particular methodological decision, to make sense of a puzzling outcome, to suggest needed directions for future research—sharpens one's thinking in a way that solitary contemplation alone could never accomplish. Such is the case when one anticipates the audience for one's work, and it is even more the case when there is an actual audience—for example, when a manuscript is submitted to a journal for publication. The publication process will involve feedback from reviewers and editors that may strengthen not only the current but also future research efforts, and the same is true for the work's reception following publication. Science is a collaborative endeavor, and the benefits from sharing one's work are very much reciprocal and not just unidirectional.

WHY WRITE WELL?

The preceding section addressed the question of why write. It did not address the question of why write well.

This is a reasonable question. Certainly the essential element in scientific communication is the content. Assuming that all the important content is included, why should we be concerned with the method of presentation? "Style" is a nicety that can be left to English classes.

There is some truth to this argument. The content is indeed the most important element of any scientific contribution. In addition, many aspects of what we often think of as "style" (e.g., setting up ambiguity, interjection of the unexpected, flashbacks or foreshadowing, use of metaphor, use of humor) are not appropriate in scientific writing. It does not follow, however, that the quality of the writing is unimportant. Indeed, just the reverse is the case. Any new contribution in psychology must compete for attention in a marketplace of publications that is far too large for any reader to come close to reading everything. One determinant of which contributions rise to the top in this survival of the fittest is the quality of the writing. The most successful publications have three attributes.

One is that they are clear. Inclusion of all the required content is a necessary, starting-point component of a potential contribution to the literature. It is not a sufficient component, however; rather, the content must be there in a form that readers can understand. And it must be in a form that they can readily understand, or the busy reader may turn elsewhere. You undoubtedly respond negatively to material whose method of presentation poses an obstacle to understanding. Researchers, reviewers, and editors have the same reaction.

A second attribute is that the most successful publications are interesting. Conceivably, clarity could be achieved by simply presenting a bulleted list of points for the reader to take away. An author who does so, however, is unlikely to achieve a further goal of scientific writing: namely, to entice the busy reader to read further. The best scientific writings tell a story, setting up the questions of interest in the Introduction, detailing the approach to studying these questions in the Method, and leading the reader gradually through to the answers to these questions in the Results and Discussion.

A final attribute is that the most successful publications are persuasive. Some people think of scientific writing as a dispassionate, facts-only enterprise. It is true that objectivity and honesty are central to scientific writing. It is not true, however, that an author cannot be an advocate for his or her work. A major element in successful writing is persuasion: persuading the reader that the issues under study are important ones, persuading the reader that the methods used to study these issues are valid and informative, and persuading the reader that the conclusions drawn from the research are novel and trustworthy.

As anyone who has done much reading in psychology knows, there is an imperfect relation between scientific eminence and ability to write. Not all of the field's major contributors have been good writers. Most, however, have been—that is one reason that their contributions have had the impact that they have.

An even more pragmatic justification can be offered for writing well. Before an article can be made available to the scientific community, it must be accepted for publication in a professional journal. Most journals are selective in what they publish, and the best journals have rejection rates of up to 80% or 90%. A poorly written article is simply much less likely ever to see the light of day than a well-written one. Busy editors and reviewers may be unwilling to make the effort to penetrate the poor writing to get to underlying content and may be unable to find the content if they do make the effort. Furthermore, because the purpose of a research report is to communicate, the quality of the writing is a quite legitimate part of the evaluation process.

The points just made are confirmed by many who have served as editors for psychology journals (Eisenberg, Thompson, Augir, & Stanley, 2002). Eisenberg (2000), for example, writes, "Many an article is rejected due to poor writing rather than to lack of a good idea . . . or good data" (p. 26). There is also some empirical evidence for a link between quality of writing and publication success. Brewer and colleagues (Brewer, Scherzer, Van Raalte, Petitpas, & Andersen, 2001), in a survey of journal editors, reported that 39% had returned a manuscript to the author because of failure to follow APA style (i.e., the rules presented in the APA *Publication Manual*, a source that I consider at length throughout the book). Onwuegbuzie and colleagues (Onwuegbuzie, Combs, Slate, & Frels, 2009) tabulated the number of errors in APA style in manuscripts submitted to the journal *Research in the Schools*. Included in the tally were several basic grammatical errors in addition to points specific to APA rules. They reported that articles with nine or more errors were three times as likely to be rejected as articles with fewer errors. The authors go on to acknowledge the familiar truism that correlation does not prove causation—in this case, that poor writing causes manuscript rejection. It is possible, for example, that researchers whose writing is relatively weak also produce research that is relatively weak. Their own belief, however—one that is probably shared by most psychologists who have been involved in the reviewing process—is that quality of writing does contribute.

WHY WRITE WELL (PART 2)?

Let me make the argument more personal. Suppose that your long-term goals do not include writing in psychology. Is there then any reason (other than perhaps a course requirement) to strive to learn to do such writing?

As you no doubt can anticipate, my answer is yes. The reason it is yes is that good writing is good writing, and what you learn about writing in psychology will carry over to other forms of writing. This point holds true even for the most psychology-specific of the things you must learn: namely, the rules of APA style.

It is possible that you may not use APA style in whatever writing you do in the future (although it is also possible that you will—APA style is used in a number of contexts in addition to psychology writing). Still, you will need to use *some* consistent style in whatever you write, such that you are not handling headings or references or footnotes in one way at the start of a paper and a different way by the time you reach the end. Working within the constraints of one style is good practice for working with any style that you may eventually need.

Again, pragmatic considerations can be added to whatever intrinsic, need-to-master motives may underlie the attempt to become a better writer. Assuming that you are still a student, then quality of writing is a definite determinant of how well you fare. Instructors may tell you that they grade on content and not on style, but you should be skeptical whenever you hear this. It is difficult (and for some of us impossible) not to be positively impressed by good writing and negatively impressed by bad. At the extreme, one can hardly reward good content if the writing is so bad that the content is impossible to discern.

I will mention just one more incentive for writing well. If you still have graduate school applications looming ahead of you, then the quality of your writing may play an important role in your future development. There are few more certain ways to sink a grad school application than to submit a poorly written essay or personal statement (Appleby & Appleby, 2006).

ORGANIZATION OF THE BOOK

As the Preface indicates, the ordering of material in this book reflects my preferred organization, and some instructors and some students will doubtless have other preferences. Although some cross-chapter checking might sometimes be necessary, it should be possible to read the chapters in any order that is preferred.

I begin in Chapter 2 with some general pieces of advice about how to approach the task of writing in psychology. Included are a variety of suggestions culled from a variety of different sources. You may find some of the suggestions easier to implement or more helpful than others, and that is fine—most are merely suggestions rather than must-follow prescriptions.

A starting point of almost every kind of writing in psychology is knowledge of the relevant research literature. An important skill for an aspiring psychologist, therefore, is the ability to search the literature to find the necessary sources. Chapter 3 discusses how to carry out a literature search.

The remaining chapters of the book are devoted to the two general challenges in writing in psychology. One is what to say. The other is how to say it.

The what-to-say question is addressed in the middle chapters of the book. Chapters 4 and 5 discuss the most common form of writing in psychology: the empirical journal article whose purpose is to report the results of research. Chapter 6 adds material on how to write a research proposal, and Chapter 7 discusses how to write review papers that summarize some aspect of the psychological literature. Because not all course assignments will fit one of these three molds, Chapter 7 also offers some suggestions with respect to how to write term papers.

The how-to-say-it question divides into two general categories. One is specific to psychology: the stylistic conventions, presented in the *Publication Manual of the American Psychological Association* (American Psychological Association, 2010), that govern writing in psychology. Chapter 8 discusses various aspects of the APA rule system. I concentrate on points that in my experience are often the source of errors in student papers.

The other part of the how-to-say-it question is both more general and more difficult: how to write good, readable prose whatever the specific style or specific context. This aspect of writing is a good deal less teachable than is mastery of a conventional rule system (if it *were* readily teachable, all of us would write well). Many of the suggestions offered in Chapter 2 are intended to aid in the task of constructing smooth and grammatical prose. In addition, Chapter 9 addresses a number of specific aspects of English grammar and word use. Again, I concentrate on points that often go astray in student papers.

In addition to its nine chapters, the book includes two appendixes. One appendix reproduces one of the tables from an article on standards for empirical journal articles that APA commissioned at the time of the most recent revision of the *Publication Manual* (APA Publications and Communications Board Working Group on Journal Article Reporting Standards, 2008). The table provides a summary of many of the points contained in the current version of the *Publication Manual*. Note that the table will be most helpful if read in conjunction with the full article in which it appears.

The second appendix presents an example of a paper in psychology, one that deliberately includes a number of errors of both APA style and English grammar. The paper appears twice: first in original form and then with the errors marked and explained. The example comes from the Onwuegbuzie et al. (2009) article referred to earlier. Assuming no specific direction from an instructor, you can, of course, use this appendix in any way you like. My advice is to take an initial look at the original (i.e., uncorrected) version soon—even if you have no familiarity with APA style, you should be able to identify some features that seem dubious. I suggest that you then return to the appendix after reading Chapter 8. Note as many of the errors as you can, and then check your reading against the corrected version provided in the second part of the appendix.

WHAT ARE YOUR REQUIREMENTS?

A point made in the Preface is important enough to be reiterated here. My assumption throughout this book is that your goal is to write an APA-style paper, either an empirical report (the subject of Chapters 4 and 5), a research proposal (the subject of Chapter 6), or a literature review (the subject of Chapter 7). If you are doing your writing as a course requirement, however, your instructor's requirements may differ in some ways from the guidelines offered here, and if so, it is the instructor's rules that take precedence.

Perhaps the most likely way in which a course requirement might differ from this book's emphases concerns the use of the APA *Publication Manual*, a topic that

I treat most fully in Chapter 8. It may be that you will be required to follow the *Manual*'s prescriptions only in part, adhering to some of its rules but not others. Perhaps, for example, you will be expected to produce a standard term-paper title page (course number, date, etc.) rather than an APA-style title page. Perhaps you will be expected to insert any tables or figures at the point at which they occur in the text, not (as in APA style) near the end of the manuscript. Or perhaps there will be a specific page limit or a minimum number of references required, neither of which is true when writing a manuscript for publication. For these and any other course-specific requirements, you may wish to note the relevant aspects of APA style for future use, but they will not be anything that you need immediately.

It is also possible that you will not be expected to have and to use the *Publication Manual* at all. If so, my advice is to try nevertheless to write your papers in APA style—apart, of course, from any aspects that you are explicitly instructed to do differently. You should follow *some* consistent style in anything you write, and for writing in psychology APA style *is* the style. Chapter 8 will not tell you everything you need to know about how to do such writing; the only way to do so would be to reproduce the entire contents of the *Manual*. The chapter will, however, give you a good starting point, especially if used in conjunction with the APA website devoted to APA style (www.apastyle.org). Or, of course, if used in conjunction with the *Manual* itself, which you should consider purchasing if you plan to continue in Psychology. For even if you do not need the *Manual* now, you will need it eventually.

2

Some General Advice About How to Write

Most of the rest of the book has to do with the two questions identified in Chapter 1: what to say and how to say it. This chapter presents various strategies that can increase the chances of being successful at both these tasks.

The strategies divide into two rough categories. Some might better be characterized as aims rather than as strategies, for they represent qualities to strive for in one's writing. The first piece of advice given in the APA *Publication Manual*, write concisely, falls in this category. So do the other qualities that I have singled out below with an "Aim for" heading (simplicity, variety, smoothness). Aiming for these qualities is, of course, not a sufficient basis for achieving them. But realizing that they are goals to strive for may well be a necessary basis.

The second category encompasses various techniques for improving one's writing. This category, as you will see, is a potpourri of different pieces of advice, some derived from my own experience and some taken from various how-to-write books or articles by others. A few of the suggestions I regard as prescriptions—that is, as strategies that should work for any author doing any sort of writing. The first suggestion, make use of available sources of help, is in this category. The "Be Careful" admonition is another example. Many of the suggestions, however, are just suggestions, things to be tried out and then kept or discarded, depending on how well they work for you.

The *Manual* expresses this point well: "The fit between author and strategy is more important than the particular strategy used" (p. 70). Authors of how-to-write books tend to present the strategies that work for them. You need to use the strategies that work for you. If you already know what these are, then put them to work whenever you write. If you do not yet know, then work to discover what they are.

SEEK HELP

A first suggestion is to make use of all the various sources of help that are available for writing in psychology. Especially if this sort of writing is new for you, there is no way to get everything right on your own—so why try to do it on your own?

Written Sources of Help

The one indispensable source of help for writing in psychology is the APA *Publication Manual*. Even if you are not expected to apply APA style to your current writing projects, you may wish to begin the task, for if you continue in psychology it is APA style that you will need to master. And if you *are* expected to apply APA style, then the *Manual* is a must. You should keep the book next to you as you write, and you should expect to consult it dozens of times between the start of a paper and the finish.

Chapter 1 identified three components of successful writing in psychology: knowing what content to include, knowing how to convey this content in clear and grammatical prose, and knowing the APA rules that govern how the content should be expressed. Of these tasks the third should be the easiest; everything that needs to be known is spelled out in the *Publication Manual*, and with sufficient care it should be possible to get everything right. Yet students often struggle to master APA rules, and few, at least in my experience, come close to complete mastery. Nor are students the only ones who find the APA system challenging; various surveys indicate that even seasoned professionals often go astray (Brewer et al., 2001; Ernst & Michel, 2006; Onwuegbuzie et al., 2009). The Onwuegbuzie et al. (2009) survey reported an average of 10.57 errors in manuscripts submitted for publication.

Why is the task so difficult? I suspect that many factors contribute, including the fact that some aspects of the system (and I am thinking now of the rules for numbers) are just plain hard to master. My guess, however, is that often the problem is not the difficulty of understanding the *Manual* but a failure even to consult the *Manual*, either because an already learned rule from some other system is assumed to apply or because of a failure to realize that there *is* a rule that applies. When I teach writing, I suggest that students begin by leafing through the *Manual*, just to get a feel for the range of topics considered. I also suggest that they look at the two sample papers in the *Manual* (which, happily, are given increased prominence in the current edition), because doing so is an excellent way to learn quickly both what is covered and where it is covered.

Various sources of help exist for those attempting to master the *Manual*. A helpful supplement to the *Manual* is a website maintained by APA: www.apastyle.org. The website summarizes the most important changes to the most recent edition of the *Manual*, gives the answers to frequently asked questions, provides updates with regard to evolving stylistic issues (e.g., how to do electronic references), and gives information about further sources of help with APA style. The importance of the website increased with the most recent revision of the *Manual*, which resulted in a book that is 168 pages shorter than its predecessor. Much of the shortening was possible because relevant information is now available on the web, on both the APA style website and the websites for the various APA journals.

There also are a number of books whose purpose is to help students master APA style. Table 2.1 lists several examples. Of course, helping students master APA style is also one of the purposes of this book, and Chapter 8 is devoted to the task. Still,

TABLE 2.1   Guides to APA Style

American Psychological Association. (2009). *Concise rules of APA style*. Washington, DC: Author.

American Psychological Association. (2009). *Mastering APA style: Student's workbook and training guide*. Washington, DC: Author.

Hacker, D., & Sommers, N. (2013). *A pocket style manual, APA version*. Boston, MA: Bedford/ St. Martin's.

Houghton, P. M., Houghton, T. J., & Pratt, M. M. (2009). *APA: The easy way!* (2nd ed.). Flint, MI: Author.

Neal, M., & Shaw, W. (2012). *Essentials of APA formatting and style*. Arvada, CO: JavaKats Publishing.

Rossiter, J. (2007). *The APA pocket handbook: Rules for format and documentation [conforms to sixth edition APA]*. Augusta, GA: DW Publishing Company.

Schwartz, B. M., Landrum, R. E., & Regan, A. R. (2011). *An easy guide to APA style*. Thousand Oaks, CA: Sage Publishing.

I mention these sources in case you would like to explore book-length and not just chapter-length sources of help.

Help From Others

If you are doing your writing as part of a course requirement, then the most obvious source of help is your instructor. At the least, you need to be sure that you are clear about the nature of the assignment. As I noted in Chapter 1, my assumption throughout this book is that your goal is to produce an APA-style manuscript, either an empirical report (the subject of Chapters 4 and 5) or a proposal or literature review (the subjects of Chapters 6 and 7). To the extent that the assignment differs from these formats, you need to be aware of the differences. If the instructor's rules and APA rules conflict, clearly it is the former that win out.

Beyond simply clarification of requirements, your instructor can be a resource in a number of ways—clarifying some point from your reading, helping you to find relevant sources, and perhaps providing feedback on a draft prior to final submission of the paper. Note that a teaching assistant can also perform these roles. Of course, instructors and assistants vary with respect to how much help they are willing to give, and you need to learn what is possible in your case. At least in my experience, however, students are more likely to fail to seek out available help than they are to ask for too much help. And at least within reasonable limits, it does not hurt to ask, especially if your questions take the form of "help me learn to do this" rather than "do this for me."

The instructor is not the only possible source of help. For particular topics it may be that other faculty members in your program have expertise that can be sought out. Or it may be that fellow students can be a resource. One helpful strategy (assuming that it does not violate course rules if you are writing your paper for a course) is to exchange drafts with a fellow student and offer critiques of each other's work. Doing so not only gives you feedback with respect to your own writing but also provides a chance to see how someone else has attempted to meet similar challenges.

I will add that there is little point in soliciting feedback on your work if you are not going to be responsive to the feedback. This point does not mean that you must adopt every suggestion that is offered. It does mean, however, that you will consider each suggestion carefully and will be willing to make changes when changes are called for. And not just immediate changes that apply only to the document in question. The main value of feedback—and the main thing that instructors hope for when they provide feedback—is that the learning will carry over to future writing efforts. Conversely, few things are more annoying to an instructor—or more grade-deflating—than to see the same errors repeated in paper after paper despite explicit advice to the contrary.

I noted that you do not need to agree with or act upon every suggestion that you receive. But of course there are situations (e.g., an instructor or committee chair says "do this") in which response to feedback is mandatory rather than optional. I offer three consolations with respect to such forced compliance. First, in the majority of cases the suggestion will be a good one that will improve your writing. Second, if you really disagree, you need not incorporate the change in your future, beyond-the-course or beyond-the-thesis writing. Finally, the experience is good practice for what will occur should you ever submit your work to a journal. Reviewers and editors are likely to offer a number of "do this" pronouncements to which you are expected to respond when you revise the manuscript. Again, you do not need to incorporate every suggestion, especially if you can provide a good reason for not doing so. Still, the eventual fate of your manuscript will likely depend on your showing at least some degree of responsiveness and willingness to change.

Going to the Source

Suppose that your study is based on the research of Researcher A and that you have some question about this research that is not answered by Researcher A's published work. Can you write to the researcher for help?

The answer is yes, but this answer comes with several qualifications. First, make certain that the answer is not somewhere in print before sending your request for help; obviously, you should not expect someone else to do your bibliographic work for you. Second, keep the request brief and also keep the asked-for-response brief. It is reasonable to ask for clarification of some procedural detail; it is not reasonable to ask for a detailed critique of your experimental design. Finally, make clear that you realize that you are asking for a favor and that the researcher may be too busy to respond quickly or fully or perhaps at all. And if you do get a response, be sure to send a thank you.

Online Help

As anyone who has typed a paper on a computer knows, sources of help with writing are no longer limited to books or other people. Various computer programs, as well as various options within those programs, are available to monitor both spelling and grammar as one writes.

Authors vary in how helpful they find these aids. My advice is to activate both spell-check and grammar-check programs while writing but to be selective in what you take from them. Even if you are a good speller, spell-check programs can catch typographical errors, as well as the occasional word that you do not in fact know how to spell. The problem with such programs, as numerous commentators have noted, is that they can tell you that you have correctly spelled *a* word but not that you have correctly spelled the *right* word. Thus spell-check programs cannot tell the difference between *there* and *their*, *lose* and *loose*, *principal* and *principle*, and any number of other homonyms or near-homonyms (a sampling of which I give in Table 9.4 when I return to the issue of homonyms). As one who graded thousands of student papers before the advent of spell-check, I can testify that such programs have made spelling errors much less common than was once the case. They have not eliminated them, however.

Grammar-check programs are also useful in catching typographical errors. And, of course, they can also perform their intended function of flagging grammatically incorrect constructions. The problem is that in their present state of development such programs also flag a number of constructions that are as grammatical as a construction can be. They produce, in other words, a high number of false positives. Doubtless the software in question will improve with time, and such programs may eventually have a much better hit-to-error ratio. At present, however, their feedback should be used *very* selectively. The odds are that your grammatical abilities outstrip those of grammar-check.

READ PSYCHOLOGY BEFORE WRITING PSYCHOLOGY

A second suggestion is to read psychology before writing psychology. A basic difficulty that many students have in writing psychology research reports is simply that they have read few such reports themselves. Writing in psychology is not fundamentally different from other kinds of writing, as I will stress shortly. Nevertheless, there is a kind of feeling for what is appropriate in a research report—for how things are said, for what should be included and what left out—that can be gained only by exposure to a number of real-life examples. Such exposure is not sufficient to ensure success, but it may well be necessary.

If you are writing a paper in psychology, then you necessarily are also reading psychology—there will be relevant literature that must be mastered as a context for the presentation of your work. The suggestion now is that you pay attention not just to the content of what you read but also to the style—to how other authors have handled the expositional challenges that you are now facing. Beyond simply required reading of this sort, I suggest that you also seek out some examples of journal articles in an area of psychology that interests you. There is no reason, of course, to seek models indiscriminately—there are plenty of bad examples in even the best journals. What makes more sense is to enlist some guidance in finding especially good examples and then learn from them. I will offer one general piece of advice here, and that is to target the journals published by the American Psychological Association, or APA (a list of which is available on the APA website: http://www.apa.org/pubs/journals/index.aspx), for these are among the strongest journals in the field.

Note that you may be able to decide yourself whether a particular example is going to prove helpful. If you read a few paragraphs and find yourself either confused or bored, then you probably do not want to pattern your writing after what you see. Conversely, notice what it is in other reports that grabs and holds your attention, and aim for similar qualities in your own writing.

Note that published articles are not a good source for one of the challenges in learning to write psychology: namely, mastering APA style. For one thing, not all journals are APA journals, and those that are not do not always require APA style. In addition, some APA rules changed with the publication of the 6th edition of the *Manual* in 2010, and so only fairly recent publications will reflect the current rules. Finally, the manuscript version of an article (the target to which the *Manual* is directed) differs in various ways from the version that eventually appears in print. The conclusion is straightforward: The only way to master APA style is to work closely from the APA *Manual*.

AIM FOR SIMPLICITY

My third suggestion is to seek simplicity in writing. The danger in a section such as the preceding one is that it may reinforce the notion that scientific writing is an abstruse business that is somehow basically different from other kinds of writing. In particular, scientific writing is *difficult,* packed with arcane technical terms, long and complex sentences, densely reasoned arguments, and so forth.

It is true that scientific writing requires a kind of formality of discourse that does not hold for writing in general. It is true also that technical terms exist in any discipline and are often preferable to less precise everyday language. (My favorite defense of technical terms in psychology is from the novelist Peter DeVries, who wrote that "Id is not just another big word.") One reason to read articles in psychology is to develop a sense of the sort of tone and sort of vocabulary that are appropriate for such writing. It is not true, however, that scientific writing should *aim* for difficulty; rather, just the reverse is the case. There will be difficulties aplenty in the content being conveyed; the goal of the writing should be to help the reader surmount the difficulties and arrive at understanding. Thus, in general the short, simple word is preferable to the long, complex one; the familiar word to the obscure one; the short, simple sentence to the long, convoluted one; and the short or medium-length paragraph to the one that stretches across two or three pages. The aim, after all, is to communicate, not to impress the reader with one's sophistication.

The value of simplicity is not limited to scientific writing. "Simplicity" is the title of the second chapter of one of the leading guides to general writing style, *On Writing Well* by Zinsser (2006). Simplicity is also a recurring theme in what is probably the best-known such general writing guide, Strunk and White's (2000) *The Elements of Style*.

AIM FOR VARIETY

The fourth suggestion is to seek variety in writing. Simple sentences may be desirable, but an unbroken string of simple sentences quickly begins to pall. The shorter word is not always the best one, and in any case an occasional long word or long sentence can impart a kind of rhythm to the prose that enhances readability. Recall that one goal of effective writing is to interest the reader. The writer who consistently uses the same vocabulary, the same sentence structure, and the same paragraph structure may succeed in being clear but is unlikely to be very interesting. Clarity of expression and grace of style are not incompatible, and both should be sought.

I should add—and this is a point I take from Bem (2004)—that varying one's wording just for the sake of variation is not always a helpful move. Consider the following two ways of summarizing a research outcome:

> "Men showed a low level of response in the low-reward condition; women, however, showed increased responding under low reward."
> "Men showed a low level of response in the low-reward condition; women, however, persisted longer at the task when the payoff was less than expected."

The second summary certainly provides more variety in wording than does the first. But it also requires more work from the reader, who must equate "less than expected payoff" with "low reward" and "persisted longer" with "increased responding." Requiring unnecessary work from the reader is never a desirable quality in writing. Variety is nice, but clarity is more important, and often it is best, especially when drawing comparisons, to use the same wording and same sentence structure rather than change just for the sake of change.

AIM FOR CONCISENESS

The first topic addressed in the APA *Manual's* "Writing Clearly and Concisely" chapter is length. As the word "Concisely" in the chapter title suggests, the emphasis is on minimizing length, an emphasis conveyed by what the *Manual* labels the "less is more" rule. It is an emphasis also found in the instructions for authors that many journals provide. For example, the web page for *Developmental Psychology* (the APA journal for developmental psychology) tells prospective authors the following: "Editors will decide on the appropriate length and may return a manuscript for revision before reviews if they think the paper is too long. Please make manuscripts as brief as possible. We have a strong preference for shorter papers." The *Journal of Consulting and Clinical Psychology* (another APA journal) limits submissions to 35 manuscript pages. Anything longer must be justified in a cover letter to the editor.

Like simplicity, conciseness is not a virtue that applies only to scientific writing. A similar emphasis is found in an often-quoted passage from Strunk and White's (2000) *The Elements of Style*: "Omit needless words! Omit needless words! Omit needless words!" (p. xv).

Although conciseness may be a general virtue, in psychology there is also a pragmatic justification for minimizing length. As I noted in Chapter 1, the number of submissions to journals far outstrips the number of available journal pages. And as we have just seen, editors are protective of their limited space. Manuscripts whose length is out of proportion to their contribution invite a negative response. If submitted to a journal they may be rejected outright; at the least, editors and reviewers are likely to demand substantial reductions in length.

The goal, then, is to produce a manuscript that is as long as it needs to be and no longer. Achieving this goal requires that authors solve two challenges. One is to say only what needs to be said. One purpose of this book is to help you make the need-to-say or not decision. Chapters 4 and 5 discuss what needs to be said in each of the sections of an empirical report, and Chapters 6 and 7 address the issue for other forms of writing.

The other challenge is to say what needs to be said as briefly as possible. The *Manual* offers various pieces of advice as to how to do so, including eliminating redundancy, cutting down on use of the passive voice, and weeding out overly detailed descriptions and irrelevancies. In part, such eliminating and weeding out can be achieved by following the aim-for-simplicity principle, for the simpler word or phrase is usually the shorter one as well. Probably the most important strategy, however, is vigilance and self-monitoring, asking yourself continually as you write (or rewrite): "Have I made this point as economically as possible?" If the answer is no, then try to say the same thing in fewer words.

Although brevity is a virtue, it is important not to overstate the need for conciseness. In the first graduate course in writing that I took, the instructor emphasized brevity so forcefully that none of us came close to including all of the necessary information in our papers. The advice to be economical does not mean that scientific writing should be telegraphic. Brevity achieves nothing if important content is lost or if the terseness of the writing makes the paper unreadable. The primary goal remains communication, not space saving. A good rule is this: When in doubt, include. It is generally easier, for both author and reader, to pare down an unnecessarily long draft than to try to make sense of a bewilderingly short one. Less may indeed be more, but only if the less is not too little.

AIM FOR SMOOTHNESS

Of all the "Aim for" goals, this one may be both the least objectionable (who would not aim for smoothness?) and the hardest to achieve.

What is meant by "smooth"? It may be easier to identify kinds of writing that are *not* smooth. The aim-for-simplicity principle is again relevant. A high proportion of multisyllable words, multiclause sentences, and page-long paragraphs is unlikely to fit anyone's definition of "smooth." In general, simpler is smoother.

The *Manual* identifies another contributor to lack of smoothness: the use of strings of nouns as adjectives. In itself, the use of words that are typically nouns as adjectives is a familiar, useful, and quite acceptable aspect of English (e.g., "test instructions," "posttest debriefing," "publication manual," "Results section").

The difficulty comes when several nouns-as-adjectives are strung together in a row—for example (to take two particularly egregious examples from the *Manual*), "commonly used investigative expanded issue control question technique," or "early childhood thought disorder misdiagnosis" (p. 66). Not only are such phrases cumbersome to read, but they lend themselves to misreading, as readers assume that they have finally reached the noun in the sentence only to find that it is another adjective. The *Manual* suggests various ways to untangle such strings, including hyphenating when appropriate (e.g., "expanded-issue, control-technique") and moving the last word to the beginning (e.g., "misdiagnosis of thought disorders in early childhood").

Another problem that the *Manual* warns against is abruptness or discontinuity in writing. Sometimes the individual elements in a manuscript are fine in themselves, but it is not clear how one element leads to the next. If so, the problem may lie more in the content than in the method of presentation; you need to be sure that the various parts of your argument are arranged in a logical, building-upon-each-other sequence. Elements of the presentation, however, can also help the reader to follow the flow of movement. In particular, various transitional terms can provide helpful links across the different parts of a manuscript. Table 2.2 presents a number of such transitional terms that the *Manual* singles out. As can be seen, different kinds of links are possible, depending on exactly how the new element relates to the old.

Let me mention one of these transition words that sometimes gets overused in student papers, and that is the word *then*. The overuse comes in Procedure sections when the author is providing a chronological account of the events of the study. What occurs is something like the following. "The tester first explained the game to the child. She then presented the warm-up item. The stimuli for the first problem were then presented. The tester then reminded the child of the rules for the game. She then. . . ." And so on. Tempting as it may be, there should never be two sentences in a row with "then," let alone half a dozen. Often at least some of the sentences in such an account do not need a specific temporal marker. When they do, other possibilities (e.g., "After this," "Next") can help to avoid the ubiquitous "then."

I will conclude this section on smoothness by pointing ahead to one of the strategies to be discussed shortly: namely, reading a draft of the manuscript aloud to oneself. There are various ways that reading one's writing aloud can be helpful, but one is as a test for smoothness. If you find yourself stumbling over words or

TABLE 2.2 Transitional Terms

Type of link	Terms
Time	then, next, after, while, since
Cause-effect	therefore, consequently, as a result
Addition	in addition, moreover, furthermore, similarly
Contrast	but, conversely, nevertheless, however, although

passages, needing to pause for breath, or wondering when a particular sentence will ever end, then your writing is not yet as smooth as it needs to be.

USE THE ACTIVE VOICE

A quick reminder. The term *active voice* refers to a sentence structure in which the actor is stated first, followed by the action, followed by the object of the action—for example, "The man read the book." The passive voice refers to a sentence structure in which the order of the actor and the object is reversed—for example, "The book was read by the man."

One of the prescriptions in the *Manual* is to prefer the active voice, because use of the active voice generally results in a more vigorous, direct communication. The pair of sentences that the *Manual* uses to make this point is not the clearest possible example: "We conducted the survey in a controlled setting." "The survey was conducted in a controlled setting" (p. 77). Note, though, that the actor is assumed in the second of these sentences; if it had to be stated explicitly ("was conducted in a controlled setting by us"), the superiority of the active voice would be more obvious. Becker (2007) provides a clearer contrast: "Every writing text insists that you substitute active verbs for passive ones when you can" rather than "The necessity of replacing passive verbs with active ones is emphasized in every book on writing" (p. 79).

A preference for the active voice is yet another suggestion that is not limited to writing in psychology. One of the first "Principles of Composition" in Strunk and White's (2000, p. 18) *The Elements of Style* is "Use of the active voice." In the words of another style authority, "The active voice has palpable advantages in most contexts: It saves words, says directly who has done what, and meets the reader's expectation of a normal actor-verb-object sentence order" (Garner, 2009, p. 613).

The admonition to use the active voice does not mean that the active voice should *always* be used. Recall that variety (if it is not overdone) is one quality to aim for in one's writing, and an occasional use of the passive is one way to provide variety. Also, as the "in most contexts" in the Garner passage indicates, there are some instances in which the passive voice is preferable to the active. Probably the most common such instance comes when the writer wishes to focus on the object or recipient of an action rather than on the actor. "The president was shot" is a natural wording for such a message, because the emphasis is on the information that is most important to convey, namely, who it was who was shot. The *Manual's* example is "The speakers were attached to either side of the chair" (p. 77), also a natural wording because the interest here is in where the speakers were attached, not in who attached them. Garner (2009) lists five other reasons for employing the passive, including the fact that in some cases the passive simply sounds better.

Despite the exceptions just noted, the advice here is straightforward. Write primarily in the active voice. Mix in an occasional passive sentence, but be aware that you are doing so and do so only when there is a good reason for using the passive. The passive voice should not be overused. Or better: Do not overuse the passive voice.

BE CAREFUL

This next suggestion should fall in the goes-without-saying category. Unfortunately, as anyone who has read many student papers knows, it does not. Especially if this kind of writing is new for you, there are certain to be missteps and omissions that are beyond your control. You need to make sure that there are no mistakes in what you *can* control.

How might lack of sufficient care lead to problems? Failing to respond to feedback is one example. Getting something wrong once is often understandable. Getting something wrong a second time, after being told the first time that you got it wrong, is simply lack of effort.

Some mistakes should not happen even once. At a basic level, there is no excuse for not proofreading a paper before submitting it. A paper replete with typographical or grammatical errors is not only an insult to the reader but also a sure stimulus for negative reactions. Spell-check and grammar-check programs can be helpful in this regard; as noted earlier, however, they are not sufficient. Whatever spell-check and grammar-check tell you, you still need to reread carefully to be sure that there are no remaining errors.

As you will see when you attempt the task, getting every aspect of your references in proper APA style can be a challenge, and some errors may be inevitable on the first few attempts. There is no reason, however, not to get certain basic aspects of the citations and references correct. Being sure that every source you cite in the text appears in the References list is simply a matter of effort. Being sure that the entry in the References matches that in the text (same names, same dates) is simply a matter of effort. Getting these things wrong is a clear sign that you have not put in sufficient effort.

Finally, at a higher level, it is important to reread papers for ideas as well as for grammar and spelling and citations. Many papers contain blatant misstatements, contradictions, inconsistencies, and so forth that obviously would never have survived if their authors had simply taken the time to reread what they had written.

I will add here a suggestion that both the *Manual* and many how-to-write guides offer. It is not simply to reread your paper but to do so after a delay. Most of us have difficulty reading our own work as objectively as we can read that of others; we know what we intended to say, and when we read we tend to process the intent rather than the actual product. Returning to the manuscript after a delay makes it easier for an author to put himself or herself in the perspective of a first-time reader. This makes it easier to see what is actually there rather than what was supposed to be there.

READ ALOUD

Here is another suggestion found in both the *Manual* and many writing guides. It is not simply to reread what you have written but to read it aloud to yourself.

One reason to do so was noted earlier: as a test for the smoothness of the writing. More generally, reading aloud serves the same purpose as reading the manuscript after a delay: It forces attention on what is actually there, rather than on what the author intended to be there. Sometimes student papers (and, to be fair, papers by others also) contain passages that clearly did not come out as intended—something is missing, something is repeated, something is contradictory, or whatever. The passage is obviously not something that the author would ever *say*, assuming that he or she were simply talking about the research. The simplest way to pose the would-I-say-this test is in fact to say aloud what you have written. If the passage fails the test, then it needs to be changed. (Note that the reverse direction does not hold: The fact that you would say something in a particular way does not mean that you can write it that way. If it did, many papers would feature the word *like* in every sentence.)

PLAN AHEAD

The most important entry under this heading is "allow sufficient time." If you are a student, you may well have had a skeptical reaction to the advice in the preceding sections. Who has time for multiple rereadings of a paper when half a dozen papers and exams are coming due at the same time? The answer is that you have to make time. The most serious error I see students make (and most instructors would probably second this observation) is to wait too long to begin working on a paper. The time to begin work on a paper is as soon as (a) you know that you will be writing it and (b) you have enough information about what you will be writing to begin. Not only will such use of the available time reward you in the present case, but it is good practice for whatever beyond-the-classroom writing you may do. Multiple responsibilities and deadlines are not limited to college classes; they are the norm for most of the writing that most of us do.

Using the available time is, of course, just one component of planning. You also need to plan *what* you will write.

Let us consider for a moment the various decisions that must be made in the course of writing a paper. You must decide, out of all the potentially usable material that you have to work with, what will be included in the paper and what will be left out. You need to decide on relative emphases, what material will receive a relatively expansive treatment and what material will be handled more briefly. You need to decide on the order of presentation, what will come first in each section of the paper and what next and what after that. Beyond simply the order of material, you need to decide on the organizational structure for the paper, what the different sections or headings will be and which subsidiary topics will be embedded within which more general topics.

How much of this organizational decision making should be done in advance of writing? Advice-givers vary in their views on this question. For some (e.g., Silva, 2007; Sternberg & Sternberg, 2010), the answer is quite bit—a detailed in-advance outline is *the* way to begin the writing process. In Silva's (2007) words, "You can't write an article if you don't know what to write. . . . Get your thoughts in order before you try to communicate them to the world of science" (p. 79). Others, however, disagree. Peterson (2006), for example, writes, "I think that the notion of planning out one's writing before one starts has been given too much emphasis" (p. 362).

And personally, I doubt that I have generated a formal, detailed outline since the last time that a high school teacher forced me to.

The preceding is not meant to suggest that an article can somehow materialize with *no* in-advance planning. But how much is necessary, as well as what form it takes, varies across authors. If you find a detailed outline helpful, then generate one (Sternberg & Sternberg, 2010, provide a helpful discussion of how to do so). If note taking or perhaps simply thinking the problem through is sufficient, then take that approach. Again, you need to use the strategies that work for you.

I should qualify this somewhat skeptical view of outlining by noting that the value of outlining may vary across different kinds of papers. Suppose that you are writing an empirical report (the subject of Chapters 4 and 5). In this case you do not need an outline to decide on the basic organizational structure for the paper; you already know that the Introduction will come first, followed by the Method, followed by the Results, followed by the Discussion. You do not need an outline to decide on the sequence of material within the Method; that section will open with Participants or Subjects, followed by (if necessary) Materials or Apparatus, followed by Procedure. Furthermore, as Chapters 4 and 5 discuss, well-established guidelines exist for deciding on sequence and emphases within each of the other sections of the paper. There will still be decisions to make about the specifics of your paper, and an outline may be helpful in that regard. But for many of us it is not necessary.

Suppose, in contrast, that you are writing a literature review (the topic of Chapter 7). In this case the organizational possibilities are a good deal less constrained than is true for empirical reports, and there consequently will be many more decisions to make about what headings to use, how to order the material, and which specific topics to embed within which more general topics. Even if you do not begin with an outline, a literature review is likely to require more in-advance planning than does an empirical report. The same is true, I will note, for the amorphous category of "term paper" that dots the syllabi of many Psychology undergraduate courses. Outlines, then, may be an it-depends decision in a couple senses: It depends on the author, and it depends on the paper.

Rosnow and Rosnow (2012) add an interesting point about outlines. Even if you do not begin with an outline, you may want to finish with one—that is, generate an outline after you have completed a draft of the paper. Doing so is one way to check—along, of course, with rereading—that you have included all that you need to include and that your organizational structure is clear and consistent.

GETTING STARTED (PART 1)

Where should you begin your writing? A famous answer to this question appears in *Alice's Adventures in Wonderland*. It is advice offered by the White King: "Begin at the beginning and go on till you come to the end: then stop."

It may be that you, like the White Rabbit in *Alice*, will have no choice with respect to whether to follow the White King's advice. An instructor may require that the Introduction be submitted first, followed by the Method, and so forth, and if so, this is the order that you will follow.

Suppose, however, that you do have a choice. You may, of course, always decide to adopt the expected beginning-to-end order. The point for now is that you do not have to.

Why would you not begin at the beginning? The answer is that Introductions are often one of the more difficult parts of a paper to write, and the opening paragraph of the Introduction can sometimes be especially difficult. Rather than sit for days agonizing over the search for the perfect opening, you might find it more adaptive to start with a part of the paper that you feel more ready to tackle. For many of us, for example, the Method is the easiest section to write, for it is mainly just straight factual reporting—you know what you did, and your task now is to convey what you did to the reader. Assuming that you understand your statistics, parts of the Results section may also be relatively easy to write, given that there are standard ways to summarize statistics in the text and that you can apply these general templates to your data. The point is that it may be important (especially with a deadline looming) to *start*—to be able to tell yourself that you are under way. Once you are, the harder-to-write sections may come more easily.

GETTING STARTED (PART 2)

The preceding section addressed where to begin. This section discusses how to begin. The basic question is how close does what you write initially need to be to what you will write finally.

One approach has been labeled the "spew method" (Peterson, 2006, p. 362). As this rather inelegant label suggests, the goal of the spew method is to get words on paper quickly, concentrating on the content that needs to be conveyed and not worrying yet about the style with which it is conveyed. In Peterson's (2006, p. 362) words, "The only rule governing the spew method is not to rewrite as one goes along." Silva (2007, p. 75) concurs, in a section labeled "Write First, Revise Later": "Generating text and revising text are distinct parts of writing. . . . The quest for the perfect first draft is misguided."

The spew method is another example of a strategy that works for some authors. If it works for you, by all means use it. If you are not sure whether it works for you, by all means experiment with it. Again, the approach is simple: Think about what you wish to write (perhaps having first generated an outline) and then write it as quickly and as without interruption as you can. Later, you can go back and work on the style.

How well this approach works for you probably depends on how easily you can separate, albeit temporarily, content and style. Advocates of the approach are no doubt correct that an attempt to make every sentence perfect before moving on may keep some authors from ever getting beyond the first few sentences. Not every author, however, suffers from this kind of perfectionist paralysis; for some, rewriting as they go may work perfectly well. Note that the issue is not whether rewriting will be necessary—few of us get much in final form on first attempt. The issue is *when* the rewriting will occur. For some authors the best strategy may be an extreme version of the spew method—that is, generate a first draft of the entire manuscript and only then go back and rewrite. For others a less extreme version may work better—perhaps generate a section of the manuscript (e.g., Introduction, Method) and then rewrite, or perhaps a section within a section, or perhaps a paragraph within a section. Whatever the approach, the constant element is the need to rewrite—to revisit each sentence and make it as strong as you can.

The discussion to this point has focused on how to produce a complete version of a manuscript, one that is ready to submit to either an instructor or a journal. If the latter is the case, then further rewriting may eventually be necessary in response to feedback from reviewers and the editor. Rewriting of this sort poses some further challenges beyond those present in self-generated rewriting. Among the helpful sources with respect to how to revise a journal submission are Liben (2010), Nagata and Trierweiler (2006), Osipow (2006), and Warren (2000). Note that the advice in these sources is not limited to journal submissions; it can also be helpful if you are required to submit multiple drafts of a course paper in response to feedback from the instructor or multiple drafts of a thesis in response to feedback from the chair.

KNOW YOUR AUDIENCE

So far we have been discussing writing without addressing a key question: For whom are you doing the writing—that is, who is the intended audience for the paper?

If you are writing your paper for a course, then the immediate audience is, of course, your instructor. Assuming, however, that the assignment is to write an APA-style report, then the broader audience is the readership for whatever journal would be appropriate given the topic of your paper. How general or how specialized should you be in writing for such an audience? What sorts of knowledge can you assume, and what kinds of information do you need to spell out?

The answer is that you want to aim for somewhere in between on the general to specialized continuum. On the one hand, you do not want to write exclusively for the relatively few specialists who do the kind of research you are reporting. Any paper should be of interest to a broader audience and should be comprehensible to a broader audience. On the other hand, you are not writing for *Time* or *Newsweek* or even *Psychology Today*. Thus you do not need to start from ground zero; you can assume some basic background knowledge in anyone who would seek out an article such as yours.

As an example (and this is an example I refer to in Chapter 4), imagine that you are writing an article about theory of mind in young children, an article that would be submitted to a journal of developmental psychology. Your readership will consist primarily of developmental psychologists but may also include researchers from other areas of psychology and perhaps other disciplines (e.g., education) who have an interest in the topic. Such readers can be assumed to bring various kinds of relevant knowledge to such an article—knowledge, for example, about major figures in developmental psychology, or about the verbal limitations of young children, or about standard statistical procedures for analysis of data. Material of this sort, therefore, should not require any explanation. Most readers will probably also already know something about the topic of theory of mind. Not all will, however, and even those familiar with the topic may not possess the specific background knowledge that is necessary to understand your work. The discussion of theory of mind, therefore, *will* require some basic expositional material, prior to a focus on the specific aspects of the literature that led to your study.

The challenge, then, is to judge what your likely audience already knows (and thus you do not need to explain) and what it does not know (and thus you do need to explain). Making this judgment can be difficult, especially if you are relatively new to the field of psychology. Here is another way in which reading psychology can inform your own writing of psychology. As you read, note what sorts of knowledge are assumed at various points in the papers you read and what sorts of things are spelled out. Look especially at the cases that are closest to the decisions that you need to make. If neither Author A nor Author B takes the space to explain a particular point, then probably you do not need to do so either. Conversely, if other authors treat particular kinds of material as in need of explanation, then probably you should also.

There may still be instances in which you are uncertain about whether the material that you are presenting requires an explanation. Earlier I suggested a default assumption for whether to include material: When in doubt, include. I suggest a similar default assumption for whether to explain material: When in doubt, explain. It is best to err in the direction of making your paper more rather than less accessible to potential readers. Depending on the content, there may still be aspects of the presentation, perhaps especially in the Method and the Results, that not every reader will fully comprehend. Nevertheless, the broad outlines of your message—what you did, why you did it, why we should care—should be accessible to any interested reader.

The know-your-audience principle is not limited to writing papers for classes or articles for journals, nor is the need to write for an audience that varies in the expertise they bring to what you have written. If you complete a master's thesis or a dissertation, you will need to produce a document that works for both your committee chair (presumably an expert in the topic) and an "outside" member from some other discipline (presumably a good deal less expert). Similarly, if you write a grant seeking funding for your research, you will need to communicate with evaluators from a range of different backgrounds and disciplines.

USE OF SOURCES

Any paper in psychology has some original element—something that makes it a new contribution, something that makes it the author's own. But no paper—not even the most groundbreaking effort by the field's most eminent theorist—is ever totally new; rather, every paper is grounded in and made possible by what came before. It is the job of the author to make clear the sources for his or her work.

Proper use of sources divides into three general tasks. One is finding the sources in the first place. I address this task in Chapter 3. A second is using the correct APA style for citing a source in the text and for spelling it out in the References list. Chapter 8 discusses these tasks.

The third task is the one that I consider here. It is how to make fair use of one's sources.

Plagiarism

The basic rule is simple: You need to cite anything that you are in some way making use of. To do so, you need to remember what you are making use of, which is one reason to take careful notes when you read your background sources. If source A was the basis for point X, you need to be able to recapture this fact when you come to write about X. Failure to cite a source that contributed to your paper constitutes one form of plagiarism. And plagiarism, as you should be aware, is one of the most serious breaches of both academic and professional ethics.

Using someone's work without attribution is one form of plagiarism. Using someone's *words* without attribution is another form of plagiarism. If you want to use someone else's words, you need to indicate that you are quoting. I discuss quotations shortly. Generally, however, rather than quoting, the way to summarize the sources you read is by *paraphrasing*—that is, convey the points that you want to take away from the source, but do so in your own words rather than those of the original author.

Paraphrasing presents two challenges. One is coming up with original wording that departs sufficiently from the original. The goal is to change the wording enough so that the meaning is retained but the resulting passage really is your writing and not that of the original author. Table 2.3 reproduces a passage from the *Manual* that I quote in Chapter 8. It also provides two paraphrases of the passage.

TABLE 2.3   Examples of Paraphrases

Original passage

As an organization, APA is committed both to science and to the fair treatment of individuals and groups, and this policy requires that authors who write for APA publications avoid perpetuating demeaning attitudes and biased assumptions about people in their writing. Constructions that might imply bias against persons on the basis of gender, sexual orientation, racial or ethnic group, disability, or age are unacceptable.

Unacceptable paraphrase

As the *Publication Manual* (American Psychological Association, 2010) indicates, APA is committed not only to science but also to the fair treatment of people. This policy affects authors who write for APA publications. Such authors need to avoid perpetuating demeaning attitudes and assumptions about people. Wording that might imply bias against people based on factors such as gender, sexual orientation, race or ethnicity, disability, or age is unacceptable.

Acceptable paraphrase

As the *Publication Manual* (American Psychological Association, 2010) indicates, APA has a dual commitment: to scientific research and to the fair treatment of people who might be affected by research. Articles intended for publication in APA journals must not employ wording that conveys negative attitudes about the groups being discussed. Among the dimensions for which the choice of wording can be important are age, gender, race, ethnicity, sexual orientation, and disability.

The first is too close to the original to be acceptable, because it reuses too many elements from the original. The second paraphrase is distinct enough to pass the own-writing test.

The second challenge follows from the first. The more you change the wording in the material you are drawing from, the greater the risk that you may be changing the meaning as well. The way to guard against this possibility should be obvious. You need to be certain that you understand what you have read before attempting to paraphrase it, because only then can you safely translate the material into your own words. And, of course, understanding should be a goal with respect to all of your background reading.

The preceding advice is meant to guard against unintentional plagiarism. I assume that most readers of this book do not need to be warned against intentional plagiarism—that is, deliberately presenting someone else's work as one's own. For the few who might need such a warning, I will add a pragmatic argument against plagiarism to go along with the ethical argument (which, of course, should be a sufficient reason for avoiding the practice). The penalties when plagiarism is detected are severe, and plagiarism is in fact often not difficult to detect. A number of electronic programs now exist precisely for this purpose. And even before the development of such programs, any experienced instructor could often spot writing that clearly was not the student's own. In short, if you deliberately present someone else's work as your own, you will not learn how to do such writing yourself, you will be violating a basic ethical principle, and you will run an appreciable risk of detection and severe sanctions.

Quotations

As noted, if you are going to quote rather than paraphrase you need to indicate explicitly that you are doing so. Chapter 8 discusses the APA rules for presentation of quotations. The main point that I want to make about quotations here is not to overuse them—a point that I make because many students do overuse quotations. If you are going to quote, there should be some *reason* for doing so. Quotations should not be used for standard passages that you could easily put in your own words; they should be reserved for material that is in some way especially vivid or informative or memorable. Quotations should not be used for material that is peripheral to the main themes of your paper; they should be reserved for material that is central to what you want to say. Finally, although any author may be the source for a quotation, quotations tend to be skewed toward the major figures in the field. Thus, other things being equal, quote Freud or Skinner or Piaget before quoting Researcher A, B, or C.

How often then should you quote? There is no set figure. For most empirical articles, however, the answer is somewhere between not at all and twice.

One of the pieces of advice offered earlier was to read psychology before attempting to write psychology. If you follow this advice, one thing that you should note as you read is how rarely quotations appear in psychology articles. I can provide a little data on this point. I did a quick scan of the first two issues of the journal *Developmental Psychology* from 2012, a total of 53 articles. Of these, 37 contained no quotations at all, 15 contained one quotation, and one contained two quotations. Again, if you find yourself with multiple quotations, force yourself do without some of them.

It may have occurred to you that the preceding advice falls under the heading of "do as I say and not as I do," given the frequency of quotations in this book. There is no contradiction, however. A book is not an empirical journal article, and in some respects (use of quotations being one) the two kinds of writing differ.

SUMMARY

This chapter has discussed a variety of ways to improve one's writing. It may be helpful to have a brief reminder of the points discussed. That is the purpose of Table 2.4.

The table divides the entries into the two categories identified at the start of the chapter: aims to strive for in one's writing and strategies to make the writing as effective as possible. I will reiterate just one point here. Realizing that strategies such as those in the table can be helpful is a starting point; often, however, further decisions must be made about exactly how to apply the strategy (how to plan, how to begin, how to reread, etc.). No single approach will work for all authors, and you need to discover the approaches that work best for you.

TABLE 2.4   Summary of Advice With Regard to Writing

Qualities to aim for:

  Simplicity

  Variety

  Conciseness

  Smoothness

Strategies to follow:

  Use available sources of help.

  Learn from examples of writing in psychology.

  Plan ahead.

  Be careful.

  Start with material with which you are comfortable.

  Use the active voice.

  Write for the intended audience.

  Reread and rewrite frequently.

  Make appropriate and fair use of sources.

  Review carefully after writing, including reading aloud.

EXERCISES

1. Find a term paper that you have written while in college—ideally, a fairly recent paper written for a Psychology course. Identify all the passive sentences in the paper and change as many as possible to the active voice. (This exercise is adapted from Dunn, 2011.)

2. Obtain a copy of the Strunk and White book (Strunk, W., Jr., & White, E. B., 2000, *The Elements of Style*, 4th ed., New York, NY: Longman) and read the chapter entitled "Elementary Principles of Composition." Find a recent paper that you have written and evaluate how well the paper adheres to the principles set forth by Strunk and White.

3. Table 5.2 presents the concluding paragraphs from three of the classic studies in psychology. For each, write a paraphrase of the passage that preserves the meaning but expresses it in your own words. If you are not certain that you have fully grasped the meaning, consult the full article before writing.

4. One emphasis of this chapter is the need to write as concisely as possible. Consider the following example of a possible concluding paragraph from an empirical report, one that has been deliberately inflated beyond the original passage on which it is based. Rewrite the passage so that the same meaning is expressed in at most half as many words. Once you have done so, compare your version with the original paragraph on which the passage is based (McCrae et al., 1999).

Like all human beings, personality psychologists are necessarily prisoners of the time in which they live, whether that time be the mid 20th century or the present moment of the dawn of the 21st century. All the development that such psychologists study, whether the study is cross-sectional or whether the study is longitudinal, necessarily occurs in the particular historical era in which the research takes place. In other words, research findings are always embedded in a specific historical context. The historical grounding of their research means that in principle psychologists cannot replicate their studies in other eras to assess directly the generalizability of their conclusions. The impossibility of such a direct test threatens one of the major goals of the discipline, the quest for a cumulative science of psychology (Gergen, 1977). Unless they are prepared to abandon this quest, psychologists must turn to indirect methods in an attempt to verify the generalizability of their conclusions. What might such methods be? The present study offers one answer to this question. The study of personality development in cultures with different recent histories—the approach taken in the present research—provides one method for surmounting the time-bound nature of any particular finding. What does such research show? The evidence so far suggests that there are lawful patterns of adult personality development that are likely to hold in all times and places.

3

Conducting a Literature Search

Writing in psychology takes a variety of forms, several of which we will consider across the remaining chapters of the book. As we will see, writing a research proposal is in some respects different from writing the report of a completed study, and both kinds of writing in turn differ in some ways from the writing that goes into a literature review. One important feature, however, is common to almost every kind of writing in psychology, and that is a grounding in the relevant empirical and theoretical literature. Anyone who wishes to write successfully in psychology must identify the relevant literature for his or her topic and must convey the conclusions from this literature clearly and accurately to the eventual reader. The chapters to come discuss ways to achieve the "clearly and accurately" goal. This chapter considers the first of these tasks: how to search the literature to identify relevant sources.

TYPES OF SOURCES

A first point is that relevant sources come in many forms, and the forms vary in how useful they are likely to be. Table 3.1 lists and briefly describes the most common types. In what follows I discuss ways to evaluate the trustworthiness and usefulness of the different sources. Note, though, that if you are doing your writing to fulfill a course assignment it is important to be clear about your instructor's expectations. You may be required to use only certain kinds of sources, and if so you can limit your search to these types.

A basic distinction divides the entries in the table, and that is the distinction between primary sources and secondary sources. In most instances, a primary source is a report of original research written by the researcher or researchers who carried out the research. Empirical journal articles are the main entry in this category. Papers or posters presented at conferences are another example. Primary sources also include theoretical statements written by the theorist himself or herself, statements that may take the form of a journal article, a conference talk, or part or all of a book.

TABLE 3.1   Sources for Information About Research in Psychology

Source	Strengths	Weaknesses
Journal article: empirical report	The major primary source for reports of research. Peer review guarantees generally high quality.	Despite peer review, articles (and journals in general) vary in quality. There is typically a delay between completion of research and publication.
Journal article: review	Generally the most trustworthy source for review articles. Such articles perform a service to the field by synthesizing large bodies of research literature.	Same as above.
Conference paper	A primary source for reports of (usually quite recent) research.	Not as detailed as journal reports and typically of more variable quality.
Textbook	A generally reliable source of information on a wide range of topics.	The breadth of coverage is at the expense of detailed, expert-level treatment of specific topics.
Specialized book	In contrast to a textbook, provides a detailed treatment of the topic under review. Expertise is generally higher, especially if different authors contribute different chapters.	Typically not as up to date as a review article in a journal. Also of more variable quality than a peer-reviewed journal article.
Magazines and newspapers	Provide an easily accessible and generally up-to-date coverage of a range of topics.	Generally written at a simplified level more appropriate for a lay audience than a professional audience. Lack the controls for accuracy and absence of bias that characterize journal articles.
Internet	Provides multiple sources of information on virtually any topic in psychology.	Different sites vary markedly in the trustworthiness of the information they provide. As with the popular press, most sites lack controls for accuracy and absence of bias.

Secondary sources, in contrast, are summaries of primary sources, written by authors who carried out at best some and often none of the work being summarized. Textbooks are one example in this category. So too are review articles published in journals and newspaper or magazine stories.

Secondary sources, as I discuss shortly, can be valuable in a number of ways. For most papers in psychology, however, the bulk of the supporting literature should consist of primary sources. The reason for this prescription is straightforward. Secondary sources are at least one step removed from the original work, and any conclusions they provide are winnowed through the perspective of someone who typically was not involved in creating the work. The admonition "go to the source" is generally a good one, and for writing in psychology the primary source *is* the source.

The preceding does not mean that any primary source must be accepted without question. A critical reading of any source you plan to use is part of your responsibility as both psychologist and author. In addition, primary sources vary in how trustworthy they are likely to be. The gold standard in this respect is the journal article. The great majority of journal articles in psychology have undergone what is known as "peer review" prior to being published. Peer review means that at least one and typically two or three psychologists with expertise in the topic under study have read the submission to the journal and have agreed that it merits publication. Peer review is thus a kind of quality control, a mechanism to ensure, via objective evaluation by disinterested experts, that only work that deserves to be published gets published. As I noted in Chapter 1, for the best journals this can mean that 80% or more of submissions go unpublished.

In addition to its gate-keeping role, peer review serves another important function. The reviews of manuscripts submitted for publication typically contain a number of comments and suggestions that are conveyed to the author, comments and suggestions that the author can take into account if he or she decides to revise the manuscript and resubmit it for publication. The result is that the final, published manuscript is in a sense a collaborative effort, and it is generally stronger than it would have been without the feedback from peers.

Earlier I referred to "best journals." This phrase raises a further point, and that is that journals vary in quality. In general, and as you would expect, journals with the most stringent criteria for acceptance tend to publish the best papers. For this reason, those who are knowledgeable about a discipline may pay special attention and give special credence to articles that appear in the most prestigious journals. Among the strong journals across many areas of psychology are those published by the American Psychological Association (a list of which is available at http://www. apa.org/pubs/journals/index.aspx) and those published by the Association for Psychological Science (a list of which is available at http://www.psychologicalscience. org/index.php/publications). A general ranking of journals, based largely on the number of times in which articles in the journal are cited in other articles, is provided by the Social Science Citation Index (http://thomsonreuters.com/ products_services/science/science_products/a-z/social_sciences_citation_index/).

Journal articles are not the only form of primary report. Every year thousands of research projects in psychology are presented at professional conferences. Conference presentations typically feature quite recent, often ongoing, research, and they therefore can be valuable sources if you can gain access to them (an issue that I discuss shortly). They do, however, have two limitations in comparison to journal articles. First, they typically are a good deal less detailed, a limitation that makes them harder to evaluate and harder to summarize accurately. Second, although most conference presentations have undergone peer review, the review is less rigorous than that for journal articles, and it typically does not include feedback to which the author can respond. Given the choice, therefore, you should always opt for the published version of a study rather than the conference version. In particular, if you encounter a reference to a conference report in your reading, check to see if the work has been published before settling for the conference version. The same point applies, obviously, to any unpublished manuscripts that you see cited.

Let us turn now to secondary sources. Two entries in this category need to be treated with special caution. One is newspapers and magazines. Although there may be a surface similarity, a story in a newspaper or magazine differs in important respects from a journal article on the same subject. A newspaper or magazine story is not only not a primary report; it is usually written by a journalist and not by a scientist with expertise in the topic. A newspaper or magazine story does not undergo peer review, it is intended for the lay public and not for a professional audience, and it typically concentrates on the conclusions from research without saying much or anything about the methods on which the conclusions are based. For all of these reasons, you should not plan to include such sources in the References list for any paper you write (the only exception being if popular-press accounts of the phenomenon in question are one of the topics that your paper addresses). Such stories, however, can be helpful in a couple senses: They may suggest an interesting topic that would not have occurred to you otherwise, and they may direct you to primary sources on the topic.

The second treat-with-caution entry is information on the internet. Such information, as you no doubt know, comes in a dizzying variety of forms, and some forms are much more trustworthy than others. To begin at the trustworthy end, most of the primary sources that you use will probably be obtained via the internet, given that virtually every psychology journal is now available electronically (indeed, some *only* electronically). Most of the search that you carry out to locate such sources will probably also occur via the internet, given that the main databases for such search (which I discuss in the next section) are electronic databases. In such cases the internet locus of the information is obviously not a concern.

In addition to the uses just described, many internet sites provide reliable secondary-source treatments of a range of topics in psychology. As an example, let us imagine that you type "autism" into Google's search engine. Among the first entries identified by the Google search are two sites provided by the National Institute of Health (http://www.ncbi.nlm.nih.gov/pubmedhealth/PMH0002494/http://www.ncbi.nlm.nih.gov/pubmedhealth/PMH0002494/; http://www.ninds.nih.gov/disorders/autism/detail_autism.htm), both of which are solidly grounded in relevant research and both of which cite a number of primary sources that an interested reader can seek out. In general, sites with a "gov" URL are relatively trustworthy, as are "edu" sites (those with a university affiliation) and "org" sites. Note that the last of these categories includes the sites for professional organizations such as the American Psychological Association (APA) and the Association for Psychological Science (APS).

On the other hand, as you progress through the Google pages for autism you will encounter a number of sites whose trustworthiness is a good deal less certain—therapists marketing a particular kind of treatment, groups arguing that vaccines are a cause of autism, one site that identifies cow manure as a possible cause. It is good to remember that virtually anyone can create a home page or blog or participate in a chat room—no credentials at all are necessary.

I have already suggested one way to evaluate the likely credibility of internet sites: pay attention to the domain name (e.g., gov, edu, org, com). Further tips are available in several helpful guides to internet use, some in book form (e.g., Ford, 2011; Tate, 2010) and some on web pages (e.g., http:/lib.nmsu.edu/instruction/ eval.html; http://www.vuw.ac.nz/staff/alastair_smith/evaln/evaln.htm). Table 3.2 presents five criteria for evaluating the credibility of websites, taken from the first of these web sources. Obviously, these are criteria that apply to any source, not just those obtained on the internet. The point, however, is that it is often more difficult to answer these questions with internet sources than it is with other sources. In comparison to a journal article, it is also less likely that the answers, assuming they are discovered, will be positive ones.

Because of its ubiquity these days, Wikipedia deserves a special mention. As of this writing, a search of Index of Psychological Articles on Wikipedia yields 121 entries—for the letter A alone. Clearly, Wikipedia is a rich source of potential information. As is true of the site in general, the psychology articles on Wikipedia are unsigned, they have not undergone peer review (although they may have been modified by multiple contributors), and they definitely vary in quality and reliability. For these reasons, such sources are dubious entries on the References list for any article you write. They can be helpful, however, in terms of alerting you to issues or ideas that you may have been unaware of, as well as directing you to primary sources for the topic in question.

It is worth noting that the Association for Psychological Science recently launched an initiative to improve the quality of psychology articles on Wikipedia (Banaji, 2010). You can follow the course of this initiative—and perhaps eventually contribute yourself—by monitoring the website devoted to the effort: http://www. psychologicalscience.org/index.php/members/aps-wikipedia-initiative.

Having emphasized the potential unreliability of secondary sources, I should say something about the more reliable entries in this category. Journal articles

TABLE 3.2   Criteria for Evaluating the Credibility of Internet Sources

Criterion	Specific Question
Authority	Is there an author identified? Is the author qualified? Is there a sponsor, and if so is the sponsor reputable? If neither an author nor a sponsor is identified, is there any way to determine the article's origin?
Accuracy	Is the information reliable and error-free? Is there anyone (e.g., an editor) who verifies the information?
Objectivity	Does the information show a minimum of bias? Is the page designed to sway opinion? Is there advertising on the page?
Currency	Is the page dated? If so, when was the last update? How current are the links?
Coverage	What topics are covered? What does the page offer that is not found elsewhere? How in-depth is the material?

Note. Adapted from "The Good, the Bad, and the Ugly, or Why It's a Good Idea to Evaluate Web Sources," by S. E. Beck, 2009. Retrieved from http://lib.nmsu.edu/instruction/eval.html. Adapted with permission.

are again the source of choice. Many journals in psychology are devoted to review articles that summarize the literature on important topics in the field. *Psychological Bulletin* is the most general of these sources, and more specialized journals exist for most of the major subareas of psychology (e.g., *Developmental Review* for developmental psychology, *Review of Educational Research* for educational psychology, *Personality and Social Psychology Review* for personality and social psychology). Books and book chapters are another possibility. Most books, it is true, do not undergo the rigorous review process that characterizes the best journals, and the reviews they offer tend therefore to be more variable in quality. Some, however, are outstanding. The *Annual Review of Psychology* has long offered in-depth reviews on a range of topics (different from year to year) written by leading researchers of the topics in question. Note that the *Annual Review* is available online (http://www.annualreviews.org.lp.hscl.ufl.edu/loi/psych). Similar expertise and depth characterize the chapters in various handbooks devoted to different areas of psychology, handbooks that typically receive new editions every few years (e.g., *Handbook of Child Psychology*, *Handbook of Clinical Psychology*).

I indicated earlier that most of the sources you cite should be primary sources. This advice does not mean, however, that secondary sources should not appear in your References list. Indeed, just the reverse is the case. If some secondary source played a role in your understanding of the topic, then you need to give proper credit by citing the source in your paper. In addition, it is a service to your readers to make them aware of helpful reviews of the topics to which your paper is directed. As I discuss in Chapter 4, there is seldom enough space to provide an exhaustive review of relevant literature in the Introduction to an empirical report. By citing further, more detailed sources you will enable interested readers to go beyond the information that you have space to provide.

SEARCH STRATEGIES

The preceding section discussed how to evaluate the different kinds of sources that underlie writing in psychology. This section discusses how to find the sources in the first place.

We can begin with the simplest (and probably the oldest) search strategy: Ask someone. If you are writing your paper for a course, then the instructor or teaching assistant is an obvious resource. For particular topics other faculty members or graduate students in your department may have expertise and may be willing to help. Note also that reference librarians can be a wonderful resource at various points in the search process.

I will add that such help-seeking probably should not be the first step in your search process. You do not want to ask someone to do something that you could easily have done yourself; in addition, one of your goals should be to learn how to conduct a search on your own. Help from others, therefore, is most appropriate when you have gotten under way and have specific questions to ask—how to select keywords on PsycInfo, perhaps, or how to weigh the credibility of conflicting sources, or how to locate an unpublished work. The specific questions, of course, will vary, but your aims should always be two-fold: to learn the answer for your immediate needs and to learn how to find the answer on your own in the future.

A second strategy is also a long-standing one: Use one source to direct your search to other sources. Whenever you find a relevant source you should check its References section for other potentially usable sources. Clearly, this strategy will be most helpful when the source you have found is a recent one. It will also be most helpful when the source contains many references, something that is more likely for a review article than for an empirical report. This, in fact, is a prime purpose of review articles: not only to give you the author's assessment of the literature but also to make you aware of primary sources that you can then read yourself.

A further point is that if you are going to cite a source in your paper, you *should* read it yourself. It is fine, assuming you give proper credit, to rely on a review article for a general summary of the literature. But if a specific source is important enough to appear in your paper, your description of it needs to be based on your own reading and analysis, not on what someone else has said about it. If you cite Smith (2010) in your paper, you are telling the reader that you read Smith (2010). Do so—do not depend on what Jones (2012) says about Smith.

The kind of snowball approach to literature search just described, in which one source leads to other sources, is valuable, but it is unlikely to identify all the sources that you may need to be aware of. For that, you need a more exhaustive search strategy, and this brings us to the various electronic databases that exist for this purpose. Table 3.3 summarizes the databases that are most likely to be helpful for someone writing in psychology. Of these, I concentrate on *the* most helpful one: PsycInfo.

PsycInfo is a database maintained by APA. It is an electronic successor to the hard-copy version that existed for 80 years, a journal called *Psychological Abstracts*. As of this writing, PsycInfo includes 3.4 million records drawn from nearly 2,500

TABLE 3.3   Sampling of Electronic Databases

Database	Description
PsycInfo	Provides abstracts of the published literature in psychology
PsycExtra	Provides access to unpublished sources in psychology of a variety of sorts (e.g., conference papers, technical reports, newsletters)
PsycArticles	Provides the full text of articles published in APA journals
PsycBooks	Provides full-text access to books published by APA as well as a number of historical and classical works
ERIC	Provides abstracts and in some instances full texts of both published and unpublished literature in education
Medline/PubMed	Provides abstracts of the biomedical literature
Social Science Citation Index	Provides abstracts and citation information for a wide range of publications in the social sciences literature

journals and thousands of books and dissertations. The oldest record dates from the 16th century, and the coverage is comprehensive from the 1880s on.

Numerous guides to PsycInfo use are available, including a website maintained by APA (http://www.apa.org/pubs/databases/psycinfo/index.aspx). If you are new to PsycInfo, I suggest visiting this website before attempting your first search. If you have experience with internet searches, however (and these days, who does not?), you should find that PsycInfo has a familiar feel. Many of the same rules and strategies learned for other search engines and databases apply here as well.

As an example (an example drawn from Reed & Baxter, 2006), imagine that your favorite area of psychology is industrial/organizational psychology and that you are interested in the topic of ethics and leadership—specifically, how ethics are developed in senior managers of organizations. One way to search on PsycInfo is by entering key terms, and you therefore begin by identifying key terms for your topic. There are various ways to identify key terms, including searching abstracts of relevant works and consulting the *Thesaurus of Psychological Index Terms*, which is available in both hard-copy (Tuleya, 2007) and online forms. You identify four key terms, along with synonyms and related terms: *ethics* (*values, morals*), *developed* (*development, socialization, change*), *senior managers* (*leaders, CEO, president, chair, CFO*), *organization* (*business, corporation*).

The first entry in Table 3.4 shows one way that these terms might be entered into PsycInfo. The AND operator means that you are interested only in sources that include both of the terms being linked. Thus, you do not want all sources that deal in some way with ethics, only those that also concern leadership. AND thus functions to narrow a search. Although it is not shown in the example,

TABLE 3.4   Example of a Search on PsycInfo

#	Modification	Search Structure	Citations
1	Original search	(ethics **OR** moral° **OR** value°) **AND** (develop° **OR** social° **OR** change) **AND** (CEO **OR** president **OR** CFO **OR** chair° **OR** lead°)	3,701
2	Limit to journal articles; add *er* to *lead*	(ethics **OR** moral° **OR** value°) **AND** (develop° **OR** social° **OR** change) **AND** (CEO **OR** president **OR** CFO **OR** chair° **OR** leader°)	973
3	Delete *value*; delete *change*	(ethics **OR** moral°) **AND** (develop° **OR** social°) **AND** (CEO **OR** president **OR** CFO **OR** chair° **OR** leader°)	305
4	Add **AND** business	(ethics **OR** moral°) **AND** (develop° **OR** social°) **AND** (CEO **OR** president **OR** CFO **OR** chair° **OR** leader°) **AND** business	10

Note. From "Bibliographic Research" (p. 52), by J. G. Reed and P. M. Baxter, 2006. In F.T.L. Leong and J. T. Austin (Eds.), *The Psychology Research Handbook* (2nd ed., pp. 41–58). Thousand Oaks, CA: Sage. Reprinted with permission of Sage.

the operator NOT is another way to narrow a search. If, for example, you wanted sources with the term *ethics* but not those with the term *moral*, you would enter "ethics NOT moral." In fact, however, you want sources with either of these terms, and so you use the OR operator. OR functions to broaden a search, because it means that you want all of the linked terms—in the example, not only those with *ethics* but also those with *moral* or *value*. Finally, the asterisk is sometimes referred to as a "wild card." It means that you want any terms that begin with the designated letters—thus, for example, not only *lead* but also *leader*, *leading*, and *leadership*.

As the table shows, the original search identified 3,701 citations (as of 2003, when the search was conducted). Because such a pool of sources is clearly too large, further narrowing is necessary. One of the options in PsycInfo is to search for only certain kinds of sources, and the second search takes advantage of this option by specifying that only journal articles are of interest (and not, for example, books or dissertations). The result is a substantial reduction in the number of citations. Subsequent searches reduce the number still further, both through deletion of terms and through use of the AND operator.

The general sequence just described is a typical one. Often an initial search will prove too broad, and if so, subsequent searches can be carried out to narrow the range. The opposite problem can also occur: an initial search that identifies too few sources. In this case subsequent searches can be structured to aim more broadly, most obviously through the addition of key terms.

The example was a search based on key terms, and this approach is probably the most common form of PsycInfo search. It is possible, however, to search under a variety of other headings, including author, title, age group, and date of publication. Probably the most useful of these additional options is an author search. If you know the major researchers for your topic, a search under author is an easy way to identify a number of relevant sources.

As we have seen, a PsycInfo search generates a list of sources. Clicking on any entry in the list brings up an abstract and related information for the work in question (in some cases there is also a link to the entire article). As an example, Table 3.5 shows one of the items that the search described in Table 3.4 would generate. I return to one of the pieces of information in the figure, the Digital Object Identifier, when I discuss References in Chapter 8. (I should note that PsycInfo is provided by different vendors, and its appearance varies some depending on the vendor. The example shows the EBSCO version of PsycInfo.)

PsycInfo offers a further option that is worth noting. Earlier I mentioned the strategy of using the References list in any source you find to direct you to earlier relevant sources. Such a strategy is referred to as a backward search. With PsycInfo it is also possible to perform a forward search—that is, to use an older source to find newer sources. Each of the sources identified in a PsycInfo list of sources has a "Cited by" link. Clicking on the link will bring up a list of more recent publications that cited the source. Another of the databases listed in Table 3.3, the Social Science Citation Index, also allows for such forward searches.

TABLE 3.5 Example of a PsycInfo Record

Leading questions: **Leadership**, **ethics**, and administrative evil.

Authors:

Reed, George E., Department of **Leadership** Studies, School of **Leadership** and Education Sciences, University of San Diego, San Diego, CA, US, george.reed@sandiego.edu

Address:

Reed, George E., University of San Diego, School of **Leadership** and Education Sciences, 5998 Alcala Park, San Diego, CA, US, 92110, george.reed@sandiego.edu

Source:

Leadership, Vol 8(2), May, 2012. pp. 187–198.

Page Count:

12

Publisher:

US: Sage Publications.

ISSN:

1742-7169 (Electronic)

1742-7150 (Print)

Language:

English

Keywords:

leadership, **ethics**, administrative evil, public administration

Abstract:

Administrative evil is a relatively new ethical concept that originated in the field of Public Administration with the publication of Guy Adams and Danny Balfour's 1998 book Unmasking Administrative Evil. It describes the phenomenon whereby otherwise well-intentioned individuals participate in systems that cause harm to innocent people. This essay explores the concept and suggests that the implications for **leadership** studies and practice are worthy of additional exploration. A critique of the concept is provided along with questions that could point the way to additional research. (PsycINFO Database Record (c) 2012 APA, all rights reserved)

Subjects:

°Ethics; °Evil; °Government Agencies; °Government Personnel; °Leadership

Classification:

Social Structure & Organization (2910)

Population:

Human (10)

Format Covered:

Electronic

Publication Type:

Journal; Peer Reviewed Journal

Document Type:

Journal Article

Release Date:

20120528

Copyright:

The Author(s). 2012.

Digital Object Identifier:

10.1177/1742715011429589

Accession Number:

2012-09876-006

Number of Citations in Source:

32

Database:

PsycINFO

Result List Refine Search Result 2 of 1371

One other database listed in Table 3.3 deserves brief mention. PsycExtra is a source for what is sometimes referred to as "gray literature"—that is, unpublished documents of a variety of sorts that fall outside the standard peer-review literature. Among other types of documents, the site includes conference papers, technical reports, position papers, newsletters, and pamphlets. If you can gain access to it (for it is a for-pay site, although many university libraries provide access), PsycExtra is a wonderful way to learn about recent and otherwise hard-to-find work.

The discussion of how to find sources has concentrated on one meaning of the term "find"—namely, how to identify the sources that are relevant for the paper being written. To be useful, however, any sources identified in this way must also be found in a second sense—you must be able to track down and access any relevant sources so that you can in fact make use of them. Because most journal articles are available electronically, this step is usually straightforward when a journal article is the target: Simply click on the relevant link on the university library's website. This approach may not work in all cases, however. Sometimes the older volumes of a journal are not available electronically, and sometimes the newest volumes are not yet available electronically. In such cases the old-fashioned approach of navigation through the library stacks in search of a hard copy may be necessary. Because books are less likely than journal articles to be available electronically, literal library use may also be necessary when books are the target for the search. Furthermore, in some instances the library may not own the particular journal or book being sought, in which case the resources of interlibrary loan must be called on. Note that the possible need for such an approach—and the concomitant delay in getting one's hands on a needed source—provides yet another reason to begin work on a paper as soon as possible.

RECORDING THE RESULTS OF YOUR SEARCH

We have discussed (although not in order) two of the three components of the search process. The first step is finding relevant sources. The second step is evaluating these sources and deciding which ones to use. Clearly, however, these first two steps will come to naught if you do not remember what you have read when it comes time to write. And this brings us to the third step: recording the results of your search.

I begin with a point made in Chapter 2. Various strategies for note taking exist—this chapter mentions a few, and other treatments of the topic (e.g., Reed & Baxter, 2006) provide a fuller discussion of the possibilities. Again, however, you need to find and to use a strategy that works for you.

Whatever your particular strategy, two features should be mandatory components of any note-taking process. One is to record the source fully and accurately whenever you come upon material that you may want to use. If you reach a place in your writing in which you wish to make a point that you found in Smith (2010), you need to remember that Smith was your source and you need to give proper credit in the manuscript. Furthermore, you need to have recorded not just Smith (2010) but the full, APA-style bibliographic information, because this is the information that you will need when you compile your References section. If you have typed this information into a word processing file, then you can simply paste it in when you come to do the References.

The second requirement is to put quotation marks around any material that you are copying verbatim from the source. Put the page number as well, because you will need it if you decide to reproduce the quotation in your paper (Chapter 8 discusses the APA rules for quotations).

The preceding does not mean that a string of quotations is the best way to take notes. As I said in Chapter 2, you should plan on using few if any quotations when you write your paper. In addition, your goal should be to understand any source you read, and if you understand it you can put it in your own words, both when you take notes and when you write your paper. For this reason, it is probably best to read a source through completely at least once before attempting to make any notes. Sometimes, however, it is difficult, when first grappling with a source, to be sure that you have fully understood what you are reading, and in such cases you may want to reproduce the relevant sections for later rereading and, if you use them, eventual paraphrasing in your own words.

The prescription to put quotation marks whenever your notes reproduce a passage is one way to guard against inadvertent plagiarizing—that is, forgetting, when you come to write, that these were the author's words and not your own. The advice not to paraphrase too soon is a way to guard against another form of inadvertent plagiarizing—using a wording that is too close to the original to qualify as your writing rather than the author's. Such a misstep is most likely when your grasp of the material is still shaky and your paraphrase therefore does not depart sufficiently from the original source.

Let us turn now to the mechanics of note taking. Two general approaches exist: writing notes by hand or typing them on the computer.

Clearly, handwritten notes can be recorded on any writable surface. One time-honored approach, however, makes use of index cards. Index cards have at least two attractive features: They are highly portable, and they can be easily rearranged in different combinations or different orders. They also lend themselves to various note-taking strategies. Simplest is the one-source-per-card approach: Record everything you wish to remember about a source, including bibliographical information, on a single card. Some authors prefer a two-card approach: Record the bibliographical information on one card (typically a 3 by 5 card) and record the notes on a separate card (typically 4 by 6 or 5 by 8) that can be yoked to the source. With both approaches, of course, additional cards can be added if necessary. Still a third possible approach is to record in terms of facts or ideas that you may wish to use in your paper. In this case each card is used to record a specific fact or concept, along with the source for that fact or concept; related cards can then be grouped as you work on the paper.

What about the computer? Clearly, any of the approaches just described could be adapted to word processing on a computer. Beyond such self-created strategies, a number of note-taking programs are available, some free (e.g., jjot, Evernote) and some that must be purchased (e.g., EndNote, RefWorks). Many of these programs not only support note taking but also manage citations and references, including applying a desired style when the references are compiled in a References list (which for psychology writing is APA style). If you have not explored the possibilities, you may wish to do so.

Whatever the specific medium and specific approach you use, your note taking should have several goals. The starting-point goal, of course, is to identify all the sources that may be relevant to the paper you are planning to write. You need to record the full, APA-style bibliographic information for any source that you may eventually use. If you quote a passage from a source in your notes, you need to remember that you have done so, which means that quotation marks should surround any quote. Eventually, however, you need to be able to put what you have learned in your own words—ideally in your note taking and certainly in the final paper. Doing so requires that you understand the source, and for some sources this may require multiple readings. Finally, when in doubt, record more rather than less. It is difficult to know in advance what material you may use, and it is better to learn too much rather than too little about your sources.

EXERCISES

1. Select some general topic in psychology that interests you (e.g., self-esteem, peer relations, creativity, ADHD—any broad, general topic). Begin a PsycInfo search by entering the general topic and then progressively narrow the search, specifying the topic more and more precisely, until you have obtained an adequate and manageable number of references (at least 30 and not more than 100).
2. Although PsycInfo is typically the most valuable database for Psychology students, it is not the only helpful electronic resource. Select two of the other databases listed in Table 3.3 and perform a search for some topic of interest to you.
3. Table 3.2 presents five criteria for evaluating the credibility of internet searches. Do a Google search for some topic in psychology that interests you. Evaluate the first five sources identified by the search in terms of the five criteria in the table. Jump to page 20 of the search and evaluate the first five sources listed there.
4. As the text notes, numerous online programs for note taking are now available. The following website lists almost two dozen such programs that can be downloaded for free: http://www.snapfiles.com/freeware/productivity/fwnotetaking.html. Select at least three of these programs, experiment with them, and decide whether you will use any of them for your future writing projects.

4

Sections of an Empirical Report
Title Page, Abstract, Introduction, and Method

As I noted in Chapter 1, two general questions underlie the writing of an empirical report. One is what to say. The other is how to say it. Chapters 8 and 9 will consider a number of specific elements of writing style. This chapter and the three that follow are devoted to the what-to-say question.

As with most of the topics addressed throughout this book, the APA *Manual* is the first and most important source for further reading. It is true that the bulk of the *Manual* is devoted to the specific elements of style that I discuss in Chapter 8 and thus to questions of how rather than what. Nevertheless, the *Manual* also provides a number of helpful suggestions (and in some cases prescriptions) with respect to what should go into each of the parts of an article. I summarize these suggestions in what follows; as always, however, my treatment is meant as a supplement to rather than replacement for the *Manual*. Other helpful sources include APA Publications and Communications Board Working Group on Journal Article Reporting Standards (2008), Bem (2004), Cooper (2011), and Sternberg (2000a). Recall that Appendix A reproduces one of the tables from the Reporting Standards article. The Cooper (2011) book is an expanded version of the original 2008 Journal Article publication.

Table 4.1 provides an overview of the components of an APA empirical report. Although I say something about each of the components in the next two chapters, there will be more to say (especially about the last four entries) in Chapter 8.

TITLE PAGE

Table 4.2 presents an example of an APA-style title page. The example is taken from one of my recent publications.

The center piece of the title page is, of course, the title. As can be seen from the example, the "center" is in part literal, for the title is centered between the

TABLE 4.1   Order of Pages in an APA Manuscript

Section	Formatting
Title page	Page 1.
Abstract	Start on a separate page, numbered page 2.
Text	Start on a separate page, numbered page 3. Type the four sections of the text consecutively.
Introduction	
Method	
Results	
Discussion	
References	Start on a separate page.
Tables	Start on a separate page.
Figures	Start on a separate page.
Appendices	Start on a separate page.

TABLE 4.2   Example of a Title Page

Running head: THEORY OF MIND AND SELF-CONCEPT

Theory of Mind and Self-Concept: A Comparison of Korean and American Children
Sunghee Ahn and Scott A. Miller
University of Florida

Author Note

Sunghee Ahn, Department of Psychology, University of Florida; Scott A. Miller, Department of Psychology, University of Florida.

We are grateful to Hyeyoung Ahn and Kiyoung Chung for their help with recruitment and testing. We also thank James Algina for his advice with regard to statistics.

Correspondence concerning this article should be addressed to Scott A. Miller, Department of Psychology, University of Florida, Gainesville, Florida 32611. E-mail: samiller@ufl.edu.

Note.   From "Theory of Mind and Self-Concept: A Comparison of American and Korean Children," by S. Ahn and S. A. Miller, *Journal of Cross-Cultural Psychology, 43*, pp. 671–686. Copyright 2012 by Sage Publications. Reprinted by permission of Sage Publications.

left and right margins (although only about a third of the way down the page). All major words in the title are capitalized (the *Manual* defines what is meant by "major"). Also capitalized are all words of four or more letters and any word that follows a colon or dash.

Construction of an effective title is one of the most important tasks that an author has. The title is typically the first thing that potential readers see, and if it does not spark their interest it may be the only thing they see. Titles should therefore be informative, and if possible they should be interesting—should do their job, as the Manual says, "with style."

I am not sure that the example in the table demonstrates any particular "style." It is, however, informative—any reader should come away with a fairly good idea of what the research is doing. The title also fulfills another function of a good title: namely, to provide key terms that can aid the search process. Titles are indexed in a variety of search programs (such as PsycInfo) and reference works, and a search by key terms will be fruitful only if the key terms are there.

How long should a title be? The *Manual* suggests no more than 12 words. This is a suggestion, not a rule, and some reports will require more than 12 words if the title is to do its job. Authors should try, however, to ensure that every word is in fact necessary (a point that applies, of course, not just to the title but to the entire paper). One space-saving suggestion in the *Manual* is to avoid phrases such as "A Study of" or "An Experimental Investigation of." Readers, after all, already know that they are reading the results of a study; they do not need to be told this.

Should you try to come up with a clever title? Doing so has both plusses and minuses. Assuming that a title really *is* clever (and failed attempts probably out-number successful ones), it is likely to attract a reader's attention, and it may increase the chances that the work will be talked about and remembered. On the negative side, space devoted to being clever may detract from space devoted to being informative, and a potential reader searching under key terms may encounter some of no relevance (because they come from the clever part of the title) and miss others that should have been there (Cooper, 2011).

A book entitled *Forty Studies That Changed Psychology* (Hock, 2013) discusses, as its name indicates, 40 of the most influential publications in the history of psychology. Many have titles that are likely to pique a reader's interest (e.g., *Superstition in the Pigeon?*, *On Being Sane in Insane Places*). None, however, has a title that is in any way clever or cutesy. (For more about titles, see Roediger, 2007, and Sternberg, 2000b.)

As Table 4.2 shows, the title is just one of the components of the title page. The running head is an abbreviated version of the title that succinctly (50 characters maximum, counting spaces) conveys the nature of the paper. It appears, in all capitals, in the upper left corner of every page of the manuscript (although the "Running Head" label goes only on the title page). In the published version the authors' names appear on one of the facing journal pages, and the running head appears on the other. The running head is thus another way for a hurried reader to get a quick initial impression of a paper and then decide whether to look further.

Clearly, the authors' names part of the title page should pose no problems. I will, however, note a few points. No titles are included with the names. The institutional affiliation is at the level of university (or some comparable institution) and not department. Finally, authors should be consistent across different publications in whether they use initials as part of their name; otherwise they will frustrate the attempts of others to search and to document the literature (e.g., Is J. Smith the same person as J. A. Smith?).

A discussion of the mechanics for handling authors' names presupposes an answer to a prior question that I do not attempt to address: that of authorship. Who deserves to be listed as an author, and in what order should the authors' names appear? The *Manual* provides guidelines for making these decisions.

The Author Note has two main functions. One is to provide contact information for readers who may wish to learn more about the research. The other is to acknowledge the contribution of those who have helped in some way with the research. Although the example does not show it, the latter would include the funding agency in cases of research supported by a grant.

Note finally that the title page is numbered. It is page 1 of the manuscript, and the page number (here and throughout) goes in the upper right corner.

ABSTRACT

The Abstract is a brief summary of the paper. It appears on page 2 of the manuscript, typed as a single paragraph without indentation. Although it is one of the first things a reader sees, it is usually one of the last things written, for an obvious reason: One cannot summarize a manuscript without knowing what the manuscript says.

The length limit for the Abstract varies across journals, but it is typically between 150 and 250 words. Clearly, this is not much space within which to summarize an entire study or perhaps series of studies. It is important, therefore, to make every word count.

The body of the paper that follows the Abstract will have four main sections: an Introduction that presents the background and rationale for the research, a Method section that discusses subjects and procedures, a Results section that presents findings, and a Discussion devoted to interpretation and implications. The Abstract should say something about each of these four components of the research. It is not necessary to devote equal space to each; typically, methods and findings make up the greater share of the Abstract. Still, the proportions devoted to the four components should not be markedly discrepant. An Abstract that spends five sentences on methods and a single sentence on results and their implications needs to be rewritten.

The *Manual* offers several further guidelines for preparation of Abstracts. An Abstract should be nonevaluative, reporting rather than commenting on the material that is to come. An Abstract should not include any information that is not in the body of the manuscript. Because an Abstract must be selective, the *Manual* suggests limiting oneself to the four or five most important concepts, findings, or implications of the research. Finally, the Abstract, like the title, should include key words that can be indexed and will aid the search process. In addition to key words embedded in the Abstract, many journals (including all APA journals) require that a list of three to five key words be provided immediately below the Abstract.

I noted that the title is typically the first opportunity to entice the reader to read further. The Abstract is typically the second. In the words of the *Manual*, "A well-prepared Abstract can be the most important single paragraph in an article" (p. 26).

INTRODUCTION

The Introduction begins on page 3. Because it is obvious that it *is* the Introduction, the word *Introduction* does not appear at the start. The title of the manuscript, however, does appear. Be sure that the title given here matches the one on the title page. Although this point seems obvious, it is one that sometimes goes astray in student papers.

Just as it is obvious that the Introduction opens the article, so it is obvious what the general purpose of the Introduction is: namely, to orient the reader to the study to follow. The kind of orientation that is appropriate will vary across different kinds of study, however, and even for similar studies different authors may take different approaches. There is, as Kendall, Silk, and Chu (2000) say, "no formula" (p. 41), and any advice you encounter, including that given here, should be taken simply as advice rather than a must-follow template.

Getting Started

This being said, the usual direction of movement in an Introduction is from general to specific. The opening paragraph typically presents the general problem that is under investigation, and the close of the Introduction typically provides an overview of how the present study will address the problem. The material in between moves us from general to specific, progressively building the case for why this particular approach to the problem will be interesting and informative.

Let me say a little more about opening paragraphs before considering the subsequent development of the Introduction. I have identified the title as the first opportunity to entice a prospective reader into reading further and the Abstract as the second opportunity. Assuming that our hypothetical reader has made it this far, the opening paragraph is the third opportunity. Although the main function of the opening is to be informative, a further goal is to be interesting. Consider the examples in Table 4.3, taken from four of the 40 "studies that changed psychology" (Hock, 2013). In each case it would be hard to stop reading after this initial taste of what the article is going to do (in case you do want to read further, the References section gives the sources).

How can an author come up with an interesting opening paragraph? Kendall et al. (2000) identify six general strategies, summarized in Table 4.4. It can be seen that the examples in Table 4.3 use a mixture of these approaches. The Harlow opening, for example, takes a familiar phenomenon from everyday experience and goes on to point out the paucity of relevant research. Both Milgram and Darley and Latane also address familiar phenomena (obedience, responsibility) but tie their work to well-known historical examples of the phenomena in question.

Identification of the problem under study is of course just the starting point. The *Manual*, drawing from the JARS document cited earlier (see Appendix A), identifies five further questions that the Introduction should address: Why is this problem important? How does the study relate to previous work in the area? What are the primary and secondary hypotheses of the study? How do the hypotheses and research design relate to each other? And what are the theoretical and practical implications of the study?

Review of Literature

Answering the first two questions requires a review of relevant research. Such a review typically begins soon after the opening paragraph and continues through the first half or so of the Introduction.

TABLE 4.3   First Paragraphs From Classic Articles in Psychology

Love is a wondrous state, deep, tender, and rewarding. Because of its intimate and personal nature it is regarded by some as an improper topic for experimental research. But, whatever our personal feelings may be, our assigned mission as psychologists is to analyze all facets of human and animal behavior into their component variables. So far as love or affection is concerned, psychologists have failed in this mission. The little we know about love does not transcend simple observation, and the little we write about it has been written better by poets and novelists. But of greater concern is the fact that psychologists tend to give progressively less attention to a motive which pervades our entire lives. Psychologists, at least psychologists who write textbooks, not only show no interest in the origin and development of love or affection, but they seem to be unaware of its very existence. (Harlow, 1958, p. 673)

Human infants at the creeping and toddling stage are notoriously prone to falls from more or less high places. They must be kept from going over the brink by side panels on their cribs, gates on stairways and the vigilance of adults. As their muscular coordination matures they begin to avoid such accidents on their own. Commonsense might suggest that the child learns to recognize falling-off places by experience—that is, by falling and hurting himself. But is experience really the teacher? Or is the ability to perceive and avoid a brink part of the child's original endowment? (Gibson & Walk, 1960, p. 67)

Obedience is as basic an element in the structure of social life as one can point to. Some system of authority is a requirement of all communal living, and it is only the man dwelling in isolation who is not forced to respond, through defiance or submission, to the commands of others. Obedience, as a determinant of behavior, is of particular relevance to our time. It has been reliably established that from 1933-45 millions of innocent persons were systematically slaughtered on command. Gas chambers were built, death camps were guarded, daily quotas of corpses were produced with the same efficiency as the manufacture of appliances. These inhumane policies may have originated in the mind of a single person, but they could only be carried out on a massive scale if a very large number of persons obeyed orders. (Milgram, 1963, p. 371)

Several years ago, a young woman was stabbed to death in the middle of a street in a residential section of New York City. Although such murders are not entirely routine, the incident received little public attention until several weeks later when the New York Times disclosed another side to the case: at least 38 witnesses had observed the attack—and none had even attempted to intervene. Although the attacker took more than half an hour to kill Kitty Genovese, not one of the 38 people who watched from the safety of their own apartments came out to assist her. Not one even lifted the telephone to call the police (Rosenthal, 1964). (Darley & Latane, 1968, p. 377)

Note.   From "The Nature of Love, by H. F. Harlow, 1958, *American Psychologist, 13,* p. 673. Copyright 1958 by the American Psychological Association. Reprinted by permission. This content is in the public domain. From "The 'Visual Cliff,'" by E. J. Gibson and R. D. Walk, 1960, *Scientific American, 202*(4), p. 67. Copyright 1960 by Nature Publishing Group. Reprinted by permission. From "Behavioral Study of Obedience," by S. Milgram, 1963, *Journal of Abnormal and Social Psychology, 67,* p. 371. Copyright 1963 by the American Psychological Association. Reprinted by permission. From "Bystander Intervention in Emergencies: Diffusion of Responsibility," by J. M. Darley and B. Latane, 1968, *Journal of Personality and Social Psychology, 8,* p. 377. Copyright 1968 by the American Psychological Association. Reprinted by permission.

The word "relevant" is important. The Introduction to an empirical report is not the place for an exhaustive review of all the research that relates in some way to the topic under study. Not only is there insufficient space for such a review, but the audience to whom the paper is directed can be assumed to be already familiar with the general content area. Note that this point does not mean that you should

TABLE 4.4   Possible Strategies for the First Paragraph of an Empirical Report (Kendall, Silk, & Chu, 2000)

Strategy	Example of an opening sentence
Pose a rhetorical question.	Do we know what children would eat if they could determine their own diets?
Relate to everyday experience.	Choices of what to eat are one of the most common decisions that we make, occurring thousands of times in the course of a life time.
Cite a statistical fact.	The average American child consumes almost a ton of candy in the years between 4 and 14.
Cite an historical fact.	Prior to 1970, most research on children's diets was funded by cereal companies.
Use an analogy or metaphor.	Many choices in life pit immediate pleasure against long-term benefit.
Note the lack of research.	Despite the importance of dietary choices in children's development, we know little about how such decisions are made.

Note. The "facts" in this table are fictitious, created solely for purposes of illustration.

write only for specialists in your area of study; any paper should address a wider audience within the psychology community. But it does mean that you can assume some prior knowledge.

Let me take as an example the manuscript whose title page appears in Table 4.2. The topic of theory of mind has been the most studied aspect of children's cognitive development for at least 20 years now. We could assume, therefore, that any reader who would seek out such a paper would need at most only a brief reminder of the general topic, after which we could concentrate on the subset of the literature that was most relevant to our research. Even with this delimitation, there were still too many studies to consider each individually—in particular, too many studies with Asian or Asian American children. Fortunately, we were able to draw from two recent review articles for our summary of this literature, allowing us space for concentrated attention on the studies that were most directly relevant to our own (e.g., any with Korean children, any with measures of both self-concept and theory of mind).

The approach just described is a standard one. For any empirical report there are some prior studies that *must* be discussed, because they are the ones that led to the present research and they are the ones in terms of which the results of the research will be discussed. It is a basic responsibility of the author to identify all such studies and to convey them clearly and accurately to the reader. More tangentially relevant work can be covered more briefly, with reliance on general reviews whenever possible.

Note that the advice to concentrate on the most directly relevant research does not mean that you have unlimited space to talk about such research. Just as you need to be selective in the sources you cover, so you need to be selective in what you say about any given source. The challenge is to determine what the reader needs to know about the past work to see how your study fits within the literature.

If, for example, a particular procedural variation is part of the basis for your study, then the results of this variation should be included in your review; if the variation is irrelevant to what you are doing, then there is no need to spend space on it. Similarly, if the nature of the subject group is an important issue for your research, then specify the group for all studies you review; if the research is all with college sophomores, then there is no need to keep detailing that fact.

Here is another case in which your reading of psychology can guide your own writing. As you read, note the kinds of information that other authors have included in their discussions of the studies that led up to their own. This strategy will not solve all the problems in your case; still, it should help you make the do-I-need-to-include-this decision.

As noted, general reviews can be cited for conclusions about the literature in general. This point brings up the question of what constitutes an appropriate source for a general review. Students sometimes cite a textbook from one of their courses as the source for some statement in their Introduction. Textbooks (and I say this as a textbook author) are not a good source in this context. Precisely because they cover so much, textbooks do not provide the depth of coverage and the degree of specialization that are wanted here. What is needed is a more specialized treatment by an author or authors with expertise in the topic being addressed—the kind of paper that appears in the journal *Psychological Bulletin*, for example, or a chapter from one of the many handbooks in the field.

It is important to be clear about what a good review article can and cannot do for your Introduction. What it can do is provide a summary of tangentially relevant work that you do not have space to cite directly in the paper. What it cannot do is provide you with sufficient information about the articles that you do plan to cite directly. This is a point that was made in Chapter 3. If you cite "Smith (2010)," you are telling the reader that you read Smith (2010), not just Jones's (2012) summary of Smith.

Suppose, however, that you do not have access to Smith (2010), and Jones (2012) is therefore your only source. In this case you would use what the *Manual* calls a "secondary source" citation—you would discuss Smith but make clear that Jones is the source you read. Do this only if Smith is impossible and not just difficult for you to find. Especially in this age of the internet, use of secondary sources should be rare.

Whatever your sources, one task for your literature review is to make clear what is already known about the topic under study. A further task is to make clear what is *not* known and thus why we need the study that you are about to report. In my experience, student papers often do a competent job of handling the first task—they identify relevant studies, they review the studies accurately, and they state some defensible general conclusions. The problem is that this is all they do. Their discussion thus leaves the impression that research on the topic is complete—we know what we need to know. If this were really the case, there would be no need for your study. Your Introduction needs to spell out what the need is, that is, how you are going beyond what is already known. Perhaps you are attempting to resolve a hitherto unresolved conflict in the literature. Perhaps you are extending a line of study to a new subject group, perhaps a new age group or a new culture. Perhaps you are modifying an existing measure or creating a new one. Perhaps you are combining measures that have not been examined together in the same study. There typically are many ways to build upon the existing literature. You need to make a case for the novelty and potential value of your way.

Note that this part of the Introduction should not require any new critical thinking on your part. The critical thinking came when you put together the study that you are now reporting. Your task at this point is to convey your thinking to the reader.

I will make two more points before leaving the Review of Literature section. The first is an application of the Aim for Variety discussion in Chapter 2. It is easy when reviewing a series of studies to lapse into repetitive wording, in particular, into a string of "founds": "Smith (2010) found . . . ," "Jones (2012) found . . . ," and so forth. Such lapses should be avoided. Synonyms or near synonyms can replace the "found"—for example, "Smith reported," "Jones demonstrated." Different sentence structures can also add variety—for example, "Similar results emerged . . . ."

The second point concerns citations and references (the mechanics of which I discuss in Chapter 8). First, with two (seldom occurring) exceptions, every source you cite in the paper must appear in the References. The exceptions are classical works such as ancient Greek or Roman texts and personal communications—for example, an interview with a psychologist whom you quote in your paper. Second, just as (almost) every source cited in the paper must appear in the References, so must every entry in the References appear in the paper. You are compiling a References list, not a bibliography, and the issue is therefore not what you read but what you used. Finally, the text citation and the References entry must match—same authors, same dates. Do not put "Smith (2010)" in the paper and "Smith (2012)" in the References.

Overview of Method

Up to this point (assuming you are following the suggested sequence), your Introduction will have identified the issues under study, reviewed the relevant research on these issues, and spelled out the gaps or uncertainties in the literature that your study is intended to address. If so, it is time to say something about *how* you would address them—that is, to provide a brief overview of your method.

It is important to note that what you say at this point about methods should be fairly brief and fairly general; after all, you will have an entire Method section devoted to this question. Nevertheless, some overview and preview of methods is a necessary part of the Introduction. The reader needs to know not only that you have identified interesting questions but also that you have devised methods that will allow you to answer these questions. If your goal is to resolve a conflict between Theory A and Theory B, what sorts of data will you collect that will allow you to do so? If you are extending a measure to some new populations, which populations will you examine and why? If you are modifying an existing measure, how will you modify it and why? The specifics you provide will depend on the study, and they will still leave many details for the Method section to spell out. Still, a reader should come away from your Introduction knowing, at a general level, what sort of subjects you will be studying, what you will be doing with them, and why.

Hypotheses

Some preview of methods is also a necessary prelude to what is typically the concluding part of the Introduction: presentation of the hypotheses or questions that the study is designed to address. Recall that one of the goals that the *Manual* identifies for the Introduction is to specify the relation between research design and hypotheses. Doing so requires that elements of the research design be presented in the Introduction. Suppose, for example, that you have a hypothesis of the following sort: Brief training and extended training will lead to equivalent performance on an immediate posttest, but extended training will result in better performance on a delayed posttest. Clearly, such a hypothesis is possible only once we know some essential elements of your design: namely, that there will be two forms of training, brief and extended, and two posttests, immediate and delayed.

One point about hypotheses, then, is that the Introduction should indicate how they will be operationalized—that is, what are the methods that will allow us to test each hypothesis? A further, perhaps prior, point about hypotheses is that it is not necessary to have them. Not all studies fit the hypothesis-testing mode, and if yours does not there is no need to generate hypotheses just for the sake of having hypotheses. If not hypotheses, however, a study must at least have *questions*— that is, unresolved issues of importance for which the study can provide further data. Your reading of the available evidence determines whether your Introduction provides hypotheses or questions. If you believe that the evidence is sufficient to justify a prediction of the outcome, then you have a hypothesis. If you believe that the evidence is not sufficient, then you have a question. And, of course, any report may offer a mixture of hypotheses and questions.

As noted earlier, the *Manual* suggests distinguishing between primary and secondary hypotheses. This is another suggestion that is not a rule; if your hypotheses are of equal importance, present them as such. If they are not, however, then it can be helpful to make the primary-secondary distinction. Doing so prepares the reader for possible differential emphases in the Results and Discussion sections. It also makes it easier, for both author and reader, to evaluate the overall success of the study in confirming the underlying expectations.

I will conclude this section with a point that may not have occurred to you yet but probably will when you write your first Introduction. The convention in writing an Introduction is that the data have not yet been collected and the author therefore does not yet know how the study will work out. It is this convention that makes it possible to present the hypotheses or questions that motivated the study as unresolved issues. But of course this is not really the case—Introductions are typically written (or at least rewritten) after the data are in and analyzed and the fate of all the hypotheses or questions is clear. Why, then, should there ever be a disconfirmed hypothesis, given that authors are free to predict what they already know to be true? (Harlow, 1962—in an article that anyone with a sense of humor should read—suggests tossing in one hypothesis that is disconfirmed, just to keep the reader from becoming suspicious.)

In fact, there is nothing wrong about using one's knowledge of the results to inform the writing of the Introduction. Bem (2004), in fact, argues explicitly that the Introduction should be written only after the results of the study are clear. In his words, "the best journal articles are informed by the actual empirical findings from the opening sentence" (p. 186). The goal, after all, is to create the most helpful and compelling framework for the report of study that follows, and knowing the results can only help in this regard. He goes on to make a further point (one also made by Sternberg & Sternberg, 2010), and that is that the Introduction should not be an autobiographical account of the author's thinking about the problem ("I used to believe A, but now I believe B."). The focus should be on what you think now, not on "a personal history of your stillborn thoughts" (Bem, 2004, p. 187).

Note that this point does not mean that all the hypotheses you present will be confirmed. Hypotheses are formulated and justified on the basis of the theory and research available at the start of the study, and if your reading of this evidence has not changed, then your initial hypothesis will not change either, whatever your data now tell you. There is a consolation, however: Sometimes the most informative studies are those that do *not* turn out as expected.

Some General Points

Should an Introduction be divided into subsections with distinct headings? Method sections, as we will see, invariably are. With Introductions it depends. If the study is a relatively simple one—a few central issues, a straightforward design, a modest-sized literature—then no subsections may be necessary. As the complexity increases, the argument for subsections also increases. The question, as always, is what will aid the reader's task.

How long should an Introduction be? Students find the standard "as long as it needs to be" answer frustrating, but this in fact is the answer. For a simple study, three or four manuscript pages may be sufficient; for a complex one, nine or 10 pages may be required. One useful heuristic with respect to length is that the different parts of the manuscript should usually be in at least rough balance with each other. In particular, if your Results section is a lengthy one, then you probably need a relatively long Introduction to prepare the reader for all the analyses and results.

Table 4.5 summarizes many of the points made throughout this section.

TABLE 4.5   Problems to Avoid When Writing an Introduction

Uninteresting or uninformative opening paragraph
Failure to review all directly relevant research
Overreliance on secondary sources
Reliance on inappropriate secondary sources
Failure to identify the gaps in knowledge that motivated the study
Failure to provide an overview of the method
Failure to state the hypotheses or questions underlying the study

METHOD

As noted, Method sections are always divided into subsections, the first of which is labeled either *Participants* or *Subjects*. Prior to the recent revision of the *Manual*, the label depended on the targets of study, with *Subjects* used for animals and *Participants* used (with a few exceptions) for humans. The current edition of the *Manual* allows either *Subjects* or *Participants* when talking about humans, thus reinstating the terminology that had held for the first 100 or so years of psychology as a science. Because it is the more general of the two labels, I will use *Subjects* in what follows; again, however, in research with humans either term is acceptable.

Before discussing what goes into the Subjects section, I will make one more point about terminology. The fact that either *subjects* or *participants* is acceptable does not mean that these are always the best terms for talking about the people in a study. Use of a more specific label (e.g., "children," "students") is more informative than "subjects" and also adds some variety to what otherwise might be overly repetitive wording.

Subjects

Whatever the label, the job of the first subsection of the Method is to describe the sample. In this attempt some elements are common across reports and others will vary depending on the nature of the research.

In research with human participants, four elements are most common in Subjects sections. Three of these are close to universal. One is the size of the sample. If there are distinct groups, then the size is reported for each group (e.g., "thirty 25-year-olds" and "thirty 65-year-olds"). The second is the sex of the subjects. The third is age. Typically, at least the mean age is reported and in some cases the range as well. Be specific in reporting ranges—for example, "65 to 80," not simply "over 65." The degree of specificity in reporting mean ages depends on the age of the sample. With adult samples, age in years is sufficient (e.g., "25-year-olds and 65-year-olds"). With children, years and months should be reported (e.g., "6 years 4 months"). Note that months and not decimals (e.g., "6.3 years") should be used. With infants, weeks or even (for very young infants) days should be added.

The fourth element is racial or ethnic status. Relatively specific designations (e.g., "Vietnamese American") are more informative than less specific ones ("Asian American"). Exact breakdowns are also more informative than general summaries (e.g., "predominantly Caucasian").

The preceding characteristics are ones that should be reported whatever the focus of the study. Other kinds of information vary in their relevance across different sorts of research. In research comparing young adults and old adults, health status and education level will probably be important and thus should be reported. In research with preschoolers, neither health nor education is typically a concern, but something like day-care experience or family income may be. The guiding principle is to provide the information that a reader needs to understand and evaluate the study.

A further principle is a general one: When in doubt, provide more rather than less information. The more that readers know about the nature of the sample, the better positioned they are to judge the generalizability of the results. A full characterization of the sample also enhances the value of the study for later meta-analysis (a topic I address in Chapter 7). Meta-analytic reviews often examine aspects of samples as "moderator variables" that may affect results, and they can do so only if the necessary information is provided.

What about research with animals? The *Manual's* instructions are the following: "report the genus, species, and strain number or other specific information. . . . Give the number of animals and the animals' sex, age, weight, and physiological condition" (p. 30). As with research with humans, further, topic-specific information may be necessary depending on the nature of the study.

In most instances, one or two paragraphs are sufficient to characterize the sample. Occasionally, however, a table may be required. As always, a table is justified only if there is too much information to fit comfortably in the text. If there are only a few values to report—say three sample sizes and three mean ages—then the text is fine. Imagine, however, a study with four subject groups, for each of whom there are four quantitative values that must be conveyed (perhaps age, IQ, income level, and educational level). In this case a table would be preferable to a string of numbers in the text.

The characterization of the sample is not the only information that should appear in a Subjects section. We also need to know where the sample came from. What was the initial pool from which subjects were recruited, what was the method of recruitment, and what proportion of those who were approached agreed to participate? Information of this sort speaks to the question of how representative the sample is of some target population of interest, which in turn speaks to the question of how generalizable the results are likely to be. It is, therefore, important information for a reader to have. If you glance through a sampling of Subjects sections, you will find that you do not always come away with such information—authors vary in how much detail they provide with respect to sampling procedures or sampling success. The current version of the *Manual* places more emphasis on the provision of such information than did its predecessor; it may be, therefore, that the situation will improve in the future. You should be guided by the *Manual's* prescriptions in any Subjects section you write.

The initial selection is not the only determinant of the nature of the sample. In some studies there is dropout of subjects in the course of the study (also labeled *subject attrition* or *subject mortality*), and such dropout can change the nature of the sample. Some authors prefer to put information about dropout under Results rather than under Subjects. Either alternative is acceptable; the important point is that the reader must be told if any subject failed to make it through the study. If there were distinct groups in the study, then the dropout should be reported by group—how many younger or older, experimental or control, or whatever. Finally, the reasons for the dropout should also be given. The point of doing so is that reasons for dropout divide into two categories. Something like equipment malfunction or experimenter error is unfortunate but also random across subjects, and there is therefore no reason to believe that it will introduce any bias in the study. In contrast, some reasons for dropout reside more in the subject than in the experiment—a failure to understand instructions, for example, or a persistent response bias. Dropout of this sort *is* potentially biasing, especially if it is differential across groups. It is therefore information that the reader needs to know.

A final possible entry in the Subjects section is a statement about ethics. Ethical guidelines govern all research in psychology, and the *Manual* encourages authors to include information about adherence to ethical standards in the Subjects section of the manuscript. In fact, probably only a minority of manuscripts do so. Such omissions do not signal a lack of concern with ethics; the research could not have proceeded if ethical standards had not been met prior to the start of data collection. Precisely for this reason, some authors may consider a further statement about ethics unnecessary, and some may put such a statement in the Author Note or in their cover letter to the editor rather than in the body of the manuscript. Still, do note, when you write your own Subjects section, that a statement about ethics, although not required, is "encouraged."

Apparatus or Materials

If an Apparatus or Materials subheading is used, it typically comes immediately after Subjects. Such a subheading, however, is definitely optional. If a study did not use any apparatus, then there obviously is no need for an Apparatus section. Or if the apparatus can be briefly described under the subsequent Procedure heading, then again no separate heading is necessary. The same point applies to any materials used in the study. Note, with respect to the term "materials," that in almost any study the use of some materials can be assumed (e.g., score sheets on which responses were recorded, pencils used to fill out questionnaires), and materials of this sort do not require mention in the text, let alone in a separate section. Materials are of interest only when they constitute stimuli to which the subject responded. Note also that a main function of an Apparatus or Materials section is to save space when you get to Procedure. If you find yourself redescribing all of your materials as part of your Procedure, then a Materials section is not serving any purpose. The description should occur in one or the other place, not both.

If you have a very lengthy set of materials (perhaps several pages of questionnaires), then a Materials section may not be feasible. Two alternatives exist, assuming you believe that it is important for an interested reader to have access to this material. One is to present the material in an appendix. The other is to make it available in a supplemental online archive. The latter is a relatively recent option that applies to all APA journals (although not yet to all journals). Materials are not the only possible content for online archives. The *Manual* discusses a number of other possible uses, including lengthy computer code, mathematical or computational models, primary or supplemental data sets, and color figures.

Procedure

Procedure sections are usually one of the easiest parts of the manuscript to write. You know, after all, what you did; the task now is simply to convey this information to the reader. The main challenge is one of selection: deciding what is important information that the reader must have and what is irrelevant information that can be omitted. The *Manual* suggests two goals to keep in mind when making the important versus irrelevant decision. One is that the description should allow an interested reader to evaluate the appropriateness of the methods and the validity of the results. The second is that the description should allow an experienced investigator to replicate the study.

Meeting these goals does not require that readers be told *everything*. In any study there are a number of procedural minutiae (e.g., Did the experimenter sit to the left or right of the subject? Were children tested in the teacher's office or the school library?) that are so unlikely to affect results that they can be safely omitted. Other elements of the procedure can sometimes be provided in reduced form. In studies with verbal instructions, it is seldom necessary to reproduce the instructions verbatim; paraphrasing what was said is often sufficient. In studies with multiple tasks of a similar nature, it is sometimes sufficient to describe one or two tasks that can then serve as examples of the rest. And just as in the Introduction, some kinds of information can be assumed to be already familiar to any experienced reader. An often-used test, for example, need not be described in detail; a published source, coupled perhaps with a brief reminder of the contents, should be sufficient. More generally, if aspects of the procedure have been previously published, then reference to the earlier source, coupled again with a brief description, may be all that is needed.

The important details of the Method are those that the reader needs to understand and to evaluate the research. The design of the study clearly falls in this category. Was the design experimental, quasiexperimental, or nonexperimental? If an experimental design was used, were the condition comparisons between-subject or within-subject? If the comparisons were between-subject, how were subjects assigned to condition? If the comparisons were within-subject, in what order were the conditions presented? With relatively simple designs, information of this sort can be incorporated within a general Procedure section; with more complex designs, a separate Design section may be necessary.

The reader also needs to be told how the design was implemented. If there was an experimental contrast, how was this contrast conveyed to the subjects (note that verbatim presentation of instructions *may* sometimes be warranted here)? How many testers and, if relevant, observers were there, and what was the age and sex of the testers (information that is seldom reported, although it may be important for some studies)? If appropriate, were the testers or observers kept unaware of the hypotheses of the study or the experimental status of the subject (a procedure commonly referred to as *blinding*, although the preferred APA term is *masking*)?

If observational measures were taken, what was the interobserver reliability? If scoring of responses was required, what was the coding system, and how reliably was it applied? If a test or tests were given, what is the evidence for their reliability and validity, either from past research or, if appropriate, from the present study? And if multiple tests were given, what was the order of administration, and what was the reason for this order?

Not all of the questions just raised will apply to every study. On the other hand, the list of questions is hardly exhaustive, and some reports may require details not touched on here. Again, the guiding criteria are two: Has a reader been given enough information to evaluate the study, and has an experienced investigator been given enough information to replicate the study? And the guiding principle is one that applies to every section of the manuscript: When in doubt, include more information rather than less.

I conclude this section by considering a decision that typically does not arise in student papers but sometimes needs to be made, especially in studies with multiple parts. Suppose that there is some aspect of the procedure that you have decided not to include in the report. Perhaps some new measure did not work as intended. Or perhaps you have decided to save some aspect of the research for a separate publication (something that should be done only if the component really is best presented separately—the *Manual* cautions against "piecemeal publication" of results). Do you need to say anything about the part of the study that you have decided not to include?

It depends. Suppose that your procedure consisted of parts A, B, C, and D, in that order, and you have decided to omit part D. In this case there is no need to say anything about the omission, because there is no way that D, coming last, could have affected the data you are reporting. Suppose, however, that B is to be the omitted component. You may believe that it is quite unlikely that experience with B could have affected response to C and D. Still, this is not a decision you can make for the reader. Readers should be told about every aspect of the procedure that could conceivably have affected the data being reported.

Note that there is a further obligation if parts of the study are saved for a later report. Readers of the later report need to be told that they are not encountering a group of subjects who are new to the psychological literature; rather, they should know that the same subjects provided the data in an earlier report. If there was any aspect of their participation in the earlier component of the research that could affect the current results, then this fact needs to be shared also.

Table 4.6 summarizes many of the points made in this section.

TABLE 4.6   Problems to Avoid When Writing a Method Section

Failure to provide sufficient information about the sample
Failure to discuss the method of recruitment and the participation rate
Inclusion of an Apparatus or Materials section when a separate section is not necessary
Inclusion of unnecessary procedural detail
Omission of necessary procedural detail

POINTING AHEAD

The Introduction and Method take both author and reader through roughly the first half of an empirical report. If these sections have done their job, they will have set up clear expectations with respect to what is coming next: the kinds of data and analyses with which the Results section will deal and the issues and conclusions that will be the subject of the Discussion section. The next chapter considers these remaining components of an empirical report.

EXERCISES

1. As the text notes, the title of an article is the first opportunity to attract a reader's interest. The journal *Psychological Science* has long been a good source for original and attention-eliciting titles. Look through several recent issues of the journal and note the titles that you find most interesting. Select at least five articles whose titles you find less appealing and rewrite them to increase their interest value. Note that you may need to read the Abstract and perhaps parts of the article to be sure that you understand what the article says.

2. Find a recent article that interests you in any of the APA journals (http://www.apa.org/pubs/journals/index.aspx). Read the article *without reading the Abstract*. Write an abstract for the article and compare your abstract with the published version.

3. The text indicates that the Introduction to an empirical report should tell the reader what sort of subjects were studied, what in a general sense was done with them, and why. Find a recent issue of a journal in your favorite area of psychology, read the Introductions of the first three articles, and decide in each case whether the Introduction provides a satisfactory answer to the three questions. If your answer is no, write a draft of the material that you believe should be added.

4. The APA *Publication Manual* indicates that a sufficiently informative Method section should permit experienced investigators to replicate the study. Find a recent issue of a journal in your favorite area of psychology and read the Method sections of the first three articles. Decide in each case whether the description is sufficient to allow either you or (if this distinction is important) an experienced investigator to replicate the study. If the answer is no, indicate what further information would be necessary.

5

Sections of an Empirical Report
Results and Discussion

Chapter 4 took us through the first half of the empirical report. The present chapter adds the rest of the story. It begins with the part of the report that often poses the greatest challenge for students: the Results section.

RESULTS

A first point about writing a Results section is that you must understand your results yourself if you are to have any hope of conveying them to others. Making sense of dozens of pages of statistical printouts can be a daunting task, one that serves as a prime example of the seek-help-when-necessary advice given in Chapter 2. Experienced researchers often solicit statistical advice from colleagues; if necessary, you should seek help, too.

Organization

A second point about writing a Results section is that you should adopt a logical order of presentation. This point could, of course, be argued to fall in the goes-without-saying category; no one, after all, deliberately adopts an illogical organization. Still, it is easy, when faced with a mountain of findings to convey, to lapse into the assumption that the main task is to ensure that everything that should be reported does in fact get reported somewhere in the Results. Completeness is indeed one goal. A further goal, however, is to ensure that everything gets reported *in the right way in the right place*. You could, after all, achieve the completeness goal simply by reproducing the statistical printouts. That, however, would be asking the reader to do your work. You need to tell the reader what happened in a clear, orderly, understandable way.

Generally, this will mean starting with the most important results. If your Introduction identified a primary hypothesis or primary question, then begin with it and move only later to the secondary issues. If your hypotheses or questions were of equal importance, then it probably makes sense to discuss them in the same order in which they were presented in the Introduction. You adopted that order as the best way to tell your story to the reader; retaining the same narrative flow in the Results helps the reader to do the necessary matching of issues and outcomes. In any case, every question that you posed in the Introduction should receive a clear answer in the Results.

There are exceptions to the principle that one should begin with the most important results. In some studies there are preliminary or peripheral analyses that need to be dealt with before you can turn to the main analyses. Perhaps, for example, you need to report the results of a manipulation check that tested whether some experimental manipulation worked as intended. Perhaps it is necessary to report the psychometric qualities of some new measure before discussing findings obtained with that measure. Or perhaps you wish to report preliminary analyses that indicate that some secondary variable or variables (e.g., sex, ethnicity) had no effects, thus allowing you to ignore these variables in subsequent analyses. In cases such as these, a brief opening paragraph may be necessary to do the preliminary work, after which you can turn to the questions of greatest interest. Alternatively, in some instances (including the first two identified here), the preliminary information can be covered under Method rather than Results.

Most of the analyses that you report in your Results section will have been prefigured by material in the Introduction and Method. There is no law, however, that every analysis in the Results must be clearly anticipated by what has gone before; unexpected or incidental findings of interest may emerge, and if so they should be included. On the other hand, there is also no law stating that *every* conceivable analysis of the data must find its way into the Results. The goal of completeness is not to include every analysis that was run; it is to include every analysis that proved informative. Researchers should beware of cluttering their Results section with peripheral analyses that add little to the study.

What to Report

What sorts of statistical information need to be reported? In this chapter I answer this question in terms of content; in Chapter 8 I add some points concerning style of presentation.

The following passage from the *Manual* provides an example of some, although not all, of the necessary information.

> For immediate recognition, the omnibus test of the main effect of sentence format was statistically significant, $F(2, 177) = 6.30$, $p = .002$, est $\omega^2 = .07$. The one-degree-freedom contrast of primary interest (the mean difference between Conditions 1 and 2) was also significant at the specified .05 level, $t(177)$, $p < .001$, $d = 0.65$, 95% CI [.13, .37]. (p. 117)

Statistics divide into two sorts. Inferential statistics test for the statistical significance of some outcome, usually either a relation between variables or a difference among means. Descriptive statistics provide the values that go into tests of significance—for example, group means in a test of differences among means.

In the example, the F statistic is an inferential statistic, derived from a test called analysis of variance. The particular test was for possible differences among three means (we know this because the first degrees of freedom term, in parentheses, is 2). As the first sentence indicates, this comparison was statistically significant, an outcome signaled by the fact that the p, or probability level, was .002. Thus, there was a .002 chance that differences as large as those observed or larger could have occurred by chance.

The t statistic is also an inferential statistic. Because there were three means involved, the F test does not tell us which contrasts produced the significant difference. The t test is a follow-up test that answers this question by comparing all possible pairs of means. Follow-up tests are necessary whenever a significant effect is based on more than two means—something which, it is worth noting, is always true of interactions. As can be seen, it was the Condition 1-Condition 2 contrast that produced the effect. Although the *Manual* excerpt does not do so, a full treatment would go on to report the (presumably nonsignificant) comparisons between Conditions 1 and 3 and between Conditions 2 and 3. There would be no need to report the nonsignificant t values in these cases (unless, perhaps, they came close to the traditional .05 cutting point); indicating that the tests were run and proved nonsignificant would be sufficient. Note, if you do want to include such a statement, that the term to use is *nonsignificant*, not *insignificant*. The word *insignificant* can be used in other contexts to convey its usual meaning of unimportant—not, however, when talking about statistics.

The conclusions from inferential tests are not all that a reader needs to know. Also important are the descriptive data that went into the tests—in this case, the means for the three conditions. As I discuss more fully in Chapter 8, there are various ways to present this information. The means can be made part of the text—for example, "The mean for Condition 1 was . . ." They can be embedded in parentheses—for example, "Condition 1 (M = . . .)." Or if there are enough of them, they can be given in a table or figure. Whatever the method of presentation, the means need to be accompanied by the standard deviation for the group in question. The *Manual* specifies that a measure of central tendency (such as a mean) should be accompanied by a measure of variability, and the appropriate such measure in this case is the standard deviation.

I noted that the means for the three conditions should be reported. We clearly need the means for Condition 1 and Condition 2, because they are the ones that produced the difference. In general, any mean that was part of a significant effect must be reported. But let us assume that Condition 3 did not enter into any significant difference. Do we need the mean in this case? More generally, should means be reported even if they were not part of any significant effect?

The answer in the case of Condition 3 is yes. It is, after all, just one more value to report, and the Condition 1–Condition 2 difference can be interpreted most clearly if we know the Condition 3 mean. The answer to the more general question is that it depends. If the means relate to one of the hypotheses or questions that motivated the study, then they should definitely be reported, significant or not. If there are only a few means in total to report or if they can be easily incorporated in a table or figure, then also yes—more information is better than less. If there are dozens of means of minimal interest, then no.

Because the *Manual's* example does not include the descriptive statistics, it does not tell us whether the descriptive information or the inferential tests were reported first. Either order is fine, just so long as the two appear in close conjunction and the links between them are clear. Some writers, however (e.g., Grigorenko, 2000; Salovey, 2000), recommend placing the descriptive information first. This, after all, is both the more accessible and the more important information that the Results section has to convey. Once readers know what the results look like, they can be told which comparisons or which relations proved statistically significant.

The *Manual's* example is deliberately limited to certain kinds of statistical information, and it therefore does not make clear a further important point. A Results section should not consist simply of a string of numbers, statistics, and p levels. It is true that the purpose of the Results section is to present data, whereas the purpose of the Discussion section is to interpret data. It is *not* true, however, that statements about the meaning of the data are forbidden in the Results. Indeed, quite the reverse is the case. An unbroken string of ts, Fs, and ps can be both difficult to decipher and extremely frustrating to read. A much better practice is to spend a sentence or two, either in preview before the tests or in summary afterward, to say in plain English what the numbers mean. Such a concluding sentence in the example paragraph might take the following form: "Thus, as expected, performance proved better when . . ."

Let us consider now the other statistics included in the *Manual's* example. As the *Manual's* section on Results makes clear, the significance-test approach to the analysis of data has become quite controversial in recent years. Even if significance tests are regarded as a necessary part of the process (and not everyone agrees that they are), such tests clearly do not tell us all that we want to know. In a general sense, this point has always been clear—that is why we have descriptive information along with the inferential. But recent years have seen an emphasis on some further statistics that can specify the nature of an effect more precisely than just a comparison of means. The *Manual* recommends the inclusion of two such statistics, both of which are illustrated in the example.

One is a measure of effect size. As the term suggests, measures of effect size (and there are a number of different ones) provide an index of the magnitude of some effect—usually, though not always, a significant one. In the example, the ω^2 is a measure of effect size for the comparison of three means assessed by the F test, and the d is a measure of effect size for the comparison of Condition 1 and Condition 2 assessed by the t test.

The second recommended addition is the inclusion of a confidence interval for any significant difference between two means. A confidence interval expresses the range of possible values within which the true population value (in this case, the mean difference) can be assumed to fall with a given probability. In the example, calculation of a confidence interval indicates that there is a 95% probability that the true difference between Condition 1 and Condition 2 is between .13 and .37.

Tables and Figures

One decision that anyone writing a Results section must make is whether to use tables or figures to convey some of the necessary information. Several considerations are relevant.

A first consideration may not apply to students papers, but it does apply to any manuscript that will be submitted to a journal. Tables and figures are expensive to set in print, and they consume a chunk of what is always limited journal space; journal editors tend, therefore, to frown on their overuse. A table or figure should be used only if in balance it will result in a more efficient and effective presentation than would providing the information in the text.

When might this be? The *Manual* offers three guidelines. A first is to use a sentence for three or fewer numbers. The second is to consider a table if there are four to 20 numbers. The third is to consider a figure if there are more than 20 numbers.

I will add a couple amendments to these guidelines. First, I doubt that you will see many tables with just four entries, given that four numbers can be easily given in the text. Recall, however, that if the numbers are means they must be accompanied by standard deviations. Thus a table with four means is certainly a possibility, given that there will be eight numbers altogether.

The second point concerns the table versus figure decision. Tables convey exact values more clearly than do figures, which is the reason for choosing them when the number of values is in the manageable, four to 20 range. Figures, however, are especially good for conveying interactions. They are also good for conveying patterns of change over time. For these uses, therefore, a figure might be preferable to a table even when only a few means are involved.

Several further principles govern the use of tables and figures. A table or figure should not repeat data given in the text or in another table or figure. If the same information appears in two places, one of the sources should be dropped. A table or figure should be largely self-explanatory—that is, comprehensible without reference to a detailed explanation in the text. Finally, although the table or figure may be self-explanatory, discussion of what it shows is still necessary. Tables and figures supplement the text; they do not replace it.

We saw that Results sections consist of two sorts of statistics: descriptive and inferential. Tables can be used to present either sort of information, and the *Manual* provides examples from both categories. In general, however, it is more important for readers to know exact values for descriptive statistics (e.g., means and correlations) than for inferential statistics (e.g., Fs and ts), and for this reason tables should be used primarily for descriptive information. Tables of inferential statistics should be used only when the analysis is both unusually complex (and therefore difficult to summarize in the text) and of central importance to the study.

So far I have not said anything about the mechanics of tables and figures. I address this question in Chapter 8.

Some General Points

There is no need to cite sources for most statistical tests. A source is necessary only if the statistic is not well known or if the present use is in some way unconventional or controversial.

I noted that subject dropout can be covered under either Method or Results. In some cases what is lost is not an entire subject but only some of a subject's potential data—perhaps one trial or one test out of several trials or several tests. Assuming that enough usable data remain, the decision may be made to keep the subject in the study. If so, the fact that some data are missing creates the same obligations for an author as does the case of missing subjects: namely, to report how often the loss occurred, to report the reasons for the loss, and to indicate whether the loss was differential across any of the groups or measures being compared. Because there are several ways to handle missing data statistically (Graham, 2009), a further obligation is to decide among these ways and to convey to the reader what is being done. Information about missing data is typically handled under Results.

As with other sections of the paper, the decision about whether to divide the Results section into separate subsections depends on the length and complexity of the material. It may also depend on what was done earlier in the paper. If, for example, the Introduction used different headings to introduce the different issues in the study, then it may be helpful to use the same headings in the Results.

I noted earlier that supplemental online archives can be used for aspects of the Method that are too lengthy or too peripheral to be included in the text. The same point applies to aspects of the Results. In particular (although not only), primary data may be made available in this way.

Table 5.1 summarizes many of the points made throughout this section.

TABLE 5.1   Problems to Avoid When Writing a Results Section

Presentation of inferential statistics without the accompanying descriptive statistics on which the inferential tests are based

Presentation of information about central tendency (typically means) without an accompanying measure of variability (typically standard deviations)

Presentation of tests of statistical significance without supplementary measures of effect sizes and confidence intervals

Presentation of a significant omnibus test (such as ANOVA) without follow-up tests to determine the basis for the effect

Presentation of the same information in more than one place (e.g., text and table, table and figure)

Presentation of a table or figure without accompanying text to say what the table or figure means

Presentation of numbers without accompanying text to say what the numbers mean

DISCUSSION

The Discussion section is the author's opportunity to draw everything together and to state the conclusions that the reader should take away. This section should have close links to both the Introduction and the Results. The Introduction lays out the questions that the research is intended to answer; the Discussion summarizes the answers that the researcher believes have emerged. The Results presents the data that the study has generated; the Discussion interprets these data and works always within their constraints. Whatever the author may have expected or hoped would occur, the data are the ultimate determinants of what the Discussion has to say.

We saw that the usual direction of movement in an Introduction is from general to specific. The usual direction of movement in a Discussion is the reverse. Bem (2004) offers an hourglass analogy for the shape of the manuscript as a whole. The Introduction typically starts out maximally broad and progressively narrows in on the study being reported. The middle sections of the manuscript are quite narrowly focused, detailing the study's methods and its findings. The Discussion typically begins close to the study and then gradually branches out to consider the broader theoretical and pragmatic implications of the work.

How, then, should the Discussion begin? The *Manual* uses some unusually prescriptive language in its answer to this question. It states that you should "open the Discussion with a clear statement of the support or nonsupport for your original hypotheses" (p. 35). In fact, this is a good way but not the only way to begin a discussion. Cooper (2011) suggests beginning with a summary of the rationale for the research, something that may be especially helpful if the study is a complex one and many pages and many details have intervened since the rationale was first presented.

Whether or not they come first, conclusions with respect to major hypotheses or major questions should come early in the Discussion. Some students write Discussions in what has been called a "striptease" manner, beginning with peripheral points and only gradually working up to their main conclusions. Such a strategy may be effective in some contexts, but a Discussion section is not one of them. Do not make readers wait for the most important things that you have to tell them.

Depending on the results, what you have to tell them may be more or less straightforward. If you stated hypotheses, then you need to evaluate how well the hypotheses worked out; if you stated questions, then you need to indicate the answers that have emerged. Doing so will require some review of what the Results section has just said; the results, after all, are the basis for any conclusions you have. This review should be kept brief, however. The Results section should have made clear what the results are. Your goal now is to interpret them.

In this attempt, it is perfectly appropriate to be somewhat selective, concentrating more on some issues and some findings than on others. If you differentiated between primary and secondary hypotheses in the Introduction, then you have already prepared the reader for such differential emphasis. And even if not, it is fine to spend the most space on what now seems clearest and most informative. It is important, however, not to be overly selective. It may be misleading, for example, to focus on the one finding that supported a particular hypothesis, while ignoring two others that failed to support it. Even if you are comfortable with this approach, a critical reader may not be. You need to acknowledge and try to make sense of negative as well as positive outcomes.

Making sense of any outcomes will require embedding them in the literature that inspired the study. Students sometimes write a Discussion section without citing any references. This is a mistake. It is true that Discussion sections usually contain fewer citations than do Introductions. A major job of the Discussion, however, is to interpret the results in the context of past work, and it is impossible to do so without revisiting at least some of the sources that were discussed in the Introduction.

For the most part, any sources cited in the Discussion will be ones that were first cited in the Introduction. There is no rule, however, against introducing a new reference in the Discussion. Doing so may be appropriate if there was some unexpected outcome for which the Introduction did not pave the way. Or a new reference may be appropriate as part of some beyond-the-study extrapolation, for example, a discussion of the applied implications of the research.

What about introducing a new finding in the Discussion? This practice is more dubious. Although occasions for doing so may sometimes arise, they are rare. The place to introduce findings is the Results. The Discussion is the place to discuss them.

However well it worked out, your study, like every study ever conducted, will have some limitations. The Discussion is the place to identify any such limitations and to discuss the effects that they may have had on your conclusions. It is important not to go overboard in this respect—if your Discussion consists mostly of a string of weaknesses, then it is not clear why either a reader or an editor should take your results seriously. Be sure that the strengths of the research do not get obscured by an overemphasis on problems. Still, a balanced treatment of plusses and minuses is a basic form of honesty that the author owes the reader. And again, it is better to acknowledge limitations oneself rather than let readers discover them on their own.

Two limitations are a frequent enough occurrence to be worth singling out. One is a sample size that fell short of what was desired. Because statistical power relates directly to sample size, a smaller than expected sample is a possible explanation for the failure of a predicted finding to achieve statistical significance. Note, however, that a small sample is a mitigating factor only if you are working with some hard-to-recruit population; if your subjects are college sophomores, then no one is going to be sympathetic if your recruiting efforts fell short. Note also that the statistical power argument applies only if the findings showed a trend in the expected direction. If there was no trend, then there is no reason to think that more subjects would have made any difference.

The second limitation applies to studies in which at least some of the issues have been examined via correlational rather than experimental methods—that is, by simply measuring and relating outcomes, with no experimental control or experimental manipulation. In itself, the correlational approach is not necessarily a weakness—for many topics correlations are the best that we can do. Nor is it inappropriate to speculate about the causal connection between the correlated variables, especially if the various statistical analyses that are possible these days support a particular causal relation. It is important, however, to acknowledge that any causal conclusions from such data are speculative. And it is important not to lapse into causal-sounding wording ("caused," "produced," "led to," "resulted in") without qualification.

I noted that the absence of statistical significance may not always mean an absence of an interesting effect. The converse point may also be relevant: The presence of statistical significance may not always mean the presence of an interesting effect. Recall that Results sections should report not only statistical significance but also the effect size for any significant effects that occur. It is possible, especially with a large sample, that an effect may be statistically significant but also too small to mean much either theoretically or pragmatically, or perhaps too small to support some specific prediction about the size of the effect that would be obtained. It is important when writing a Discussion section not to lose track of the distinction between the statistical significance of an effect and the size of the effect. It is important also to keep this point in mind when reading a Discussion.

The latter part of the Discussion is typically the place to discuss extensions beyond the study, including possible future research. This practice is fine, as long as the suggestions are (a) specific, (b) sensible, and (c) concisely stated. Merely saying that more research is needed, however, does not tell the reader anything.

Just as the *Manual* takes a prescriptive stance with respect to the opening of the Discussion, so it does also with respect to the conclusion. The *Manual* states that authors should "end the Discussion with a reasoned and justifiable commentary on the importance of your findings" (p. 36). Especially if the Discussion has been a long and multipart one, such a summary of the take-home message can be helpful. Some authors add a Conclusions section for this purpose. Even if you do not opt for a Conclusions section, you should try to end the Discussion and the manuscript on a strong note. In the words of Bem (2004), "End with a bang, not a whimper" (p. 203).

Of course, the advice to end on a strong note falls in the easier-said-than-done category. What might a strong ending look like? Table 5.2 provides three examples, drawn from three more of the classic studies in psychology (Hock, 2013). The Fantz (1961) research that provides the first entry reported both a new method for studying visual perception in nonverbal organisms, including human newborns, and some previously unsuspected conclusions about the extent of early visual ability. The article by Bouchard and colleagues (Bouchard, Lykken, McGue, Segal, & Tellegen, 1990) summarized results from the Minnesota Study of Twins Reared Apart, the largest study of separated twins and a major source of evidence for the contribution of genetic factors to individual differences in intelligence. Finally, the third entry comes from a report of the well-known (and controversial) Zimbardo "prison study," in which college students took on the roles of jailer or prisoner with results that were both surprising and in some ways very upsetting (Zimbardo, 1972). Clearly, the final paragraphs, like the studies themselves, vary greatly in content; each, however, provides a strong statement about the importance of the work just presented.

TABLE 5.2   Concluding Paragraphs From Classic Articles in Psychology

Further research is necessary to pin down this and other implications more concretely, but the results to date do require the rejection of the view that the newborn infant or animal must start from scratch to learn to see and to organize patterned stimulation. Lowly chicks as well as lofty primates perceive and respond to form without experience if given the opportunity at the appropriate stage of development. Innate knowledge of the environment is demonstrated by the preference of newly hatched chicks for forms likely to be edible and by the interest of young infants in kinds of forms that will later aid in object recognition, social responsiveness and spatial orientation. This primitive knowledge provides a foundation for the vast accumulation of knowledge through experience. (Fantz, 1961, p. 72)

Whatever the ancient origins and functions of genetic variability, its repercussions in contemporary society are pervasive and important. A human species whose members did not vary genetically with respect to significant cognitive and motivational attributes, and who were uniformly average by current standards, would have created a very different society from the one we know. Modern society not only augments the influence of genotype on behavioral variability, as we have suggested, but permits this variability to reciprocally contribute to the rapid pace of cultural change. If genetic variation was evolutionary debris at the end of the Pleistocene, it is now a salient and essential feature of the human condition. (Bouchard et al., 1990, p. 228)

Finally, the main ingredient necessary to effect any change at all in prison reform, in the rehabilitation of a single prisoner or even in the optimal development of a child, is caring. Reform must start with people—especially people with power—caring about the well-being of others. Underneath the toughest, society-hating convict, rebel, or anarchist is a human being who wants his existence to be recognized by his fellows and who wants someone else to care about whether he lives or dies and to grieve if he lives imprisoned rather than lives free. (Zimbardo, 1972, p. 8)

Note.   From "The Origin of Form Perception," by R. L. Fantz, 1961, *Scientific American, 204*(5), p. 72. Copyright 1961 by Nature Publishing Group. Reprinted by permission. From Sources of Human Psychological Differences: The Minnesota Study of Twins Reared Apart," by T. Bouchard, D. Lykken, M. McGue, N. Segal, and A. Tellegen, 1990, *Science, 250*, p. 228. Copyright 1990 by the American Association for the Advancement of Science. Reprinted with permission from the American Association for the Advancement of Science. With kind permission from Springer Science+Business Media: "The Pathology of Imprisonment," by P. G. Zimbardo, 1972, *Society, 9*, p. 8.

In most manuscripts the Results and Discussion are separate sections. Authors do have the option, however, of writing a combined Results and Discussion section. Typically, this option is chosen only when the manuscript is relatively brief and there are not a large number of results to report. Combined Results and Discussion sections are also common in manuscripts that report multiple studies, which is the topic to which I turn next.

Table 5.3 summarizes many of the points made with respect to Discussion sections.

MULTISTUDY REPORTS

Suppose that you have at least two studies that you wish to report in the same manuscript. One issue is how to organize the material. The second of the two sample papers in the *Manual* provides an example of a multistudy report, and Table 8.1 in the chapter on APA style shows what the headings might look like in such a paper.

TABLE 5.3   Problems to Avoid When Writing a Discussion Section

Failure to begin with the most important results
Repetition of results without interpretation of results
Overly selective discussion of issues and results
Failure to embed the results within the relevant literature
Introduction of results not presented in the Results section
Failure to distinguish between statistical significance and effect size
Failure to acknowledge limitations of the study
Overemphasis on limitations of the study

How is the presentation of content affected? The Introduction section of the manuscript should provide some preview of all the studies that are being reported. Typically, the Introduction will spend most of its space on the first study, an imbalance that is justified by the fact that later studies will have their own Introduction sections. Still, the reader needs to be given some orientation to all the research that is to follow. Further orientation to later studies in the sequence will come in the separate Introductions to those studies later in the manuscript.

Each study will also have its own Method section. How lengthy the later Method sections need to be will depend on the overlap across studies. Other than noting that they are unchanged, there is no need to repeat procedural details that are common across studies. The main task for the later sections is to spell out how the current procedures differ from those reported earlier.

As noted, it is typical, although not required, to use combined Results and Discussion sections when reporting multiple studies. Whether or not this approach is employed, the manuscript ends with a General Discussion section. As its name indicates, the purpose of the General Discussion section is to provide a summary and evaluation of all the research that has been presented. Again, the goal is to end with a strong take-home message.

EXERCISES

1. Look through one of the journals in your favorite area of psychology until you find an article that especially interests you. Read the article through the Results section but stop once you reach the Discussion. Write a Discussion section for the article. Compare your Discussion section with the one in the article.
2. Table 5.1 provides a list of problems to avoid when writing a Results section. Find a recent issue of a journal in your favorite area of psychology and read the Results sections of the first three articles. For each, determine whether each of the problems listed in the table is or is not present.
3. One decision that must be made in writing a Results section is when to use a table or a figure. Select a recent issue of a journal in your favorite area of psychology, look

(Continued)

(*Continued*)

> through the Results sections of all of the articles, and do a tally of the number of tables and figures. Try to identify the principles that determine whether a table or figure is used and, if either is used, the choice between the two. Among the factors to consider are the number of data points, the nature of the data, the nature of the finding or findings, the importance of the findings to the study as a whole, and whether the information being conveyed is descriptive or inferential.
>
> 4. Imagine that you have tested 60 children, equally divided among the four groups shown in the table below, and that you have obtained the (hypothetical) data reported in the table. T-tests reveal significant differences between 3-year-olds and 4-year-olds and between boys and girls. Calculate effect sizes and confidence intervals for these differences. If you do not have a textbook that gives the necessary formulas, do an online search to find them.

Number of Aggressive Responses

	Boys		Girls		Total	
	M	*SD*	*M*	*SD*	*M*	*SD*
3-year-olds	5.60	5.38	5.00	5.88	5.30	5.55
4-year-olds	13.40	13.90	3.40	3.29	8.40	11.15
Total	9.50	11.09	4.20	4.75		

6

Research Proposals

Chapters 4 and 5 were devoted to the most common form of writing in psychology: the empirical report that presents the results of a research project. Not addressed, however, was a basic and prior question: How do you come up with a research project to report? The first part of the present chapter addresses the question of how to generate ideas for research. The second part discusses how to present one's ideas in the form of a research proposal.

DECIDING ON A RESEARCH TOPIC

Generating Ideas

If you are currently taking a course in research methods, it is possible that your text will offer some helpful suggestions about how to generate ideas for research, and if so you obviously should make use of the suggestions. It is also possible, however, that it will not—or at least that any such discussion will be brief. Most texts in research methods (and I include my own in this category) spend far more space on how to implement one's ideas than on how to come up with the ideas in the first place. In the words of McGuire (1997), "our methods courses and textbooks concentrate heavily on procedures for testing hypotheses . . . and they largely ignore procedures for generating them" (p. 2).

The preceding does not mean that helpful sources do not exist. Among the sources I draw from in what follows are Cone and Foster (2006), Leong and Muccio (2006), McGuire (1997), and Sternberg and Sternberg (2010).

Figure 6.1 is taken from Leong and Muccio (2006). As can be seen, it identifies four general sources for ideas.

The category of personal experience is self-evident. Psychology is the science of behavior, and each of us sees hundreds of instances of behavior, both our own and that of others, every day. Most of these instances, of course, are familiar and commonplace and therefore raise no questions that might spark an idea for research. Occasionally, however, something out of the ordinary occurs,

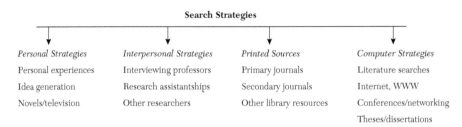

Figure 6.1 Search strategies for finding a research topic. From "Finding a Research Topic," by F. T. L. Leong and D. J. Muccio, 2006. In F. T. L. Leong & J. T. Austin (Eds.), *The Psychology Research Handbook* (2nd ed.), p. 24. Thousand Oaks, CA: Sage Publishing. Copyright 2006 by Sage Publishing. Reprinted by permission.

some behavior for which the explanation is not immediately apparent. The Kitty Genovese case (Table 4.3) is a striking example, one that stimulated the influential research by Darley and Latane (1968) on bystander intervention and diffusion of responsibility.

Personal experience is not limited to one-time events such as the Genovese case; rather, it also encompasses more long-term and cumulative experiences. Growing up as an only child might lead to an interest in how only children differ from children growing up with siblings. Noticing the variable relations that one's friends have with their siblings might spark an interest in the topic of sibling rivalry. The opportunity to live abroad might suggest a number of interesting possibilities for cross-cultural study. (All of these examples are taken from Leong & Muccio, 2006.)

As the figure indicates, the personal category also includes more vicarious experiences, such as those obtained through reading or watching television. One of Leong and Muccio's (2006) examples in this case is the movie "Twelve Angry Men," a movie whose focus on the interactions among members of a jury might spur an interest in group dynamics. An example they take from the news is the phenomenon of posttraumatic stress disorder, a topic that has in fact generated a large and still-growing research literature. More generally, stories in the news are an almost daily source of phenomena that might profitably serve as the targets for psychological research.

As the label indicates, the interpersonal category refers to other people as a source for ideas. Interviewing a professor about his or her research interests may suggest ideas that you can pursue yourself. You may even find a possible advisor should you decide to turn your ideas into an actual research project. For a broader sampling of research interests you can consult your department's website, which (at least at many universities) will include descriptions of all of the faculty members' ongoing research projects. Eventually, you may have the opportunity to serve as a research assistant for a faculty member or graduate student in your department. Doing so will give you hands-on research experience that may both sharpen your interests and make you better prepared to carry out a study of your own.

Indeed, in many departments serving as a research assistant is a common prelude to a senior thesis.

The third category in the figure, printed sources, encompasses a variety of possibilities. Primary journals are sources for empirical reports of original research, which, as I said in Chapter 3, are the most important sources for any paper you write. If you have a favorite area of psychology, a good strategy is to scan the contents of recent issues of the major journals in that area. As I noted in Chapter 3, among the major journals for most areas of psychology are those published by the American Psychological Association (http://www.apa.org/pubs/journals/index.aspx) and those published by the Association for Psychological Science (http://www.psychologicalscience.org/index.php/publications). This sort of journal scan is a quick way to learn which topics are of current interest in the field and may suggest ideas for topics that you can pursue yourself. Once you begin to read about a particular topic, another source for ideas is provided by the Discussion sections of the articles you read. As we saw in Chapter 5, suggestions for future research are a common way to end a Discussion section. It makes sense, therefore, to pay special attention to these sections of your sources as you read.

Secondary sources can also be valuable. Any textbook in psychology that you have ever read covered hundreds of studies on dozens of different issues. One way to come up with ideas for research is to think back to what intrigued you most in what you read or, of course, in what you heard while listening to lectures. If you still have the texts or the notes, you need not rely solely on memory; a quick look at the relevant sources may reawaken some earlier interest. Better yet, if you wrote a term paper on some topic that still intrigues you, then you have an excellent starting point for research, because you are already familiar with the major sources and major issues for the topic in question.

Review articles, especially those that appear in top journals, are another possible source of ideas. Because virtually no research topic is ever completely resolved, such articles almost always include discussions of needed future research. You must make sure, of course, that no one has acted on these suggestions in the time since the review was written. The more recent the review, the more likely it is that any suggestions are still in the yet-to-be-done category.

The final category, computer strategies, applies more obviously to the task of evaluating and refining an idea than to coming up with the idea in the first place. In particular, computer databases such as PsycInfo are central to a critical step in completing a research proposal: identifying all of the relevant literature on which the new study will be based. Still, computer databases can sometimes be helpful in the very early phases of topic selection. Suppose that all you know is that you have an interest in some very general topic—say self-esteem, or eating disorders, or eyewitness memory. One way to decide just what to pursue in a topic is to type the general term into PsycInfo and then look through the first several hundred entries that such a search yields. In the case of self-esteem, for example, you will see (among many other possibilities) studies devoted to various ways to measure self-esteem, studies concerned with possible antecedents of self-esteem (e.g., parenting styles, father absence, adoption, ethnicity), and studies that address possible correlates or consequences of self-esteem (e.g., depression, social anxiety, emotional intelligence, perfectionism). Once you have decided which of these possibilities most interests you, you can then use the strategies described in Chapter 3 to refine the topic further and identify the sources that you will be working from.

Evaluating Ideas

We turn now to the question of how to decide which of your ideas are worth pursuing further and which should be left behind. To some extent, of course, you can evaluate ideas as you generate them, keeping the one or ones that seem most promising and quickly discarding the others. For some researchers, however, a more adaptive strategy is to separate the generation and evaluation phases: to generate as many ideas as possible and only then turn to the task of choosing among them. Leong and Muccio (2006) describe such a "brainstorming" approach as follows:

> This general process of idea generation starts by writing down all topics that come to mind, independent of an immediate judgment of each idea's worth. Only after a substantial list of ideas has been produced should you allow yourself to eliminate an idea. (p. 25)

Brainstorming is another example of a strategy that works for some people and not for others, and, as always, you must find the strategy that works best for you. However you go about the evaluation process, the idea that survives and results in an eventual proposal must meet several criteria.

The first criterion is obvious but still worth stating. The topic should be one that interests you. Especially if the proposal is the prelude to an actual study, you will be devoting considerable time and effort to your project; doing so will be more rewarding if you have found a topic that you care about. Furthermore, a major goal of your proposal is to persuade others that your topic is an important and study-worthy one. You are more likely to achieve this goal if you yourself believe in the value of what you are proposing.

A second criterion follows from the point just made, and that is that your topic should be of interest to others as well as yourself. Most immediately, it should be of interest to those for whom you are writing the proposal—your instructor in the case of a course assignment, the committee chair and committee members in the case of a thesis or dissertation. Even if you are not required to do so, it is a good idea to consult with your instructor about your topic, both to be sure that it is acceptable and to obtain any advice that he or she might offer. If you are writing a proposal for a thesis or dissertation, then such consultation is a mandatory part of the process. Indeed, theses and dissertations are inherently collaborative efforts. Most of the ideas and most of the effort may be (indeed should be) yours, but the work proceeds always under the guidance, and with the approval, of the members of your committee, especially the chair. Cone and Foster (2006) provide an excellent discussion of how to find and work with a research advisor.

Although your instructor or advisor may be the only source whom you need to satisfy, he or she is really just a proxy for the field in general. You need a topic that is of interest to the broader psychological community. It is here that your search of the relevant literature becomes critical. Your reading must convince you—and must give you a basis for convincing others—that your research will speak to questions that are of substantive interest to members of the field. It must also convince you that it will speak to questions that are of contemporary interest to members of the field—that is, that the questions you identify have not already been answered by previous research. Unless your assignment is to replicate some study, any study you propose must have some novel element—something that makes it an original contribution, something that makes it *your* study. Note that having an original idea is not a sufficient basis for a study—the fact that no one has done what you propose may mean simply that it is not worth doing. Some degree of originality, however, is a necessary basis.

The notion of originality deserves some discussion. Some students suffer from what Cone and Foster (2006, p. 26) label the "Nobel laureate error"—namely, the belief that any study they design must be *the* definitive study that addresses and answers all the questions of interest. In fact, no study ever does this. Science is a cumulative enterprise, and hundreds or even thousands of studies may contribute to what we know about the major topics in the field. To add to this literature, a new study does not have to do everything; it merely has to do something that has not been done before.

A new study can extend the literature in various ways. Here are some of the possibilities (Table 6.1 provides a fuller listing). You might devise a new procedure to study some topic of interest. You might modify some existing procedure in an informative way. You might extend an existing procedure to some group to which it has not been applied—perhaps a new age group, for example, or a new culture or subculture. You might bring together in a single study elements that previously had only been examined separately. Or you might devise an experimental procedure to examine some issue that had only been examined correlationally. Note that this is a far from exhaustive list of possibilities. You may be able to find other ways to go beyond what is already known.

TABLE 6.1   Examples of Ways to Build Upon the Existing Research Literature To Create A New Study

Create a new measure to study some construct of interest.
Modify an existing measure to study some construct of interest.
Extend an existing measure to some group or groups not previously studied.
Combine in the same study elements that previously had been studied separately.
Modify the range of an independent variable.
Divide a dependent variable into separate components.
Devise a procedure to resolve a conflict in the literature.
Devise an experimental approach to an issue that had only been studied correlationally.
Devise a correlational approach to an issue that had only been studied experimentally.
Devise a longitudinal approach to an issue that had only been studied cross-sectionally.

One way to determine what is meant by "new" is by noting how previous researchers have answered this question. As you read, note how the more recent studies build upon and extend the studies that came before them. Doing so should give you a good idea of the balance of old and new to aim for in your own study.

A further criterion is that your proposed study must be specific. You may have decided, for example, that you wish to determine the effects of parents' child rearing on their children's moral development, a topic that certainly meets anyone's criterion for being interesting and worth pursuing. This general idea cannot become a study, however, until you also decide exactly which aspects of child rearing you will focus on and exactly which aspects of moral development you will measure. Parents, after all, do many things with their children, and moral development has many facets and forms—which of these many possibilities will you examine in your research? The need for specificity does not stop once decisions of this sort have been made. You must also decide how the constructs that you have decided to examine will be *operationalized*—that is, translated into specific experimental manipulations or measurement operations. Suppose that you have decided, for example, to study parents' use of reasoning as a technique of socialization. You must still decide exactly what you mean by "reasoning" and how exactly you will determine which parents do or do not favor this method of socialization.

The point of the preceding is that identifying important topics to study is just part of being a successful researcher. Also essential is deciding *how* to study them.

The *how* aspect includes another essential feature, and that is that any study you propose must be feasible—that is, something that someone could actually do. You might, for example, construct a study of reasoning and moral development in which you randomly assign parents to different experimental groups that will use varying degrees of reasoning across their children's early years. Such a study would be quite informative; unfortunately, both ethical and practical constraints make it impossible ever to carry out. Similarly, you might propose monthly measures of the children's moral development across an 8- or 10-year period—again informative, but also not feasible.

If you are writing your proposal as a course assignment, you need to be clear about your instructor's expectations with regard to the feasibility of the proposed project. Are you expected to create a study that you yourself could actually carry out (even if executing the study is not part of the assignment)? Or is the goal to create a study that *someone*, given proper resources, could carry out? As we have just seen, the latter does not mean that anything is possible. Still, the scope of possibilities expands greatly. You might, for example, propose a 20-year longitudinal study that follows children from infancy to adulthood, or a cross-cultural study that encompasses a half dozen or so different cultures, or a national survey study that administers multiple measures to thousands of participants. If, in contrast, you need to design a study that is doable within your own resources and timeline, then the possibilities are more limited.

Note that the personally doable study is not necessarily weaker or less informative than the maximally ambitious one—it is simply smaller. Note also that you might opt for a doable study even if the assignment does not require you to. Doing so makes sense if there is a chance that you could actually carry out your proposed study in the future—most obviously, as a senior thesis (as dozens of students in my Methods courses have in fact done over the years). Note finally that the choices are not simply dichotomous: small and doable or large and beyond your reach. You might design a study with multiple components, one of which you could break off as a stand-alone study in the future.

Research Ethics

A final criterion is important enough to single out with its own heading. Your proposed study must be ethically acceptable. With very rare exceptions, all research in psychology must be approved for ethical standards before it can be conducted. To this end, all universities at which such research occurs maintain committees whose purpose is to evaluate the ethics of proposed research projects. If the research is with human subjects, the relevant committee is the Institutional Review Board (IRB); if the research is with animals, the relevant committee is the Institutional Animal Care and Use Committee (IACUC).

If you are writing your proposal as a course assignment, the issue of ethical approval is another question to raise with your instructor. Are you expected to submit an IRB or IACUC proposal as an accompaniment to your research proposal? If you are writing your proposal as the prelude to an actual research project, then you know that an IRB or IACUC submission will be required; the only question is when. In some cases approval from the IRB or IACUC may be a condition for acceptance of the proposal. Such is often the case when a grant is submitted for funding. It may also be the case for research that fulfills an academic requirement. Approval of a thesis or dissertation proposal may be contingent on prior approval by the IRB or IACUC.

It is beyond the scope of this book to discuss research ethics at any length. Table 6.2, however, provides a brief overview of the most important ethical principles that govern research in psychology. The table is drawn in part from the Ethical Principles of Psychologists and Code of Conduct published by the American Psychological Association (http://www.apa.org/ethics/code/index.aspx). The APA code is just one of a number of sources on ethical standards in research. The United States government provides detailed standards for the use of both human and animal subjects, primarily in the form of rules supplied by the various agencies that dispense federal research grants. The websites for the Office for Human Research Protections (http://www.hhs.gov/ohrp/) and Office of Animal Laboratory Welfare (http://grants.nih.gov/grants/olaw/olaw.htm) are helpful sources with regard to these rules. Various professional societies whose members carry out research have developed their own sets of ethical standards. The APA standards apply to research in general, and the Society for Research in Child Development has added standards for research with children (http://www.srcd.org/index.php?option=com_content&task=view&id=68&Itemid=102). There are also numerous books devoted to the

TABLE 6.2   Ethical Principles That Govern Research in Psychology

Principle	Description
Institutional approval	Research can proceed only after approval from the university IRB or IACUC.
Freedom from harm	The most basic ethical principle is that subjects must not be harmed in the course of research. Although physical harm is seldom an issue in psychological research, investigators must also guard against the possibility of psychological harm.
Informed consent	Prospective subjects must be informed clearly about the nature of the research and must give their explicit consent to be included in the research. They must also be allowed to withdraw at any time without penalty.
Inducements	Investigators must avoid offering excessive or inappropriate inducements when such inducements may coerce research participation.
Confidentiality	Information obtained in research is confidential, and results from individual subjects must never be revealed in a way that could harm or embarrass the subject.
Humane treatment of animals	Researchers make reasonable efforts to minimize the discomfort or pain of animal subjects. They use a procedure that subjects an animal to pain or distress only when an alternative procedure is unavailable and the goal is justified by its prospective scientific or applied value.

question of how to maintain ethical standards in research (e.g., Akins, Panicker, & Cunningham, 2005; Panter & Sterba, 2011; Sales & Folkman, 2000).

At a local level, these principles are embodied in a university's IRB and IACUC committees. If you have not already done so, I suggest checking the websites for these committees at your university. Doing so is a good way to begin to master the two general ethical questions that you will face when you are ready to do your own research. One is the procedures to follow to ensure that your project is ethically acceptable and can go forward. The other is the ethical principles that govern the ready-to-go-forward decision. As noted, the latter question is important even if you are writing your proposal for a course assignment and do not need to seek ethical approval. You still need to be sure that your study adheres to the basic ethical principles that all research in psychology must honor.

A final point is that even if you are not required to write an IRB or IACUC submission, you may wish to gain the practice of doing so, for such a submission will be part of any future research you do. Clearly, the practice will be most beneficial if your instructor is willing to give you feedback on any drafts that you prepare.

WRITING THE PROPOSAL

Empirical reports, as we saw, have a single standard format. Proposals do not. If you are writing your proposal as a course assignment, then your instructor has presumably told you the required format (or will if you ask). If you are writing your proposal for a thesis or dissertation, then your chair (or perhaps the relevant university office) is the source for information about format. It is true that proposals for theses and dissertations have a canonical form that tends to be common across universities; still, you need to learn the local expectations. Finally, if you are writing a proposal for a grant, then the granting agency will be your source. Formats for grants vary widely, depending on the type of grant and the granting agency. Grant proposals also require various kinds of information (e.g., budget, personnel) that are not an issue for other types of proposal. Although any detailed discussion of grant proposals is beyond the scope of this book, I can cite further sources for those who are interested (Borkowski & Howard, 2006; Gerin, 2006; Locke, Spirduso, & Silverman, 2007; Sternberg, 2013). Even if you are not working on a grant, these sources include helpful advice that can be applied to *any* sort of research proposal.

In what follows I organize material in terms of what is probably the most common format for proposals, and that is a format that matches the format for empirical reports (see Table 4.1). The paper opens, therefore, with a title page and abstract; if the proposal is for a dissertation or thesis, there may also be a table of contents that immediately follows the title page. The proposal ends with references and, if there are any, tables, figures, and appendixes. What was said about these various beginning and ending components in Chapters 4 and 5 applies to proposals as well. For example, you should aim for an interesting and informative title, you should make certain that your abstract accurately summarizes the study, and you should reserve tables and figures for material that is most effectively conveyed by those formats. Here I concentrate on the middle sections that make up the bulk of the proposal.

Introduction

The Introduction to a research proposal should explain the topic under study, review previous research on the topic, point out any gaps or inconsistencies in the literature, and indicate the questions being addressed and the potential gains in knowledge from the new study. It should, in short, do the same things that an Introduction to an empirical report does. Typically, however, the Introduction to a proposal will differ in two ways from that for an empirical report.

The first difference is a minor one. It concerns tense. In both sorts of paper the review of literature is either past tense ("Smith found") or present perfect tense ("Research has shown"). In an empirical report the overview of the present study is also typically past tense ("We included three conditions," "The expectation was"). In a proposal either future tense ("We will include") or present tense ("The expectation is") typically replaces the past tense when talking about the proposed study.

The second difference is not always found, for it depends on the expectations of those for whom the proposal is being written. Often, however, the Introduction to a research proposal is longer and fuller than the comparable section of an empirical report. At the least, it is likely to be longer in a proportional sense, given that a research proposal, unlike an empirical report, has no results to present and discuss. Many of us who require proposals, however, also prefer Introductions to be longer in an absolute sense as well. In particular, the expectation may be that the review of research will be fuller than what is typical in an empirical report. Because there will be no new data to report, the justification for the research becomes even more important than is usually the case, and this justification depends on a thorough embedding of the study within all the relevant literature. There is also a more pragmatic argument for greater length, and it is that the length limitations that constrain journal submissions (the usual goal for empirical reports) do not apply to research proposals. At the extreme, some dissertation proposals—depending on the topic and the preferences of the committee chair—may include up to 100 pages of literature review.

Clearly, the know-your-audience principle discussed in Chapter 2 applies to the question of how to write an Introduction to a research proposal. You need to know what sort of literature review and what overall length are expected in your case. To the extent that this decision is yours to make, arguments exist for both a relatively brief and a relatively full approach. If you adopt a brief approach, then your Introduction will be similar (some aspects of tense aside) to that for an empirical report, which means that you will already have a draft of this section of the report if your proposal leads to a potentially publishable study. If you opt for the longer and fuller approach, you will have more rewriting to do should you eventually adapt your writing to an empirical report. On the positive side, mastering and writing about the larger literature will be a valuable learning experience in itself. In addition, it is possible that your literature review—assuming that it is strong enough and original enough—might be adapted to a stand-alone and potentially publishable contribution. The next chapter takes up the topic of how to write such literature reviews.

Method

As with the Introduction, the Method section of a proposal is similar to the comparable section in an empirical report. Again, however, one obvious difference concerns tense. The Method section of an empirical report describes events that have already occurred, and past tense is therefore appropriate. The Method section of a proposal describes events that have not yet occurred but that the author hopes to make happen in the future. Future tense is therefore appropriate—"The participants will be," "Each participant will," and so forth. The same point applies to discussions of intended analyses in a subsequent Results section ("The data will be analyzed").

I should qualify this statement by noting that some instructors or committee chairs may have different preferences—or may be open to your suggestion if you propose a different approach. Couching the Method in conditional tense ("The participants would be") or present tense ("The participants are") is a possibility. So is use of the past tense. Although obviously counterfactual (since nothing has yet occurred), such an approach has a couple virtues: It is good practice for the kind of writing required in an empirical report, and if the proposal does result in an actual study the Method section will already be in final form (at least as far as tense is concerned). Having noted these other possibilities, however, I will add that my advice is to use future tense unless instructed otherwise.

As with an empirical report, the first subsection of the Method section of a proposal is Subjects or Participants. Here you should specify all the aspects of your intended sample that a reader needs to know to evaluate your proposal, both general characteristics that are relevant in any study (e.g., number, age, gender of participants) and whatever study-specific features are important for your research. You should also address how the sample will be recruited. If the recruitment process is straightforward (e.g., college students from an Intro Psych pool), this discussion can be brief; if the sample is a harder-to-find one, then you need to provide more detail about how you would proceed. You should also address the expected participation rate (i.e., what proportion of those you solicit are likely to agree) and, if relevant, possible dropout.

The issue of sample size deserves some comment. How do you decide how many subjects you will need? You know, of course, that you will need a sufficient number to show the effects of interest—too small a sample size is a common culprit when results turn out to be nonsignificant. It does not follow, however, that bigger is always better. You could specify a sample size of 1,000 and ensure that most of your statistical tests will reach significance; it is doubtful, however, that significance would mean much in such a case. What is really of interest is the size of any effects you obtain, and you do not need 1,000 participants to determine effect size. A further problem, of course, is that a huge sample size is easy to propose but hard to achieve, and you should not propose something that cannot in fact be done. Finally, even if it *could* be done this does not mean that it should; testing a larger-than-necessary sample is a waste of your time and resources (and, of course, of the subjects' time as well).

So how do you decide on a number that is neither too small nor too large? Past studies can be a guide, especially, of course, those studies that are closest to yours. If 100 participants were sufficient for a closely related study by Researcher A, then 100 may be a good number for you.

It is also possible (for some but not all projects) to conduct what is known as a power analysis. A power analysis is based on the interrelations among four factors: the size of the hypothesized effects, the power of the statistical test to detect effects, the alpha level at which the null hypothesis will be rejected, and the size of the sample. Given knowledge or estimates of the first three factors, it is possible to determine the sample size necessary to demonstrate the expected effects. Cohen (1992) provides a brief and readable introduction to the topic of power analysis.

As with an empirical report, the section that follows the Subjects section depends on the nature of your study. If you plan to include complicated or lengthy apparatus or materials, then an Apparatus or Materials section would be appropriate. If the design of the study is sufficiently complex to warrant separate consideration, then a Design section would be appropriate. If not, you can move directly to Procedure.

Like your Subjects section, your Procedure section should provide all the information that a reader needs to evaluate your study. In Chapter 4 I suggested a default rule with respect to whether to include information in a Procedure section: when in doubt, include. If anything, that rule applies even more strongly to a proposal than to an empirical report. It is your intended procedures that provide the main basis for evaluating your project; you need to be sure, therefore, to provide the reader with all the necessary information.

As with an empirical report, this admonition does not mean that the Procedure section should be crowded with minutiae that no one needs to know. And as in an empirical report, it does not mean that every procedure or measure must be described in full. Often measures are drawn from those used in previous research, and in such instances a brief description or example, coupled with citation of the original source, may be sufficient.

There is a further point here. When possible, measures *should* be drawn from those used in previous research. Why invent something anew if a satisfactory version already exists? Several arguments can be given in favor of use of established measures. First, in such instances the validity and reliability of the measures have already been established, saving you from the need to demonstrate these properties as part of your project. The appearance of a measure in the literature, especially if it has appeared frequently, is an indication of its acceptance by the field, and this acceptance makes a positive response to your research more likely. Finally, comparison of your results with those of others is easiest when the same measures have been used.

Of course, use of established measures is not always either possible or desirable. If one goal of your project is to create a new measure, then obviously you cannot simply redo what has already been done. Also, in some instances there may be no established measure that works for your purposes. Perhaps, for example, the closest existing measure lacks some items that are central to your study, or perhaps the relevant measures have never been adapted for the age group with which you plan to work. Even in such cases, however, your starting point should be whatever existing measures you find that are closest to what you need. From this starting point you can then make whatever modifications or additions are needed. Your Procedure should make clear exactly what is new and what is retained in your proposed adaptation.

Suppose that you do not know in advance exactly how some aspect of the procedure will be handled. There may be instances in which such uncertainty is unavoidable; if so, however, you should indicate how (e.g., pilot testing, analysis of preliminary data) the eventual decision would be made. If your proposal is intended to lead to an actual study, it would be best, if possible, to carry out any necessary pilot testing prior to writing the proposal.

Results and Discussion

Not all faculty members who require a proposal of their students (whether as a course assignment or for a thesis or dissertation) require that the proposal include a Results section. There are, after all, no results to report, and the Introduction and Method clearly constitute the heart of the proposal. Nevertheless, many of us believe that it is useful to include a relatively brief Results (or perhaps Results and Discussion) section as part of a proposal. The point of doing so is not to make up results; such a section will include none of the numbers that populate an actual Results section. The point, rather, is to talk about the *kind* of results that the study would generate and about the forms of statistical analysis that would be used to make sense of the results. For this reason, some faculty members prefer Data Analysis rather than Results as the heading for such a section.

What might the Results section of a proposal look like? I use as an example a study of mine that was briefly discussed in Chapter 4 (Ahn & Miller, 2012). Table 6.3 shows what part of the Results section for a proposal for this study might say. (We did not generate a proposal at the time, and hence the example is an after-the-fact creation.) As can be seen, the attempt is to be as specific as possible about the data that the study would produce and about the statistical analyses that would be applied to the data. Of course at this point it is easy to be specific with respect to the example in the table, given the fact the actual analyses were completed some time ago. The goal of a proposal is to be specific before and not just after the fact—to know what the analyses will be prior to collecting the data and to convey this information clearly to the reader. Indeed, whenever you plan a study, even if you are not writing a proposal, you should think through the statistical analyses carefully in advance. Doing so can ensure that there *will* be an analysis for all the questions of interest, and doing so increases the chances that the most appropriate and powerful analyses will be selected.

As with the Method section, there may be some aspects of the Results that cannot be known in advance. The appropriateness of some analyses may depend on the nature of the data. In particular, so-called parametric tests, such as t-tests and analysis of variance, depend on certain assumptions about the data—for example, that the scores are normally distributed. If aspects of your proposed analyses are contingent in this way, your proposal should specify the possibilities and indicate how a choice will be made among them.

TABLE 6.3   Example A Portion of the Results Section for a Proposal

Children's responses to the false belief questions will be included only if they answer the control questions correctly. The proportion of correct responses will be analyzed via generalized estimating equation (GEE) analyses (Liang & Zeger, 1986; Zeger & Liang, 1986), which is a form of analysis appropriate for a repeated-measures design with dichotomous dependent variables. The predictors will be culture, age, and task, as well as the possible two-way interactions among the three predictors. Significant interactions will be followed up with chi squares.

On the self-concept measure children will earn 1 point for each endorsement of a High statement and 0 points for each endorsement of a Low statement. These scores will be examined in a 2 (age) by 2 (culture) by 4 (self domain) analysis of variance. The follow-up tests of significant effects will be Bonferroni post-hoc pairwise comparisons.

Possible relations among the four dimensions of the self-concept measure will be examined through Pearson correlations. These correlations will be calculated both for the sample as a whole and separately within culture.

Possible relations between the self scores and false belief performance will be examined in three sets of logistic regression analyses, first for the sample as a whole and then separately for the Korean and the American children. The predictors will be age and each of the four self scores.

As in the Results section of an empirical report, the choice of statistical tests does not need to be explained unless the test is unfamiliar or its use is in some way unusual. The example in Table 6.3 cites references for the relatively unfamiliar GEE analyses; the other analyses, however (e.g., ANOVA, Pearson correlations), are well known approaches that require no further explanation.

I noted that you should not make up results. There are two possible exceptions to this rule, however. One is if your instructor requires you to. There are various reasons that he or she might. Generating numbers for all the possible descriptive and inferential outcomes of a study (what Cone & Foster, 2006, refer to as "mock results") forces a researcher to think carefully and specifically about every measure and every analysis that is being proposed, as well as about exactly how the various hypotheses or questions will be examined statistically. Doing so is also good practice for writing the Results section of an empirical report, where, of course, numbers of many sorts will appear and it is not always easy to get the numbers in the correct, APA-style form.

The second possible exception follows from the points just made. Even if you are not required to do so, you may wish to generate a mock results section just for your own benefit. Indeed, Cone and Foster (2006) suggest generating three: one that shows the ideal case in which everything works out as expected, one that shows what a total bust would look like, and one that shows a more realistic mixture of successes and failures. In such a case the with-numbers versions serve as initial drafts; you can then drop the numbers but retain the general structure when you write the final version of the Results.

What about a Discussion section? Again, such a section is not a mandatory component of all proposals, and you need to learn what is expected in your case. My own preference, however, is reflected in the heading for this section: to include some Discussion-like material but to make it a part of a combined Results and Discussion section. Combining the two sections often makes sense when each section in itself would be fairly brief, which is usually true in a proposal. Combining the sections also allows for frequent back-and-forth movement between presentation of a particular analysis and discussion of the possible results and implications of that analysis.

In an empirical report the grist for the Discussion section is obvious: You have all the results from the study to attempt to make sense of. In a proposal the basis for a Discussion is less obvious. The Introduction, after all, has already discussed issues and hypotheses and expectations, and you have no results to add to what was said there. How can you avoid simply repeating what you have already written?

The answer is to make use of information that was *not* in the Introduction. Although the Introduction may have talked some about the proposed measures, it is only in the Method that the reader learns exactly what the measures will be and exactly what sort of scores they will yield. It is only in the Results that the reader learns how these scores will be statistically analyzed and thus how the various hypotheses or questions identified in the Introduction will examined. The discussion of possible outcomes in the Discussion can thus have a degree of specificity not possible in the Introduction—not just (for example) a greater effect of training for older than for younger children but a significant interaction of age and condition on measures X and Y.

A further distinction between the Introduction and Discussion concerns the range of outcomes that are considered. The Introduction, appropriately, will have talked about what you expect to find. Again, the Discussion can revisit these expectations at a more specific level, tying them to the measures and analyses discussed in the Method and Results. But the Discussion should also consider the implication of results that do *not* turn out as expected. What sorts of alternative outcomes are possible? Will an unexpected finding be an interesting outcome in itself, suggesting an answer, albeit a different one from that predicted, to some question of interest? Or will an unexpected finding suggest that some aspect of the method should have been decided differently, and if so, how might future research address this possibility? Because few studies work out exactly as expected, questions such as these are common foci in the Discussion sections of empirical reports. You should attempt to make them part of the Discussion section of any proposal you write. Doing so will help to persuade the reader that you have thought through and are ready to make sense of any outcomes that your study might produce. And if your proposal leads to an actual study, doing so will make you readier to make sense of whatever you do in fact find.

EXERCISES

1. The text suggests that stories in the news can be a source of ideas for research. Spend a week monitoring the news (via newspapers, television, the internet) for possible research topics and record any ideas you have.
2. Another suggestion in the text is to use your everyday experiences as sources for research ideas. Spend a week recording any puzzling or unexpected instances of behavior you encounter (including, if applicable, your own behavior). For each, generate as many kinds of relevant research as you can.
3. Find a recent article in your preferred area of psychology. Working from your university's website for either the Institutional Review Board (if the study was with human subjects) or the Institutional Animal Care and Use Committee (if the study was with animals), prepare the kind of submission for ethical approval that would have preceded the study.
4. As the text notes, recruitment of an appropriate sample is often one of the most difficult steps in research. Imagine that you wished to recruit the following samples: children of immigrant families who are just starting school in the United States, adolescents who have been treated for eating disorders, and spouses of individuals with Alzheimer's disease. In each case, write the section of a research proposal that describes how you would go about identifying and recruiting the sample.

7

Literature Reviews and Term Papers

As its title indicates, this chapter considers two topics. The first and longer section of the chapter is devoted to literature reviews. Literature reviews, like empirical reports and research proposals, are one of the major kinds of writing that psychologists do. It is important, therefore, to know what to look for when reading a literature review, as well as to begin to build the skills that will allow you to write such papers yourself.

The second topic that the chapter addresses is term papers. Term papers are not a kind of writing that psychologists do; they are a task, rather, for budding psychologists—that is, students. As I say when we reach the topic, the variety of forms that term papers can take frustrates any attempt to spell out exactly how to do such writing. Nevertheless, some helpful suggestions can be offered, and that is the goal of the concluding section of the chapter.

LITERATURE REVIEWS

Whatever else they do, almost all papers in psychology include some form of literature review. As we saw in Chapter 4, a review of relevant literature is a central component of the Introduction to an empirical report. If the report takes the form of a thesis or dissertation, then the literature review is likely to be an even fuller and more important part of the final product. And as we have just seen in Chapter 6, literature reviews are also a critical element in research proposals.

In this chapter we consider literature reviews not as components of other types of paper but as stand-alone contributions. As you have probably already discovered in your reading in psychology, literature reviews are in fact a valuable and essential part of the field's scientific literature. The following two passages illustrate this point. The first is from a discussion of literature reviews by Baumeister and Leary (1997).

> Literature reviews serve a scientific field by providing a much-needed bridge between the vast and scattered assortment of articles on a topic and the reader

who does not have time or resources to track them down. Reviews also present conclusions of a scope and theoretical level that individual empirical reports cannot normally address. (p. 311)

And here is the APA *Publication Manual*'s description of literature reviews:

By organizing, integrating, and evaluating previously published research, authors of literature reviews consider the progress of research toward clarifying a problem. In a sense, literature reviews are tutorials, in that authors

- define and clarify the problem;
- summarize previous investigations to inform the reader of the state of research;
- identify relations, contradictions, gaps, and inconsistencies in the literature; and
- suggest the next step or steps in solving the problem. (p. 10)

Literature reviews are of two sorts: narrative reviews and meta-analyses. I defer a discussion of the differences between the two approaches for a later section on meta-analysis. It can be noted, here, however, that narrative reviews are the more longstanding and familiar of the two categories. A narrative review is what you have encountered in any textbook that you have ever read; it is also what is found in the literature review section of the Introduction to an empirical report. It is worth noting also that the two kinds of review are more similar than they are different; in particular, both perform the four tasks identified in the *Manual*'s description, and in part they do so in the same way and are subject to the same sorts of critical evaluation. Our initial coverage will focus on issues and decisions that are common to any form of literature review. Useful further sources include Baumeister and Leary (1997), Bem (1995), Eisenberg (2000), and Galvan (2009).

In what follows I assume that your goal is to write the sort of review paper that might be published in a journal. If you are writing your paper as a course assignment, the expectations may differ in various ways from what is presented here—in terms of the originality of the topic, for example, or the length of the paper, or the amount of literature to be reviewed. As always, it is the instructor's requirements that take precedence.

Choosing a Topic

If you are writing your paper for a course, it is possible that the instructor will have specified the topic that must be reviewed. If not, your first task is to choose a topic for your review.

Chapter 6 discussed the criteria that underlie the choice of topic for a research proposal. Many of the same criteria apply to the selection of a topic for a literature review. Four considerations, in particular, are important. Once again, the topic should be something that interests you. Once again, it should be something that you are ready to handle. A third criterion is that the topic should be neither too large nor too small. Finally, it should not be a topic that has already received a satisfactory review.

As with a research proposal, the argument for the first criterion is twofold. Writing a review paper takes many hours of concentrated effort; putting in the effort will be less onerous (and perhaps even enjoyable) if you have found a topic that you care about it. Furthermore, one of your goals as an author is to persuade the reader that your topic is an interesting and important one, and a good start toward this goal is to work with a topic that you yourself find interesting and important.

The second criterion is also straightforward. As with the research proposal for an intended study, you need to pick a topic that your background has prepared you for. Note, though, that the feasibility criterion applies somewhat differently to the two sorts of project. Because you are not working toward a study that you can actually carry out yourself, any sort of research, no matter how large and challenging, is potentially fair game for a review—cross-cultural studies, longitudinal research, national survey projects, or whatever. Nevertheless, you still need a topic that fits your readiness. It may not make sense, for example, to focus on national survey projects if you have no background in survey construction or survey evaluation. Similarly, you should not choose a topic for which complicated statistics are important if your own statistical abilities are still limited.

What about the third criterion: finding a topic that is the right size? No topic, of course, has a single "right size"; rather, size varies with the context within which the topic is being discussed. The same topic that receives a book-length treatment in a work intended for the specialist might be allocated a single paragraph in a general psychology textbook.

What, then, about a literature review? A rough guideline is that the topic should be one that can be covered satisfactorily in 20 to 40 manuscript pages. The upper bound is probably more flexible. Some topics may require more than 40 pages, and some publication outlets (for example, handbook chapters) may allow more than 40 pages. In the other direction, a paper of fewer than 20 pages may be fine for a course assignment, and if you are in fact writing your paper for a course you should be clear about the expectations for length. Such a paper, however, is unlikely to be "big enough" to constitute a publishable contribution.

I noted that the topic must be one that can be satisfactorily covered in the available space. "Satisfactorily" means that there is sufficient space to provide a full discussion of all of the issues that have been identified as targets for the review, as well as sufficient space to review all of the literature that is relevant to these issues. The amount of relevant literature, in fact, may be the best single index of whether a topic is either too large or too small. If you have found only a half dozen or so relevant sources, then the topic is not yet ready for review. If you have found several hundred or so relevant sources, then the topic needs to be narrowed.

The latter is a more common occurrence. A progressive narrowing of scope is probably the normal course for most literature reviews. Most of us have a number of general topics that interest us, and selection of one of these often provides the starting point for a review. The challenge then becomes to decide on a doable subtopic within the overall area of interest. Chapter 3 discussed ways to use Psyc-Info to narrow and refine an initially overly large topic.

The size of the topic is one determinant of what is doable. Another is the final criterion noted earlier: The topic must be one that has not already received a satisfactory review. This point does not mean that you must find a topic that has never been the subject of a review. What it does mean is that you must find some new perspective on the topic, some way in which your review adds to what was already known. As with the creation of a new study, there are various ways in which a review can be made different from its predecessors. It might focus on a particular age group, for example, or on a particular operationalization of the target construct. It might review the literature from the point of view of a particular theoretical position, or perhaps contrast two theories with respect to the issues under study. If previous reviews of the topic appeared some time ago, it might provide an updated account of the literature, filling in what has happened in the time since the last review was completed. The particular focus will vary across topics and across authors, and the preceding list of possibilities is hardly exhaustive. The point is that there must be something both new and interesting that your review brings to the psychological literature—something that makes it *your* contribution.

The point just made should sound familiar, for it is the same basic point that was made with respect to research proposals. Any paper in psychology should not simply redo what was done before; rather, it should do something new that adds to what was already known. The next section provides a fuller consideration of how literature reviews can meet this goal.

Goals and Contributions

Every literature review has the goal of accurately summarizing some body of knowledge. Beyond this commonality, reviews differ somewhat in their specific goals, and thus also in their potential contributions. In what follows I draw from discussions of this issue by both Baumeister and Leary (1997) and Eisenberg (2000). Table 7.1 lists the goals to be discussed. Note that the distinctions among the goals are not always clear-cut, nor are the goals mutually exclusive; a particular review might make contributions under more than one of the headings.

As noted, an accurate summary of the relevant literature is a starting-point goal for any literature review. To make a genuine contribution, however, a review must do more than simply tabulate the results of existing research—must be more, in short, than simply an annotated bibliography of some collection of studies. As the

TABLE 7.1   Possible Contributions of Literature Reviews

Integration of existing knowledge
Generation of new knowledge
Identification of problems
Theory testing
Theory development

first entry in the table indicates, reviews perform a service to the field through their *integration* of the existing literature. Thus, a successful review does not simply summarize findings; rather, it identifies the important issues for the topic under consideration and organizes findings with respect to what they tell us about these issues. Similarly, a successful review does not simply report conclusions at the level of individual studies; rather, it offers general conclusions that emerge from the literature as a whole—and that are possible only when the entire body of research is taken into account. A successful review, in short, tells us what is known about a particular content area, and in so doing it saves its readers from having to discover this knowledge themselves.

As the second entry in the table indicates, a review is not necessarily limited to the integration of existing knowledge; it may also generate new knowledge. Baumeister and Leary (1997) provide a good discussion of this possibility. As they note, individual studies are necessarily limited in the scope of the conclusions that they can offer. Discussion sections, it is true, typically propose some broader, beyond-the-study extrapolations; any such extensions, however, are tentative and limited (especially since editors and reviewers may frown on too much speculation). In Baumeister and Leary's words, "Any single study will rarely yield enough data that can justify broad conclusions about human nature, human behavior, or the human condition" (p. 313). But broad conclusions are precisely what a good literature review makes possible. The problems that limit generalization from individual studies (a single subject group, a single measurement, a single experimental manipulation) disappear when conclusions are based on the literature as a whole and thus on multiple subject groups, multiple measurements, and multiple manipulations. To quote Baumeister and Leary again, "Without literature reviews, the field might remain permanently unable to answer some of its most fascinating questions" (p. 313).

Just as a review may make clear what we know about a topic, so it may make clear what we do not know. A successful review does not simply report what has been done; rather, it also tells us what has *not* been done—that is, it identifies needed directions for future research. This, of course, is the "Identification of problems" entry in the Table 7.1. The problems may include a lack of needed research—no one has done manipulation X in population Y. Or they may include contradictions or uncertainties in the research that has been done—Researcher A reported one outcome, but Researcher B reported some quite different outcome. Again, the Discussion sections of individual studies typically offer suggestions for future research. Again, however, the greater scope of a literature review makes possible a range of suggestions that go well beyond those that emerge from any individual study.

What about the remaining two entries in the table? Whether theory evaluation is a reasonable goal for a review depends on both the readiness of the reviewer and the nature of the content area, for some topics in psychology are a good deal more theory-driven than are others. For those for which theory *is* important, however, a further possible contribution of a literature review is to evaluate an existing theory or theories in light of the available research evidence. It is true that such an attempt to link theory and evidence is unlikely to be totally new—most authors who propose a theory attempt to embed their ideas in the context of relevant evidence. A literature review, however, is likely to be more all-encompassing in its consideration of the evidence than is a theoretical presentation. Assuming that the reviewer is not also the theorist, it is also likely to be more impartial in its evaluation of what the evidence shows.

Finally, in the case of theory development the researcher moves beyond a consideration of existing theories to develop a new theory of his or her own. The new theory need not be totally original; indeed, it probably will build upon and incorporate aspects of existing theories, perhaps as the culmination of a review directed to an evaluation of current theories. The distinctive aspect of this form of review is that it does not stop at the point of evaluation; rather, it goes on to extend or modify the previous theories in new and substantive ways, thus bringing a new theory into existence. Furthermore, because the new theory emerged from a review of relevant research, it already possesses one desirable quality for a theory, namely, a supportive empirical grounding.

It may be helpful to have an example or two of a review that culminates in the development of a new theory. Here are two examples from one of the field's most prolific authors: Robert Sternberg. In a 1998 article Sternberg proposed a new "balance theory" of wisdom, a theory that grew out of a review of the theoretical and empirical literature on wisdom. Earlier he and a colleague (Sternberg & Lubart, 1991) had developed a new "investment theory" of creativity based on a review of the existing research on creativity.

The goal of theory construction is the most ambitious of those listed in Table 7.1. It may also be the one that is the most rarely achieved; indeed, many of us go through our careers without publishing anything that qualifies as theory development. Theory development is, in any case, not a likely goal for a student paper (although if you are writing such a paper, and you have your instructor's approval, you might try). Still, it may be an *eventual* goal to aim for, assuming that you go on to a career as a psychologist. And in your role as reader rather than writer of psychology, the possibility of discovering a new theory upon its first appearance provides one reason to seek out review articles in your areas of interests.

Possible Problems

How might a literature review go astray? This question is a main focus of both the Baumeister and Leary (1997) and Eisenberg (2000) articles, and again I draw much of what I say from these sources. Table 7.2 lists the points to be discussed.

Incomplete or inaccurate coverage of evidence. Just as an accurate summary of research is an initial goal for any review, a failure to provide such a summary is a first possible problem. A review might fail to meet the accurate-summary goal in either or both of two ways: It may omit some studies that should have been included, or it may misstate the results of some of the studies that it does include. Such errors are certainly understandable—writing a review requires that the author identify, read, understand, and convey the results of dozens if not hundreds of studies, often (as is the case for class papers or theses) within a limited time in which

TABLE 7.2   Possible Problems in Literature Reviews

Incomplete or inaccurate coverage of evidence
Blurring of assertion and evidence
Lack of a critical appraisal
Lack of a clear organizational structure
Focusing on researchers rather than research
Stopping at the present
Lack of a clear take-home message

to complete the task. The fact that the errors are understandable, however, does not make them acceptable. Several of the pieces of advice offered in Chapters 2 and 3 apply here: Allow sufficient time for any writing project; be careful at every phase of the process; use all the resources of the available databases to identify sources; take careful notes when reading sources; and seek help when necessary, including help finding sources and help in the form of feedback on initial drafts of the manuscript.

Errors of any sort are a problem. Errors are especially problematic, however, when they are not random but rather are directional—that is, slanted in favor of a particular conclusion. The writer of a review often has conclusions that he or she wishes to argue for; indeed, a review *should* offer conclusions and not just a compilation of facts. The problem is not in having a particular perspective that the writer presents in the review; the problem is that evidence may be marshaled selectively in favor of this perspective. Perhaps, for example, studies that support the hoped-for conclusions are more likely to be included in the review than studies that do not, or perhaps the supportive findings from a study are given more weight than the nonsupportive ones, or perhaps negative outcomes receive close critical scrutiny whereas positive ones go unquestioned. If so, the review may end up saying more about what the author wishes were true than about what is actually true. The author of an empirical report is required to be objective, honest, and complete in the presentation of his or her results. The same standards apply to the author of a literature review.

The preceding discussion suggests that reviews should be all-inclusive, that is, should include all of the studies that fall within the scope of the review. In most cases they should be—an all-inclusive coverage is clearly most informative, and such an approach ensures that the author is not selectively omitting sources that fail to support some hoped-for conclusion. In some cases, however, including everything is not a reasonable goal. Suppose, for example, that there are a dozen closely related studies that all converge on the same conclusion. In such a case there is little point in taking the space to discuss all 12 studies; two or three "for example" entries may suffice. Or suppose (to take an example from Eisenberg, 2000) that a review is organized around some theoretical model with a number of different facets and that the reviewer wishes to cite evidence with respect to each facet. In such a case an exhaustive coverage of research under each heading would add unnecessary length and would distract from the main point of the paper. Again, a "for example" approach makes more sense.

Although selectivity in the coverage may sometimes be appropriate, the author who opts to omit sources has several responsibilities. First, the studies that *are* included should not be randomly selected from the various possibilities; if only some studies are to be described, it generally makes sense to make them the relatively strong entries from the literature. On the other hand, it is also important that the studies that are included are representative of the larger literature (and not, for example, only the studies with clear-cut findings). Such representativeness, of course, is what the "for example" wording implies. Note that this point means that the reviewer must be familiar with this larger literature, even if some of the sources that he or she has read do not make it into the paper. Finally, it is important to let the reader know that the sampling of sources is intentionally partial rather than complete. More generally, if certain sources are deliberately omitted from a review (e.g., works not available in English, works published prior to a particular date), this restriction should be noted at the outset of the review.

Blurring of assertion and evidence. The next entry in the table, blurring of assertion and evidence, refers to the need to be clear about the basis for any claims from the literature that are reported in the review. Baumeister and Leary (1997) use the following (hypothetical) example of a possible passage that fails in this regard: "women are smarter than men (Brown & Green, 1966)." The wording of the passage leaves an important point unclear: Did Brown and Green merely set forth the claim of female superiority, or did they provide evidence for this assertion? Better wording would be either "Brown and Green proposed that women are smarter than men" (making clear that the first was the case) or "In a sample of middle-aged adults, women scored higher on a test of logical reasoning than men" (making clear that evidence was provided, as well as what the evidence was). Note that the need to distinguish between assertions and evidence does not mean that only the latter should enter into a review. Theoretical proposals are an important part of the field's thinking, as well as frequent catalysts for research, and as such they are legitimate components of any literature review. The point is simply that the assertion of a claim and the evidence for the claim should be clearly distinguished.

The preceding discussion leaves a basic question unanswered. It tells us that evidence-based claims should be identified as such, but it does not say how much detail about the evidence should be provided. Suppose, to return to Baumeister and Leary's (1997) example, that the second possible wording had been "Brown and Green showed in their research that women are smarter than men." This sort of wording is on the minimal side; it makes clear that research supported the claim in question but does not tell us *how* the research did so. In the other direction, a detailed description of every study included in a review would make clear the basis for any conclusions, at the expense, however, of producing a book-length rather than article-length manuscript.

So what is an author to do? Several considerations can guide the decision about how much detail to provide. First, in any study there are three basic questions: Who (who were the subjects?), How (how were they studied?), and What (what were the results)? As the Brown and Green example shows, it is often possible to answer all three questions in a single sentence; at the most, a few sentences should suffice. Second, in any review some sources are more important than others, and any at all detailed descriptions should be saved for the more important sources. Third, often some methodological element is common across a number of the studies being reviewed—perhaps the same kinds of subjects, for example, or the same experimental manipulation, or the same operationalization of the dependent variable. In such cases a single description at the start of a section can suffice, coupled with an indication that the remaining studies took the same approach. Indeed, in some cases several similar studies can be covered in the same sentence. Finally, the default rule in this case is one that we have seen before: When in doubt, provide more information rather than less. You necessarily will still ask your readers to take some points on faith, given the impossibility of documenting all of the evidence for every assertion in the paper. Still, as Eisenberg (2000, p. 24) says, "You do not want your paper to have a 'Trust me' feel to it."

Lack of a critical appraisal. An elaboration of the Brown and Green example can serve to introduce the next entry in the table. Let us assume that their claim was an evidence-based one, and let us assume also that the second way of wording the claim ("In a sample of . . .") is sufficiently detailed to show its basis. Imagine, though, that the test of logical reasoning they used was of doubtful validity or that the women in their sample were more highly educated than the men. These problems do not necessarily invalidate the research, but they certainly suggest cautions in accepting its conclusions. Most readers of a review, however, will not be familiar with the original source, and thus they will know about the cautions only if the author of the review shares this information. And this brings us to the next possible problem in a literature review: failure to adopt a critical-evaluative approach to the work being reviewed. Your job as a reviewer is not simply to report what authors have claimed; it is to indicate what the research in fact shows.

Again, the length limitations of any review pose a challenge—you simply do not have space for a detailed critique of every study included in the review. Again, however, you can set priorities, focusing more on studies that are central to your conclusions than on those that are more peripheral. Again, you can group related studies; if the same critical point applies to some set of similar studies, you need make the point just once. Finally, even though a "critique" is not necessarily negative, you can be mostly one-directional in the evaluations you offer. There is no need to lavish praise on studies that you evaluate positively; the fact that you present their conclusions without qualification is praise enough. It is the studies with problems that are most in need of critical attention.

Baumeister and Leary (1997) make a further important point. Sometimes the weaknesses of one set of studies are offset by the strengths of some other set of studies. Self-report measures, for example, are subject to various forms of bias, and we might therefore be cautious about any conclusions that are based solely on self-report. Suppose, however, that the same conclusions emerge when other measurement operations are used—objective tests, for example, or perhaps physiological indices. In this case the problems of self-report recede in importance (as, indeed, do the problems of the other two approaches), because we know that conclusions are not tied to a single methodology. Similarly, a well-known limitation of correlational studies is the inability to demonstrate cause-and-effect relations; such studies can show that variables X and Y are related, but they cannot show that X causes Y. Suppose, however, that the research on some topic includes not only correlational research but also experimental studies in which manipulation of X is shown to produce changes in Y. The experimental demonstrations of X's causal efficacy make the causal interpretation of the correlational findings a good deal more plausible.

The use of multiple methodological approaches to study a particular topic is known as converging operations. The value of converging operations is a basic point in research methodology. Because any single approach has limitations, we can have the greatest confidence when multiple approaches converge on the same conclusion. Although individual studies can sometimes include more than one approach (e.g., two or three different ways to measure the dependent variable), any single study is limited in what it can show. Because they encompass the research literature as a whole, literature reviews are uniquely suited to identify instances of converging operations.

Lack of a clear organizational structure. The next possible problem is one that numerous authors have discussed (Baumeister & Leary, 1997; Bem, 1995; Eisenberg, 2000). It concerns an important question: What is the best way to organize a review? The answer, as we will see, is that there is not a single best way to organize a review but there may be a worst way. Probably the simplest organizational system is the one-study-per-paragraph approach—a paragraph on what Smith found, followed by a paragraph on what Jones found, and so forth. Eisenberg (2000, p. 27) refers to reviews organized in this fashion as "being written like an undergraduate paper." She does not mean this as a compliment.

What are the problems with the one-study-per-paragraph approach? To begin with, such an approach is likely to be boring, given the unvarying organizational structure, and it is likely to result in an unnecessarily long paper, given the fact that not every study is worth a full paragraph. Beyond these problems, the one-study-per-paragraph approach essentially abrogates the task of organization, for all the author is doing is giving back a version of whatever note cards he or she compiled when searching the literature. The task for the author of a literature review is to identify the important issues for the topic under consideration and to present conclusions with respect to these issues. Thus it is issues, not studies, that should provide the organizational framework.

As an example of the organizational possibilities, let us imagine a review directed to the question of whether perspective taking relates to prosocial behavior in children. Because there are multiple forms of perspective taking, one way to organize the review would be in terms of the different kinds of perspective taking—thus sections on cognitive perspective taking, affective perspective taking, and so forth. This approach would make sense if possible differences among the various forms are a main focus of the review. It may be, however, that a main focus is on possible differences across various kinds of prosocial behavior. In this case we might have a section on sharing, a section on comforting, a section on help giving, and so forth. Whatever the specific forms of perspective taking and prosocial behavior, possible developmental differences are likely to be of interest. Another organizational possibility, therefore, would be to group in terms of age period—thus a section on preschoolers, another on grade schoolers, and another on adolescents. Finally, some of the studies in the literature will have taken a correlational approach, measuring and looking for relations between perspective taking and prosocial behavior, whereas others will have taken an experimental approach, training perspective-taking skills and then measuring possible effects on prosocial behavior. Another possibility, therefore, would be to organize by design—thus a section on correlational studies and a section on experimental studies.

Note that the decision about organization is not an all-or-nothing one; some sections can be embedded within other, more general sections. A paper might, for example, be organized in terms of design but also contain separate subsections for different measures or different age groups nested under the design headings. Note also that the stricture against the one-study-per-paragraph approach does not mean that such paragraphs can never appear. Major sources, in particular, may deserve their own paragraph or even more than one paragraph. The point is simply that the paper should not be organized in terms of individual studies.

The main implication of the advice to focus on research rather than researchers is the organizational one just discussed. But this point also has an expositional implication, that is, an implication for how research is presented. For the most part, names of researchers should be confined to parentheses rather than appearing as part of the text. Thus rather than "Smith (2010) found that cognitive perspective taking was especially predictive for preschoolers," write "Cognitive perspective taking is especially predictive for preschoolers (Smith, 2010)." There are, of course, exceptions to this rule; in some instances a focus on a particular author is desirable, for example, when a seminal study is being discussed or when particular theorists are being contrasted. In general, however, the names-in-parentheses rule is a good one—"a valuable stylistic device for ensuring that the article focuses on ideas and research rather than on theorists and researchers" (Baumeister & Leary, 1997, p. 320).

I realize that the points made across the preceding paragraphs fall in the easier-said-than-done category. Once again, an important piece of advice is to read psychology before writing psychology—in this case, to read published reviews to see how they have handled the expositional challenges just discussed. Table 7.3 presents one example, taken from a recent review in *Psychological Bulletin* that I return to later to illustrate a further point. Note how the focus remains on issues and conclusions rather than individual researchers and studies. Note also how a dozen or so studies are summarized within the space of just three paragraphs.

Stopping at the present. What about the "Stopping at the present" entry in the table? In a sense, of course, any review must stop at the present, there being no more research to review. The point of the entry is that there *will* be more research eventually, and one contribution of a review is to suggest the directions that such research should take. Recall that suggestions for future research are also a possible contribution of the Discussion section of an empirical report. A review article,

TABLE 7.3   Example of How to Summarize Multiple Studies Briefly and With a Focus on Issues Rather Than Researchers

Early ritualized infant-caregiver interactions are powerful emotional bonding events (Bruner, 1999; Stern, 1985; Tronick, 1981). Infants become emotionally bonded to their caregivers and to the social rules they embody. This is critical to effective norm transmission because norms are not cold, detached rules of conduct. They are emotionally charged behavioral "oughts" that people are intrinsically motivated to follow. The deep emotional bonding present in infant-caregiver interactions is an outgrowth of our species' unique capacity for cognitive and emotional sharing. Among humans, infant-caregiver interactions involve both proto-conversational "turn taking" and joint attention (where infant and caregiver share attention on a third object such as a toy). These features are very likely unique to humans. Evidence for both joint attention and proto-conversation in nonhuman apes is weak (Bard & Vauclair, 1984; M. Carpenter, Tomasello, & Savage-Rumbaugh, 1995; Tomonaga et al., 2004). While infant chimpanzees can follow another's gaze (Okamoto et al., 2002), their ability to translate this into bouts of joint attention or proto-conversation is limited at best, possibly nonexistent (M. Carpenter et al., 1995; Tomasello & Carpenter, 2005; however, see Plooij, 1984, p. 142).
The behavioral turn taking found in proto-conversation involves interpersonal synchrony where gestures and vocalizations are coordinated in time. Greater interpersonal behavioral synchrony has been shown to create positive emotions between participants (Hove & Risen, 2009). The positive emotions generated within ritualized infant-caregiver interactions are but one element of a larger uniquely human cognitive/emotional sharing that also includes shared attention, intentions, and goals (Tomasello, Carpenter, Call, Behne, & Moll, 2005).

Note. From "The Essential Role of Ritual in the Transmission and Reinforcement of Social Norms," by M. J. Rossano, 2012, *Psychological Bulletin, 138,* pp. 535–536. Copyright 2012 by the American Psychological Association. Reprinted by permission.

however, can generally be more expansive in this regard—not only is there more space to work with, but the suggestions can grow out of the entire research literature and not just the literature surrounding a particular study. This was the point made earlier in the discussion of the "Identification of problems" entry in Table 7.1. As with any suggestions that a Discussion section might offer, the suggestions will be most helpful if they are specific rather than general—thus not just "more research is needed" but "theory X needs to be tested with method Y in population Z."

Lack of a clear take-home message. The final entry in the table has perhaps been prefigured by much of the discussion to this point. We have seen that a review should not be simply a recitation of one study and one finding after another. A review should identify the important issues for the topic under consideration, it should organize the discussion in terms of these issues, it should provide general conclusions when general conclusions are available and directions for further study when they are not, and it should make clear to readers why they should care about the issues being discussed. A review should, in short, present a clear take-home message—it should be clear what the review is *about.* Bem (1995) puts this point colorfully: "Authors of literature reviews are at risk for producing mind-numbing lists of citations and findings that resemble a phone book—impressive cast, lots of numbers, but not much plot" (p. 172).

Baumeister and Leary (1997) add a further point. Authors should not wait until the end of the paper to present their take-home message; rather, readers should be aware of the main themes of the review from the opening pages. In their words, "Few readers can manage to wade through 50 pages of text and dozens of facts and findings before learning what the point is" (p. 316). Although authors should not leave their take-home message until the end, they should definitely return to it at the end, at which point it can be tied to lines of research reviewed throughout the paper. Thus, the "end strong" advice given with respect to empirical reports applies to literature reviews as well. Table 7.4 provides some examples of strong endings, taken from the concluding paragraphs of three recent articles in *Psychological Bulletin*. The first example concerns firstborn children's adjustment following the birth of a sibling, the second has to do with changes in people's social networks across adulthood, and the third is from a review addressing the role

TABLE 7.4 Examples of Concluding Paragraphs From Literature Reviews

As already noted, the arrival of a newborn sibling is a normative life event for many children. The period surrounding this transition may be stressful for some children and their parents. Yet, individual differences seem to dominate the older siblings' reactions to the birth of their baby siblings. Because familial, individual, and contextual changes co-occur with the arrival of an infant sibling, it will be important for future studies to address how these changes are interrelated over time, what influences the firstborns' acceptance of their newborn siblings, and what parents can do to facilitate the development of a healthy sibling relationship—one of the longest lasting relationships of an individual's life. (Volling, 2012, p. 524)

In conclusion, the current meta-analysis shows that people's networks of social relationships change from adolescence to adulthood to old age, and these changes are similar to changes related to experiencing age-specific life events. At the same time, a stable convoy of family relationships and few close confidants accompanies people through positive and negative life events and as they grow older. The study should equip the reader with two things: (a) an answer on the initial questions of what the typical size of networks is and how it changes over the life span, and (b) first insights into how social network development relates to and informs other disciplines. (Wrzus, Hänel, Wagner, & Neyer, 2013, p. 71)

An important implication of this view is that the evolutionary foundation upon which our hominin ancestors built uniquely human levels of social organization and cooperation was not language but controlled motor movements expressed in ritual. Before language could articulate the behaviors and attitudes morally valued by a group, intentional rule-based behavior was doing so (this is true both ontogenetically and phylogenetically). Language gains or loses its credibility as a norm transmitter by its relation to intentional action. Language can specify, codify, and allow for the analysis of normative content, but ritual enacts the values of which the norms are composed. Thus, all the research herein reviewed can be reduced to one very general and simple prediction: The strongest human communities will always be those with the richest ritual lives. (Rossano, 2012, p. 544)

Note. From "Family Transitions Following the Birth of a Sibling: An Empirical Review of Changes in the Firstborn's Adjustment," by B. L. Volling, 2012, *Psychological Bulletin, 138,* p. 524. Copyright 2012 by the American Psychological Association. Reprinted by permission. From "Social Network Changes and Life Events Across the Life Span: A Meta-Analysis," by C. Wrzus, M. Hänel, J. Wagner, and F. J. Neyer, 2013, *Psychological Bulletin, 139,* p. 71. Copyright 2013 by the American Psychological Association. Reprinted by permission. From "The Essential Role of Ritual in the Transmission and Reinforcement of Social Norms," by M. J. Rossano, 2012, *Psychological Bulletin, 138,* p. 544. Copyright 2012 by the American Psychological Association. Reprinted by permission.

of ritual and ritualized behaviors in the transmission of social norms. In no case does the concluding paragraph convey everything that a reader should take away from the review—no single paragraph could. But each reiterates some of the most important themes that make up the overall take-home message.

This section has been organized in terms of various problems that may occur in literature reviews. As a complement to this emphasis on things not to do, I conclude the section by noting some of the positive points that should be taken away from the discussion—qualities to aim for when writing a literature review. A literature review should provide a comprehensive, accurate, and unbiased account of the literature that falls within its scope. In doing so, it should draw clear distinctions between assertion and evidence, and it should provide sufficient detail so that the reader knows what the evidence is. It should maintain a critical-evaluative orientation throughout, not just reporting what has been claimed to be the case but offering the author's own evaluation of what in fact *is* the case. It should offer general conclusions when such conclusions are available, and it should specify needed directions for future research when conclusions are not yet possible. It should adopt a clear organizational structure, grouping material in terms of issues and findings rather than in terms of individual studies. Finally, it should offer a clear take-home message, making clear from the outset the major themes of the paper and reiterating these themes at the end.

Meta-Analysis

Narrative reviews have been around since the dawn of psychology. Meta-analyses are a development of the past 30 or so years.

I will begin this section by noting that a meta-analysis is not a likely option for a student paper. Nor is meta-analysis an option for the literature review section of an empirical report, even the lengthy reviews that may appear in theses or dissertations. Meta-analyses are written as stand-alone contributions intended for publication. The purpose of discussing them here is not to teach you to write a meta-analysis; considerably more space and detail would be necessary to accomplish that goal. I do hope, however, to help you to read meta-analyses, for such reviews are becoming an increasingly important part of the field's scientific literature. Figure 7.1 provides a dramatic illustration of this point. In addition, writing a meta-analysis may be a future goal, and the discussion here is intended to be a helpful starting point should you ever embark on the task. Among the sources for further reading are APA Publications and Communications Board Working Group on Journal Article Reporting Standards (2008); Cooper, 2009; Cooper, Civey, and Robinson (2006); Humphrey, 2011; Rosenthal (1995); and Rosenthal and DiMatteo (2001). Note also that there is a journal devoted to meta-analysis: *Research Synthesis Methods*. Note too that one of the sample papers in the *Manual* shows a portion of a meta-analysis.

What is a meta-analysis? A brief definition is that a meta-analysis is a quantitative approach to literature reviews. Rosenthal (1995, p. 183) provides a fuller definition:

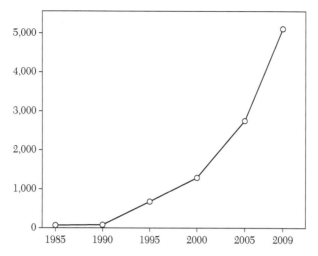

Figure 7.1   Number of meta-analyses per year from 1985 to 2009. From "Meta-Analysis in Developmental Science," by M. H. van IJzendoorn, M. J. Bakermans-Kranenberg, and L. R. A. Alink, 2012. In B. Laursen, T. D. Little, and N. A. Card (Eds.), *Handbook of Developmental Research Methods*, p. 669. New York, NY: Guilford Press. Copyright 2012 by Guilford Press. Reprinted with permission.

> Meta-analytic reviews are quantitative summaries of research domains that describe the typical strength of the effect or phenomenon, its variability, its statistical significance, and the nature of the moderator variables from which one can predict the relative strength of the effect or phenomenon.

I will pick up on the components of this definition as we go.

Steps in a meta-analysis. In discussing meta-analysis it is helpful to draw comparisons with the empirical report of an individual study, for there are in fact a number of parallels.

If you are carrying out a study, one of your first tasks is to identify and recruit your sample of subjects. Identifying and obtaining a sample is also an early step in a meta-analysis—in this case, however, the sample of studies that will be included in the review. Of course, the author of a narrative review must also begin by locating relevant studies. The attempt in a meta-analysis, however, is to take a more objective and more inclusive approach to literature search than is typical in a narrative review, as well as to share the information about the search with the reader. Table 7.5 provides an example of a typical Study Selection section for a meta-analysis, one that is drawn from one of the reviews whose concluding paragraphs were given in Table 7.3.

One aspect of the search procedure described in the example is worth singling out. Included in the review were not only published sources but also a large number of unpublished dissertations. An attempt to identify and incorporate unpublished sources is a feature of most meta-analyses. The argument for doing so is to guard

TABLE 7.5 Example of Information About Identification of Sources for a Meta-Analysis

An extensive literature search was conducted in 2008–2009 and updated in 2012 using the databases PsycINFO, Web of Science/Social SciSearch, Science Direct, Psychology and Behavioral Science Collection (including Dissertation Abstracts via EBSCO), and also PSYNDEX to retrieve German publications. No restriction was set regarding the earliest year of publication. Furthermore, we searched in the journal Social Networks for studies from 1978 to 2012. We used a routine procedure of two steps. First, we looked for publications on social networks, excluding neurological networks. Keywords were network, personal network, and social relationship with exclusion terms mind, brain, semantic, and neural. Second, we searched for publications focusing on social networks and life events. For this search we combined keywords for networks (network, personal network, social relationship, and close relationship) and life events (life-event, normative transition, transition, puberty, marriage, parenthood, entering work life, retirement, widowhood, death, divorce, relocation, and move), yielding 48 combinations in all. English and German terms were used.
This search yielded 5,423 hits, from which we read abstracts to decide on the suitability for the aims of the meta-analyses. This preselection resulted in 916 articles, 68 books or book chapters, and 126 dissertations to read. From these, we excluded 702 articles, 65 books or book chapters, and 71 dissertations from the final analyses because

1. they did not report statistics on either network size or age of sample (k = 285 articles, k = 55 books, k = 18 dissertations), or
2. they did not assess any kind of social network because they focused, for example, on parent–child relationships (k = 277 articles, k = 8 books, k = 30 dissertations), or
3. they focused on unsuitable samples, such as psychiatric patients or animal samples (k = 140 articles, k = 2 books, k = 23 dissertations).

For dissertations not retrievable through ProQuest or the Internet, we tried to contact the authors and found no contact information (k = 18) because the dissertations dated back to 1969, or did not receive an answer (k = 28). This left 214 articles, three books, and nine dissertations to code, which amounted to 277 studies. The number of studies slightly exceeded the number of sources because some articles and books reported on more than one study or sample. They were therefore included as separate studies.

Note. From "Social Network Changes and Life Events Across the Life Span: A Meta-Analysis," by C. Wrzus, M. Hänel, J. Wagner, and F. J. Neyer, 2013, *Psychological Bulletin, 139,* p. 57. Copyright 2013 by the American Psychological Association. Reprinted with permission.

against possible bias. It seems reasonable to predict (and for some topics there is supporting evidence) that published studies are more likely to report significant effects than are unpublished studies; that is one reason that the former have been published and the latter have not. Including only published studies in a review could therefore lead to overestimation of the certainty or the size of effects.

As the preceding paragraph reminds us, determination of statistical significance is a basic issue in an individual study. Determination of statistical significance is also an issue in a meta-analysis. In a meta-analysis, however, statistical procedures can span the entire research literature, which means that tests for significance can be based on dozens or perhaps hundreds of studies rather than just one. Because of this broader scope, a meta-analysis has considerably greater statistical power than does an individual study and therefore a greater chance of detecting genuine effects (Cohn & Becker, 2003).

We saw that in an individual study determination of significance is often just an initial step; also of interest is the size of any effects that are obtained. Effect sizes are also a basic issue in a meta-analysis—indeed, are what Rosenthal and DiMatteo (2001, p. 70) label "the chief coins of the meta-analytic realm." Again, however, a meta-analysis allows us to move beyond a single value based on a single sample to an average of dozens or hundreds of effect size values. We can be much more confident, therefore, that we really have identified the strength of the relation between the particular independent and dependent variables under study.

Although various measures of effect size exist, the measures group into two general "families" (Rosnow & Rosenthal, 2009). One family is based on differences between the means being compared. Chapter 5 discussed one such measure: Cohen's d, which is the difference between means divided by their standard deviation. The other family consists of effect size measures derived from correlational relations. Most commonly used is the Pearson r, which is a direct measure of the strength of a relation between two variables; it is thus one of the most immediate and interpretable measures of effect size. If desired, mean differences can be converted to r or vice versa.

In addition to establishing the existence and size of an effect, a third goal of most individual studies is to explore factors that might influence the nature or extent of any effects that are identified. In other words, what other variables influence the results? This is also a goal of meta-analysis. The usual starting point is the discovery that there is variation in the magnitude of effect sizes across studies. Such variation suggests the operation of so-called *moderator variables*—that is, variations among studies that are affecting the results. Further analyses then test for the effects of possible moderator variables. We might test, for example, to see whether effects vary for children compared to adults, or in cross-sectional comparisons compared to longitudinal, or for one operationalization of the dependent variable compared to another.

In most cases moderator variables will be ones that were examined in individual studies. They need not be, however. Even if no study has included a cross-country comparison, we could test for possible variations across countries, assuming that different countries appear in the literature as a whole. Indeed, a meta-analysis can examine variables that not only were not examined in individual studies but *could* not be examined in individual studies. For example, we might test to see whether results vary as a function of the date of publication of the research or the sex of the principal investigator (both factors that *have* proved important in some meta-analyses). Neither factor could be examined in an individual study; it is easy, however, to incorporate them in a meta-analysis.

Challenges. A first point under this heading is that not all research domains lend themselves to meta-analysis. A meta-analysis is feasible only if a number of studies have taken a quantitative approach to the same research question, have done so in ways that are similar enough to permit aggregation, and have provided the kinds of data that a meta-analysis requires. For research areas that do not meet these conditions, a narrative review is the only option. Van IJzendoorn and colleagues (van IJzendoorn, Bakermans-Kranenberg, & Alink, 2012) provide a fuller discussion of this issue.

A second point concerns the statistics required to do a meta-analysis. At the least, anyone embarking on a meta-analysis is committing to do a considerable amount of statistical work. Not only must every study be scoured for the necessary statistical information, but in some cases the meta-analyst may have to calculate values (e.g., effect sizes) not included in the original report. Various decisions must be made at various points in the process, and in some instances the statistics can get complicated. On the other hand, for many meta-analyses the statistics are not necessarily complicated—or at least no more complicated than those found in the Results section of an individual study. Rosenthal and DiMatteo (2001) warn against taking an overly complicated approach to a meta-analysis, with respect to statistics or any other dimension. In their words, "The simpler a meta-analysis, the more likely it is to be accurate; it is not possible to present one that is too simple" (p. 68).

A final point is that the statistics are important but not all-important. This is a point that Eisenberg (2000) makes. As she notes, some authors seem to feel that their work is done once they have located studies, carried out analyses, and reported the resulting values for statistical significance, effect sizes, and moderator variables. In fact, at that point they have produced the Method and Results section for their paper. Just as in the report of an individual study, these middle sections must be accompanied by an Introduction that spells out the rationale for the research and a Discussion that presents the general conclusions that the reader should take away. In this respect, of course, a meta-analysis resembles not just an empirical report but also a narrative review. The empirical facts are part of the story, but there must also be a compelling narrative and a clear take-home message.

Possible problems. What about possible criticisms of meta-analysis? There *have* been criticisms, and the most common objections can be summarized in three phrases (Sharpe, 1997): "apples and oranges," "garbage in, garbage out," and the "file drawer problem."

The first phrase ("apples and oranges") refers to the charge that meta-analyses lump together studies that are too disparate to be classified together—perhaps, for example, several quite different operationalizations of a particular independent variable. The result would be what is always the case when either the independent variable or dependent variable is inadequately specified: uncertainty about exactly what has been found.

The "garbage in, garbage out" criticism is perhaps self-explanatory. It refers to the criticism that meta-analyses take an uncritically egalitarian approach to research synthesis, weighting bad studies equally with good.

Finally, the "file drawer" problem refers to the issue of publication bias mentioned earlier. The criticism is that meta-analyses concentrate mainly on published studies, and thus miss the mostly nonsignificant unpublished outcomes that reside in researchers' file drawers.

Proponents of meta-analysis offer two general replies to these criticisms. The first reply is that the problems are not unique to meta-analysis—narrative reviews also may group studies inappropriately, may fail to adjust for quality, and may distort the literature by an overemphasis on published work. Indeed, at least for the last of these issues, meta-analyses are probably less susceptible to the criticism than are narrative reviews.

The second reply is that the problems are not intrinsic to meta-analysis. Thus a well-executed meta-analysis will group studies appropriately, will weight studies with respect to quality, and will incorporate unpublished as well as published work. How successfully these goals are achieved in particular cases can still be debated, of course. Rating of quality is a challenging enterprise, and it is probably never possible to find all of the unpublished work on a topic. Still, the general argument seems reasonable.

Some General Points

Apart from some of the specifics in the discussion of empirical reports in Chapters 4 and 5, almost everything that has been said to this point in the book applies as well to the topic of literature reviews. I will single out just a few points for reiteration here.

One is the need for headings that organize the manuscript. The opening and closing sections of a literature review are the same as those for an empirical report: title page and abstract at the start, references and (if needed) tables and figures at the end. As we saw, in the body of an empirical report the basic division into parts (Introduction, Method, etc.) follows a standard template, although there are still decisions to make about further divisions within the parts. There is no standard template for literature reviews, however. It is true that the opening and closing sections tend to be roughly analogous to those in an empirical report: a general overview of the topic at the beginning and some general conclusions at the end. The movement from beginning to end, however, depends on the topic and the author and thus takes different forms across different reviews. The common element is the need for headings to help the reader understand the organizational structure and the sequence of movement from one topic to the next.

I can provide some data with respect to headings, drawn from the reviews quoted in Table 7.3. Summing across all levels of heading, the Volling (2012) article used 50 headings in 21 journal pages of text, the Rossano (2012) article used 18 headings in 16 pages, and the Wrzus et al. (2013) article used 34 headings in 18 pages. As these examples suggest, if you find yourself writing several pages without a heading, you may want to rethink your organizational plan.

A second point is related. Headings are of limited use if they do not reflect a coherent organizational structure. Deciding on the most effective organization for the paper may be the most challenging task that the author of a literature review faces. Even if you (like me) do not find outlines necessary for much of your writing, you may want to consider an outline if you are writing a literature review. At the least, some careful planning, whatever form it takes, should precede any serious attempt to get words down on paper. It may also be helpful, once a draft is completed, to generate the kind of reverse outline that was discussed in Chapter 2. Doing so is a way to check whether you yourself find your organizational structure a clear and satisfying one. Your positive evaluation does not guarantee a similar response from the reader; it should, however, make it more likely.

Headings are one way to break up a lengthy string of text. Tables and figures are another. Of course, the main reason for including a table or figure is not simply to break up text; it is to convey material that is most effectively and efficiently conveyed in that format. For almost any literature review, there will be such material—typically material for which tables are appropriate, but occasionally uses for figures as well (Figure 7.1 is one example). One of the exercises at the end of the chapter is directed to the question of when and how to use tables in a literature review. If you find that you have written a review with no tables, reread and rethink—there almost certainly will be places where the presentation would benefit from the inclusion of a table.

A final general point concerns the need to acknowledge any limitations or uncertainties in the arguments being presented. We saw in the discussion of empirical reports that such an acknowledgement should be a part of any Discussion section. It should also be part of any literature review. It may be, of course, that some of the general conclusions you offer are so firmly supported that they can be presented without qualification. Often, however, this will not be the case—there will be some contradiction in the literature, some uncertainty in interpretation, some research step not yet taken. You owe it to the reader to share any such gaps and uncertainties. And as with an empirical report, there is also a pragmatic reason for such honesty: It is better to present any limitations yourself than it is to let readers discover them on their own.

TERM PAPERS

Unlike the other kinds of writing considered in this book, term papers do not have a common goal or a common format. A term paper, rather, is whatever your Psychology professor says it is. Table 7.6 lists some of the most frequently occurring forms that term papers take. As a running example, the table uses the Milgram obedience research, one of the "classic studies" quoted in Table 4.3.

The list of forms provided in the table is hardly exhaustive. For one thing, variants are possible for any of the types listed. A book review, for example, might

TABLE 7.6   Types of Term Paper (With the Milgram Obedience Research as an Example)

Type	Example
Historical figure	Write an account of Milgram's life and career.
Classic study	Write a summary and critique of the Milgram obedience study.
Book review	Write an evaluative review of Milgram's book *Obedience to Authority: An Experimental View* (Milgram, 1974).
Literature review	Write a review of research inspired by the Milgram study.
Research proposal	Propose a study to address some unresolved issue in the obedience literature.
Research report	Report a study of your own directed to some issue in the obedience literature.

take a comparative approach, comparing two or more books directed to the same subject. Any article of interest, and not just a "classic study," might serve as the basis for a critique. Furthermore, various kinds of papers that appear on course syllabi are not listed in the table. Miller and Lance (2006), for example, include 12 different types of papers in their compilation, a list that overlaps only in part with the one provided here. Both they and other authors, I should note, include some kinds of assignment that I do not attempt to discuss. Collaborative group projects are one example. Oral presentations in class are another.

In what follows I offer various pieces of advice with respect to how to write a term paper. The most important piece of advice, however, is the first one offered: Know your requirements. Because "term paper" can mean so many different things, it is critical to be clear about what your instructor means by the term. Read the requirements carefully when they are first announced (presumably on the course syllabus), ask questions if anything is not clear, and ask further questions if necessary as you work on the paper.

Choosing a Topic

As with any paper, the first step is to choose a topic. This assumes, of course, that the instructor has not specified the topic for you, something that may be more likely for a term paper than for the other kinds of writing that I consider. If you are told to write a review paper on "aggression in preschoolers," then clearly that is the paper you will write.

Note that there are two decisions to be made when setting out to write a term paper. One is the topic, such as aggression in preschoolers. The other is the type of paper that will be written to address the topic. The example in the preceding paragraph was of a review paper. But you might instead write a review of a book directed to preschool aggression, or propose a study to examine the topic, or report an actual study based on your observations at a local preschool. Sometimes an instructor will specify one but not the other of these components. Perhaps you will be told to write about preschool aggression, but the type of paper will be left up to you. More commonly, perhaps, the instructor might specify the format (write a book review, propose a study, etc.) but let you decide on the particular topic.

To the extent that the topic is under your control, the same strategies for coming up with an idea that were discussed in Chapter 6 apply here as well. Because term papers, unlike other papers, are always written as part of an ongoing course, the course material that most intrigues you is one obvious source for ideas. In any case, you will need a topic that fits the particular course—thus a paper on clinical psychology if you are taking a clinical psychology course, a paper on developmental psychology if the course is developmental psychology, and so forth.

Once you have generated some possible topics, the same criteria for evaluating your ideas that were discussed in both Chapter 6 and earlier in this chapter apply. Again, the topic should be one that interests you. Not only will the effort that you put in be more enjoyable if you care about the topic, but you are also more likely to achieve one of the goals of any psychology paper: namely, convincing others that the topic is an interesting and important one. Again, the topic should be one that you are ready to handle. If you discover on your initial foray into a topic that you are awash in theoretical complexities or high-powered statistics, then you probably should select a different topic—or at least a different aspect of that particular topic.

The size of the topic is again important. Probably the most common error is selection of a topic that is too large to cover in the available time and space, both of which are typically limited in a term paper. A paper on aggression would clearly be in the too-large category, as would a paper on aggression in childhood. Preschool aggression is more thinkable, although even here some further delimiting (e.g., types of aggression in the preschool, gender differences in preschool aggression) would be possible. Chapter 3 talked about how to use PsycInfo to narrow an initially overly large topic. Note that your instructor or teaching assistant can also be helpful in this regard. So can your textbook. If you are interested in aggression, for example, a glance at the relevant pages in the text should give you a good idea of the subtopics that fall under this heading.

Still not addressed is one of the criteria that was discussed for all of the types of papers considered to this point: namely, originality. Any paper should not simply duplicate what has been done before; rather, there should be some original element that is the author's contribution. A term paper should also be original in the sense that it should reflect your own effort and thinking and writing. The expectations with regard to the novelty of the contribution, however, are likely to be lower than is the case for the other kinds of writing that I discuss. Term papers are typically among the first forms of writing that students do, and they almost always are written under limitations of both time and length. No instructor expects a publishable contribution under such circumstances. Still, you should aim high, trying, as far as possible given the constraints of time and readiness, to apply the points discussed across the last several chapters. Doing so should reward not only your immediate effort but also your future writing in psychology.

Types of Paper

I have already discussed three of the types of paper listed in Table 7.6 at length, and I will not repeat those discussions here. I will note again, however, that there may be some adjustment in what is expected given the constraints of a term paper. If you are writing a review paper, for example, the instructor may set a limit on the number of pages or number of sources. Even if no limit is set, the expectations with regard to the comprehensiveness of the coverage are likely to be less than they would be if you were writing a paper intended for publication (which does not mean, of course, that you cannot try to exceed your instructor's expectations). Similarly, if your paper reports the results of a study that you have carried out, a simpler study than one intended for a journal may suffice. It may be sufficient, for example, to report tentative results based on just a handful of participants. Or it may be sufficient to report the replication of a published study. Although a replication clearly does not meet the original-contribution goal discussed in Chapter 6, it can provide valuable experience in both carrying out and writing up a study, which is the reason that instructors sometimes make such an assignment. If a replication is not an explicit paper option for your course, you may nevertheless want to ask whether it is an option in your case.

What about the other types of paper identified in the table? If you are writing a book review and have never attempted such writing before, you may want to look at some examples of how book reviews are written. If so, check the APA journal *PsycCritiques*, a journal that consists solely of book reviews. *PsycCritiques* is available online through the APA website (http://www.apa.org/pubs/databases/psyccritiques/index.aspx). I will add that you probably should not (or, if your instructor forbids it, definitely should not) read the review of the book that you yourself are reviewing—or at least should not do so until you have turned in your paper. The danger is that your paper, despite your best efforts, may end up consisting too much of the reviewer's critical thinking rather than your own.

The reference to critical thinking brings up a point that applies to both a book review and a critique of an article. Both types of paper have two goals. One goal is to summarize the main points of the work being reviewed. The summary will necessarily be selective, especially in the case of a book review; still, the reader of your paper should come away with an appreciation of the main themes of the work being discussed. The second goal is to offer your own critical evaluation of the work. Note that "critical" does not necessarily mean negative (although of course it may be negative), but it does mean evaluative—what you liked, what you disliked, and why.

In my experience, student papers that consist of reviews or critiques often go astray in either of two ways. One way is that the paper consists too much of straight summary and not enough of critical evaluation. The summary component *is* an important part of such papers; it provides information that a reader needs, and it demonstrates to your instructor that you have understood what you have read. It is not all-important, however; what is also needed is your critical assessment of the work being reviewed. If you find that you have written nine pages of summary followed by one or two paragraphs of evaluation, then you need to rethink and rewrite. There needs to be more of you in the paper.

The second problem that decreases the value of many papers is that the evaluation is there but the reasons for it are not. What is wanted is not just what you liked or disliked; it is the basis for these evaluative judgments. At the least, what you write should be grounded in relevant course experience; you have, after all, had a dozen or so weeks of such experience before your paper is due. This point does not mean that you need to work course experience into every paragraph. It does mean, however, that your instructor should feel that your paper is in some way different from what you could have written before the course even began.

What about the use of additional sources? This question, clearly, is another entry under the know-your-requirements heading. If your analysis is supposed to be based solely on your own thinking (along, of course, with what you have learned in the course), then clearly you should not seek out other sources. If background sources are allowed, however, then the various search strategies discussed in Chapter 3 become relevant. If your paper is a critique of a specific study, recall the forward-search option in PsycInfo. Pulling up the PsycInfo entry for the study will give you a list of every more recent source that has cited it, which, in the case of classic studies, is likely to number in the hundreds. Indeed, many of these studies are so well known that typing the author's name into Google will bring up a long list of citations. Of course, a point made in Chapter 3 applies here: Any information obtained from the internet needs to be used selectively. Table 3.2 provides a summary of the considerations to keep in mind.

I will make one more point about the mixture of summary and evaluation that should characterize a book review or a study critique. One approach, which is probably most common in student papers, is to order these components one after another: perhaps seven pages of summary, followed by two or three pages of evaluation. This approach is fine, but it is not the only possibility. An alternative approach, which often makes for a more original and more interesting paper, is to weave the two components together as you write, stating some theme from the work, offering your opinion of it, moving on to another theme and related opinion, and so forth.

Strategies for Writing

In this section I return to some of the points discussed in Chapter 2. Although all the forms of advice offered there are meant to apply to any kind of writing, including term papers, I settle here for revisiting four of the points.

Two have already been touched on. One is a version of the know-your-audience principle—in this case, know your instructor and the requirements and expectations that he or she has for the paper. You will need to make a number of decisions about your paper as you write—how long the paper should be, how many sources should be used, what the level of presentation should be, how much should be summary and how much should be evaluation. There is no point in guessing about these matters—get clear about what your instructor expects.

The second point follows, and it is to seek out whatever help you need. Clarification of instructions is one form of help, but it is hardly the only assistance that an instructor or teaching assistant might provide. In my experience (and, I would guess, that of most instructors), failing to seek needed help is a far more common problem for students than is seeking unnecessary help. Note also that help includes printed as well as interpersonal sources. Use the articles you read as models of how to do this type of writing. If you are attempting to follow APA style, work closely from the *Publication Manual* and also the APA style website (www.apastyle.org).

A third point is to be careful. No one has ever written a perfect paper, and your paper will not be an exception. You want any mistakes you make to be things that you could not have done differently, given your current development as a writer of psychology, not things that you could have gotten right if you had just expended sufficient care. If, for example, you commit a grammatical error, the error should reflect some aspect of grammar that you have not yet mastered (but, one hopes, will master if you receive helpful feedback), rather than something that you simply missed because you failed to proofread your paper. Similarly, if you miss some important source in your search of the literature, the error should be an understandable result of your inexperience with such searches, not a result of the fact that you spent only 10 minutes exploring the database.

The final suggestion is to plan ahead. One aspect of planning is the use of time. Careless mistakes of the sort just noted are often the result of trying to fit too much work into too short a time period. It is undoubtedly unrealistic for an instructor to expect students to begin work on a paper the moment they know of its existence. Still, if 15 weeks separate the announcement of a required paper and its due date, you should plan to spread your work across at least most of the available time. Doing so will result in both a more successful paper and a more pleasant writing experience than if you try to cram everything into the two or three days before the paper is due.

In addition to planning the use of your time, you need to plan what you will write. We saw in Chapters 4 and 5 that empirical reports follow a standard template that reduces (though does not eliminate) the need for in-advance planning of the organizational structure. Term papers, for the most part, do not have a common template. It is true that most have a very general three-part structure: introduction, evidence, conclusions. Within this general framework, however, there are numerous possibilities and related decisions for how to order and how to relate the various elements. You should think through the organizational possibilities carefully before writing, and you should reread your paper after writing to be sure that your organizational structure is what you want.

You should also make sure that the organizational structure is clear to the reader. Students sometimes write terms papers, even fairly lengthy ones, without any use of headings. This is a mistake. If the paper is at all successful, it will have distinct sections, and the sections will follow from and relate to each other in the ways necessary to express what the paper has to say. Headings are a way to convey this underlying structure. Why not share this information with the reader?

Style of Presentation

Clearly, whether you are expected to apply APA style or any particular style as you write falls under the know-your-requirements heading, and therefore is something to be clear about before you begin to write. As I have said at various points, if the instructor's rules and APA rules conflict, it is the former that win out. As I have also said, however, if the instructor does not impose any style requirements, then my advice is to try, as best you are able, to apply APA style. You should always use *some* consistent style when you write, and APA style is the style that you will need if you continue in psychology. It is a good idea to begin to practice it as soon as you can.

The gist of the preceding is that Chapter 8 of this book may be more or less relevant to your term paper writing, depending on your specific requirements. Chapter 9, however, will be relevant for any form of writing in any context. For many instructors, the quality of the writing is an explicit component of the grading process, and even when it is not, the quality of the writing is likely to affect how your work is evaluated. As I have stressed, quality of writing is also important beyond the bounds of the classroom—for grad school essays, for theses or dissertations, for work submitted for publication. In addition to the specific aspects of grammar and word use discussed in Chapter 9, pay attention to the aim-for qualities discussed in Chapter 2: simplicity, variety, conciseness, smoothness. As you read over what you have written (another strategy discussed in Chapter 2), ask yourself how well your writing has achieved these four qualities. If the answer is not as well as possible, then rewrite.

EXERCISES

1. Find a recent review article on some topic that interests you. Evaluate the review with respect to how well it avoids the various problems identified in Table 7.2.
2. Do a PsycInfo search on some topic that interests you. Find five sources that are similar but not identical in what they do—that is, they address the same general issue but do so in at least partly different ways. Imagine that you are writing a review paper that incorporates these studies. Write a passage that summarizes the studies in no more than one page and two or three paragraphs.
3. One of the challenges in writing a literature review is knowing when to use tables. Look through the reviews (preferably narrative reviews rather than meta-analyses) in a recent issue either of *Psychological Bulletin* or of a more specialized journal of reviews in an area of interest to you (e.g., *Developmental Review*, *Review of Educational Research*, *Personality and Social Psychology Review*). Note the uses to which tables are put. If possible, develop a classification system for the different types of tables (e.g., presentation of issues, summary of methods, summary of findings) and tabulate the number of entries under each type.
4. One way to begin to learn the differences between a narrative review and a meta-analysis is to read examples of the two approaches that are directed to the same general topic. Two reviews of the literature on gender differences in posttraumatic stress disorder were published in close conjunction in *Psychological Bulletin*, one a narrative review (Olff, Langeland, Draijer, & Gersons, 2007) and one a meta-analysis (Tolin & Foa, 2006). Read both articles and note similarities and differences between them. Which approach, if either, do you prefer?
5. Although a critique of an article may encompass the entire article, it may also focus on one aspect of the work. Two of the *Forty Studies That Changed Psychology* (Hock, 2013) have been quite controversial from an ethical standpoint: the Milgram (1963) obedience study and the Zimbardo (1972) prison study. Read both the Milgram and Zimbardo articles and write your own evaluation of the ethics of both studies. Once you have done so, use PsycInfo to find other commentaries and compare their evaluations with yours.

8

Rules of Writing
APA

This chapter has to do with the mechanics of writing in psychology—with the rules for handling headings, references, quotations, and a dozen or so other stylistic issues. There is no single "right" way to do most of these things, and you have undoubtedly encountered a number of different approaches across different books or articles or college courses. Precisely because various possibilities exist, however, it is important for members of a discipline to agree on a common approach. Thus, in psychology there *is* a right way to handle headings, references, and numerous other stylistic conventions, and this way is spelled out in the APA *Manual*. In the words of the *Manual*,

> Uniform style helps us to cull articles quickly for key points and findings. Rules of style in scientific writing encourage full disclosure of essential information and allow us to dispense with minor distractions. Style helps us to express the key elements of quantitative results, choose the graphic form that will best suit our analyses, report critical details of our research protocol, and describe individuals with accuracy and respect. It removes the distraction of puzzling over the correct punctuation for a reference or the proper form for numbers in the text. Those elements are codified in the rules we follow for clear communication, allowing us to focus our intellectual energy on the substance of our research. (p. xiii)

In what follows, I first consider what is perhaps the most general issue addressed by the *Manual*: the language to use in referring to the people who participate in research or who may be affected by the results of research. I then discuss the remaining topics in the order in which they are presented in the *Manual*. Appendix B provides a reminder of many of the points made throughout the chapter.

USING UNBIASED LANGUAGE

Scientific writing must be clear and accurate. It must also be unbiased—that is, fair and respectful toward the people who are the subjects of study or who might be affected by the results of study. The *Manual* summarizes this goal as follows:

> As an organization, APA is committed both to science and to the fair treatment of individuals and groups, and this policy requires that authors who write for APA publications avoid perpetuating demeaning attitudes and biased assumptions about people in their writing. Constructions that might imply bias against persons on the basis of gender, sexual orientation, racial or ethnic group, disability, or age are unacceptable. (pp. 70–71)

This statement in the *Manual* is followed by seven pages of guidelines with respect to how to achieve the goal. In what follows I summarize the most important principles.

One principle is to be specific in designating groups. The term *Hispanic*, for example, encompasses individuals from a wide range of countries of origin. More informative, and also more respectful of group membership, is a term such as *Mexican American* or *Cuban American*. Similarly, *Vietnamese* or *Vietnamese American* is more informative than *Asian* or *Asian American*. If the group can be described at a still more specific level (e.g., a specific geographical region, a specific ethnicity), then the more specific description should be given.

A second principle is to be sensitive in designating groups. Language use changes, and some labels that were once acceptable (e.g., *retarded*, *Oriental*) no longer are. The *Manual*, as well as the APA style website (www.apastyle.org), is a source for currently acceptable designations. Whenever possible, authors should use the label that is preferred by the group members themselves.

In addition to selection of labels, authors need to be alert to more subtle ways in which their wording may favor one group over another. A constant ordering when presenting groups (e.g., "men and women," "Whites and Blacks") may suggest that the first named group is in some way more typical or dominant. Use of the term *minority* suggests that the group in question can be defined in terms of its lesser status with respect to some majority group. If *minority* is used, it should be accompanied by an adjective that indicates what sort of minority (e.g., *ethnic*, *racial*).

Another principle is the "put people first" maxim. Especially when referring to individuals with clinical conditions or disabilities, it is important not to equate the individual with the condition. Thus rather than "autistic children" or "autistics" write "children with autism." Similarly, write "group diagnosed with schizophrenia" rather than "schizophrenics."

Handling of gender presents special challenges. Asymmetrical wording (e.g., "man and wife") should be avoided. Wording that incorrectly suggests that some occupation or role is limited to one gender (e.g., "chairman," "policeman") should also be avoided. So should the use of the generic "man" or "mankind" to refer to humans.

The absence of a gender-neutral pronoun in English exacerbates the problem. If you have read any psychology (or, really, anything) from 30 or so years ago you

TABLE 8.1 Alternatives to Use of a Single-Gender Pronoun

Sample sentences: When a participant receives honest feedback, he benefits most.
A researcher should ensure that his subjects are well motivated.

Change	Example
Make the sentence plural.	When participants receive honest feedback, they benefit most.
Replace "his" with "his or her."	A researcher should ensure that his or her subjects are well motivated.
Use a noun rather than pronoun.	When a participant receives honest feedback, the participant benefits most.
Omit the pronoun.	A researcher should ensure that subjects are well motivated.
Reword the sentence.	When honest feedback is given, the participant benefits most.
Replace the pronoun with an article.	A researcher should ensure that the subjects are well motivated.

know that the generic "he" was routinely used. This device is no longer acceptable. In its place, the *Manual* offers various strategies for handling the pronoun issue. Table 8.1 summarizes the possibilities. I will add two points here. The first is that the search for gender equality should not be allowed to impair the readability of the presentation. Thus sentences of the "He or she . . . his or her . . ." sort should be minimized. The second is that constructions of "the child . . . they" form solve the gender issue but at the cost of a serious grammatical violation. Such constructions should never be used.

A different sort of gender error sometimes occurs in student papers. Having introduced a study by Smith (2010), the student wishes to replace the author's name with a pronoun in further references to the study and therefore writes "He also found . . ." Such a substitution is fine—only, however, if Smith is in fact a man (as some students seem automatically to assume) and not a woman. If you want to use a gender pronoun in referring to an author, be sure that you know the author's gender.

I will conclude by noting two rules from this section of the *Manual* that may be counterintuitive; at the least, these are points that often come out wrong in student papers. One is that the words *White* and *Black* should be capitalized when used to designate racial groups. The other is that no hyphen is necessary in terms such as *African American* and *Asian American*, even when the term is used as an adjective (e.g., "African American participants").

HEADINGS

APA style permits five levels of heading. These levels are shown in Table 8.2. When only one level of heading is needed, Level 1 is used. When more levels are needed, the additions are made in numerical order: Levels 1 and 2 for two levels; Levels 1, 2, and 3 for three levels; and so forth.

How many headings should a manuscript have? The answer depends on two things. One is the complexity of the material. A single level is likely to be sufficient only for relatively short papers, for example, reviews or commentaries. Most empirical reports require at least two levels, and some may use three or even four. Use of all five headings is rare, being confined mainly to reports of multiple studies or to lengthy reviews or theoretical articles.

The second determinant is the preferences of the author. In many instances use of a heading is optional, and some authors are more likely to opt for a heading than are others. Even when they are not mandatory, however, headings can undoubtedly be helpful. Not only do they help to identify the organizational structure of a manuscript, but headings also serve to break up strings of text that might otherwise be daunting and interest-deflating. It is reasonable to argue, therefore, that the default assumption should be a positive one: When in doubt, use a heading. Or, more accurately, use at least two headings. A basic organizational principle is that any instance of a heading at some level must be matched by at least one other instance at the same level. Thus with respect to the example in Table 8.2, if we wish to use a Level

TABLE 8.2   Levels of Heading in APA Journals

Level of Heading	Format
Level 1	Centered, Boldface, Uppercase and Lowercase Heading
Level 2	Flush Left, Boldface, Uppercase and Lowercase Heading
Level 3	Indented, boldface, lowercase paragraph heading ending with a period.
Level 4	*Indented, boldface, italicized lowercase paragraph heading ending with a period.*
Level 5	*Indented, italicized lowercase paragraph heading ending with a period.*

Example of all five headings in the same manuscript:

Experiment 1

Method

   Apparatus and materials.

   Executive function tasks.

   Younger children.

   Older children.

   Theory-of-mind tasks.

   Younger children.

   Older children.

   Procedure.

Results and Discussion

Experiment 2

3 heading for **Apparatus and materials**, then we need to include at least one other Level 3 heading—which, of course, has been done with the heading for **Procedure**.

A further point about headings is that they must follow a logical hierarchy. Those in Table 8.2 do. Thus, **Apparatus and materials** and **Procedure** are both aspects of **Method** and are therefore appropriately grouped under this more general heading. In contrast, it would not work to place all three headings at the same level, for that would result in a mixture of parts and whole. For the same reason, **Executive function tasks** and **Theory-of-mind tasks** cannot be grouped with **Apparatus and materials**; rather, these categories are separate entries under the more general heading and thus must receive a heading one level higher in the one-to-five ordering.

I will note finally that there are some exceptions (not explained in the *Manual*) to the five-level system for headings. The heading for Abstract, the title of the manuscript on page 3, the heading for References, and the heading for appendixes are all centered headings and thus look like Level 1 headings. None, however, is bold-faced.

SERIATION

Sometimes you may have a set of items that you wish to present in list form. APA style offers three ways of doing so.

If the list is presented within a paragraph, then the elements are identified by lowercase letters in parentheses—for example, "The criteria for selection were (a) a vaginal birth, (b) a full-term birth, and (c) an Apgar score of 8 or higher." Letters are used both for elements within a sentence (as in the example) and for elements in separate sentences, assuming that the sentences are in the same paragraph.

If the elements of the list are in separate paragraphs, then they are identified by numbers, as in the following example. Note that no parentheses are necessary around the numbers.

> The children selected for participation met the following three criteria:
>
> 1. Each had been enrolled in the school for at least 2 years.
> 2. Each had a full-scale IQ score of at least 90.
> 3. Each had a reciprocated "best friend" in the sample.

The third option is to identify the elements by bullets rather than letters or numbers. The main reason to do so is to avoid the suggestion of ordinality that both letters and numbers convey (e.g., item 1 is in some way prior or most important). A bulleted list should be typed as a single sentence with appropriate punctuation.

It is possible, of course, to forgo all of these options and to present a set of items simply as a series in the text, and thus without letters, numbers, or bullets. The formats described here should be used only when the writer wishes to give special prominence to the series of items.

I will conclude this section by noting a basic grammatical point that applies to series of any sort, and that is that the items in the series should be parallel in form. Thus in the first example, it would not work to end with "(c) achieving an Apgar score of 8 or higher" because there is no matching verb in either (a) or (b).

ANTHROPOMORPHISM

Anthropomorphism is the attribution of human characteristics to animals or to inanimate sources. It is something to be avoided in writing. Thus do not write "rat couples"; write "pairs of rats." Similarly, do not write "The program was instructed"; write "The staff for the program was instructed."

Perhaps the most common context in which the issue arises is in talking about an experiment or a theory. An experiment cannot hope or wish or desire. A bit less obviously, an experiment also cannot attempt to demonstrate, control unwanted variables, or interpret findings, nor can tables or figures compare (all of the examples in this sentence are taken from the *Manual*). Experiments, tables, and figures can, however, show or indicate.

The *Manual's* discussion makes clear the general issue with respect to anthropomorphism. The examples it provides, however (all of which I have given here), still leave a number of possible applications unsettled and thus dependent on the judgment of the writer. Some writers interpret the guidelines as ruling out virtually any sort of verb with a nonhuman subject. Kline (2009), for example, regards both "research found" and "theory says" as anthropomorphisms.

Personally, I have no problem with research finding something or a theory saying something. Nor, as this book makes clear, do I have a problem with the *Manual* (certainly an inanimate entity) saying, prescribing, discussing, or doing any of the other actions that I attribute to it. (Note, therefore, that I would not regard Error 19 in Appendix B as an error.) My advice is to use common sense when confronting the anthropomorphism issue. Whenever you follow "experiment," "study," or "theory" with a verb, think carefully about whether the verb implies a human actor—as "hope," I would say, does and as "say," I would say, does not. When in doubt, be conservative and reword.

PUNCTUATION

Most of what follows concerns general rules of punctuation and thus might have gone as well in the next chapter. In some instances, however, style guides differ in their treatment of punctuation, and in those instances I give the APA prescriptions. My coverage will be selective, focusing on points that go astray most often in student papers.

Commas

Among the uses for commas are to separate items in a series—for example, "red, white, and blue," or "first, second, or third." In such instances there needs to be a comma before the "and" or "or." This is a generally followed principle in American (although not English) writing.

Commas are also used to separate two independent clauses that are linked by a conjunction—for example, "Participants first filled out the demographic questionnaire, and then they began the first task." Or "Smith discusses the issue at length, but Jones largely ignores it." The *Manual* presents this stricture as a rule without exception. In fact, when the clauses are short, some writers omit the comma—for example, "She played and he slept." It will be safest, however—and also most APA-like—to include a comma between independent clauses joined by a conjunction.

As the preceding suggests, although the use of a comma is sometimes mandatory, in some instances it is optional, and some writers like commas more than others. In a sentence such as the following, the commas are fine, but they also could be omitted: "The participants were signaled at random, and therefore impossible to predict, intervals." Note, though, that this is an all-or-nothing decision. If a comma is placed after "random," there needs to be a matching comma after "predict."

The *Manual* also specifies some instances in which a comma is not needed. One is to separate the parts of a compound predicate—for example, "All subjects completed the first phase of the experiment and returned the following week for Phase 2." Another (which may run counter to what you have seen in other styles) is to separate the parts of measurements or ages. Thus write "3 min 40 s," not "3 min, 40 s," and "8 years 2 months," not "8 years, 2 months."

I will add a further not-needed case, and that is following a lengthy, multipart subject. Consider the following sentence: "The instruction to repeat the digits backwards whenever they saw a red, blue, or yellow light on the screen placed in front of them posed a problem for many of the children." Some students are tempted to insert a comma after "them." Do not do this. No matter how long the subject, a comma should not be used to separate subject and predicate.

In addition to knowing what commas can do, it is important to know what they can*not* do. There are, of course, many things that they cannot do, but I will concentrate on the one that I see most often in student papers, and that is to connect independent clauses when there is no conjunction linking the clauses. A construction like "Smith agrees with the theory, Jones disagrees" is a run-on sentence and therefore not really a sentence at all. Various corrections are possible. We could make it into two sentences by replacing the comma with a period. We could add an "and" or a "but" after the comma. We could put the necessary linking element at the beginning of the sentence ("Although Smith . . . ," "Whereas Smith . . ."). Or we could replace the comma with a semicolon. What we could *not* do—and this is the error that I see most often—is to place a "however" after the comma. In this context *however* is an adverb, not a conjunction, and thus cannot perform the linking role. The same point applies to a number of other transitional terms; among them are *therefore, moreover, furthermore,* and *otherwise.*

Semicolons

The previous section mentioned one use for the semicolon: to connect independent clauses. Another use is to connect items in a series that already contain commas—for example, "The order of colors was red, yellow, blue; blue, yellow, red; or yellow, red, blue."

Like commas, semicolons are sometimes misused. Semicolons should not be used to introduce a list; for that, use a colon. They also should not be used to introduce a phrase that is not an independent clause—for example, "The youngest children solved none of the problems; an unexpected outcome." Depending on the desired emphasis, a comma, colon, dash, or parentheses could work here—not, however, a semicolon.

Colons

One use for colons is to introduce a list. More generally, colons serve to introduce material that in some way completes a thought expressed in the preceding clause—for example, "The theorists agree on one point: Early experience can be especially important."

It is important to note that such two-part constructions do not always require a colon. No colon is necessary when the first clause is not an independent clause. Thus write "The order was red, blue, green," not "The order was: red, blue, green."

Is it necessary to capitalize following a colon? The answer is that it depends. If the material that follows the colon is an independent clause (as in the first example in this section), then the capital is necessary. If the material that follows the colon is not an independent clause, then no capital is necessary.

Parentheses

The *Manual* lists nine uses for parentheses. Among the more familiar of these uses are to set off structurally independent clauses (as in the preceding paragraph), to set off reference citations in the text, to introduce an abbreviation, and to enclose statistical values. The *Manual* also identifies cases in which parentheses should *not* be used. One is to enclose material that is already within parentheses; for that, use either brackets or commas—for example, "(the range of scores for the youngest third of the sample [n = 10] was 0 to 9)." Parentheses should also not be used back to back. The following shows one way to avoid back-to-back use: "(an outcome that is only sometimes obtained; Smith & Jones, 2000)."

Students are sometimes uncertain about whether to put a period inside or outside parentheses that come at the end of a sentence. This is another it-depends situation. If the material within the parentheses is a complete sentence, then the period goes inside. If the material is not a complete sentence, then the period goes outside (as shown in this sentence).

HYPHENS

Decisions about when to hyphenate can pose a challenge, and the Manual devotes four pages to the issue. Included in the discussion is a list of prefixes that do *not* require hyphens in APA style (some exceptions will be noted shortly). Table 8.3 shows what these prefixes are. Note that the list includes a number of entries (e.g., mid, multi, non, pre, post) that are often hyphenated in other contexts—not, however, in APA style.

The items in the table do not exhaust the no-hyphen-needed category. Among the other constructions that require no hyphen in APA style are compounds that include an adverb ending in *ly* (e.g., "widely used test"), compounds that include a comparative or superlative adjective (e.g., "better written paper"), foreign phrases used as adjectives or adverbs (e.g., "post hoc comparisons"), and common fractions used as nouns (e.g., "one third of the participants").

Of course, in some cases a hyphen *is* required. The following constructions fall in this category when they precede the term they modify: a compound with a participle (e.g., "role-playing technique"), a phrase used as an adjective (e.g., "trial-by-trial analysis"), an adjective and noun compound (e.g., "middle-class families"), and a compound with a number as the first element (e.g., "12th-grade students"). Note that the "precede" part of the rule is important. When the compound follows the term no hyphen is necessary (e.g., "The families were middle class." "The students were in 12th grade.").

As noted, there are some conditions under which some of the prefixes in Table 8.3 do require a hyphen. Table 8.4 spells out what these conditions are.

TABLE 8.3 Prefixes That Do Not Require a Hyphen in APA Style

after	mega	pseudo
anti	meta	quasi
bi	micro	re
co	mid	semi
counter	mini	socio
equi	multi	sub
extra	non	super
infra	over	supra
inter	post	ultra
intra	pre	un
macro	pro	under

TABLE 8.4 Prefixes That Do Require a Hyphen in APA Style

Compounds in which the base word is capitalized (e.g., pro-Freudian)

Compounds in which the base word is a number (e.g., post-1970)

Compounds in which the base word is an abbreviation (e.g., pre-UCS trial)

Compounds in which the base word is more than one word (e.g., non-achievement-oriented students)

All *self*-compounds (e.g., self-report technique; self-esteem)

Words that could be misunderstood (e.g., re-pair, re-form)

Words in which the prefix ends and the base word begins with the same vowel (e.g., meta-analysis, co-occur)

In my experience, students often have difficulty knowing whether hyphens are needed when presenting ages. If you write "The children were 4 years old," no hyphens are necessary. If you present the age in the form of an adjective, however (e.g., "4-year-old children"), then you need hyphens. Similarly, if you present the age in noun form (e.g., "4-year-olds"), you also need hyphens. Note that two hyphens are required in both cases.

The discussion to this point may give the impression that any question about hyphenating can be solved by simply looking up the relevant example in the *Manual*. Although many in fact can, there is no way (especially in four pages) to anticipate every instance that may arise. The *Manual* therefore provides several "general principles" to guide decision in doubtful cases, along with two further pieces of advice. One is to consult a dictionary if necessary (APA follows Webster's Collegiate Dictionary). The other is to use a hyphen when in doubt, because doing so is likely to promote clarity.

CAPITALIZATION

I have already made some points about capitalization in earlier sections, and some more points will be made in some of the sections to come. I add a few others here.

We saw the rules for capitalization in the title of the manuscript: first word of the title and subtitle, major words, any words of four letters or more. The same rules apply to titles of books or articles that are given in the paper. Note that if a word is a hyphenated compound both parts of the compound are capitalized (e.g., "Short-Term Memory"). But note also that this rule does not apply in the References list; there, only the first part of the compound is capitalized (assuming that it is the first word of the title or subtitle).

Many of the remaining rules present a challenge to master, in that they apply in some instances but not in other, closely related instances. For example, nouns should be capitalized when they are followed by a number or letter that denotes a specific place in a numbered series—thus "on Day 2 of Experiment 4," "as shown in Table 2," "as discussed in Chapter 4." Nouns are not capitalized, however, when they denote common parts of books or tables—thus "page 4," "row 3." Names of conditions or groups are also not capitalized (thus "experimental and control groups") unless they fit the numbered-series rule, in which case they are capitalized (thus "Condition 1 and Condition 2"). Similarly, references to effects or variables are not capitalized (thus "a small age effect") unless they appear with multiplication signs, in which case they are capitalized (thus "the Sex x Age x Weight interaction").

My advice with respect to capitalization is the same advice that applies to the even more challenging topic of numbers (which we will consider shortly): Whenever you have a decision to make, check the *Manual* to find the case that matches yours.

ABBREVIATIONS

Abbreviations are of two sorts: those that are optional and those that are required. The main consideration with regard to the first category is whether on balance an abbreviation will help or hinder the reader's attempt to make sense of the material.

If the term in question is both long (e.g., "dimensional change card sort") and frequently used, then an abbreviation (in this case, DCCS) will probably be helpful. On the other hand, if an unfamiliar abbreviation is seldom used, especially in a long paper, the demands on the reader's memory may outweigh the savings in length.

Assuming that an abbreviation *is* used, it must be explained. On first use the term should be written out in full, followed by the abbreviation in parentheses. The abbreviation can then be used without explanation throughout the rest of the paper.

As noted, in some instances the use of abbreviations is automatic. Such is the case for most units of measurement when they are accompanied by a numerical value—thus "10 s," "25 cm," and so forth. The exceptions are the words "day," "week," "month," and "year," which could be misread if abbreviated and so are always written out. As the examples show, in most instances it is not necessary to follow an abbreviation with a period. Again, there are exceptions (a.m., p.m., in.) to prevent misreading.

Latin abbreviations are another exception to the no-period rule. Table 8.5 shows the Latin abbreviations that appear in APA-style writing. Note that with two exceptions these abbreviations should be used only in parentheses; in the text the English translation should be written out. The exceptions are *et al.* and *v*, which

TABLE 8.5   APA Style for Latin Abbreviations

Abbreviation	Meaning	Example	Notes re APA Rules
cf.	"compare" or "consult" (used to provide contrasting information)	Smith found supportive results, unlike those of previous research (cf. Jones, 2008).	Use only in parentheses. Never put a comma after.
e.g.	"for example"	Some studies (e.g., Brown, 2010; Jones, 2008) have supported this conclusion.	Use only in parentheses. Always put a comma after.
etc.	and so on" or "and so forth"	Students ranked their school subjects (chemistry, math, etc.) in order of preference.	Use only in parentheses. Put a comma before if used to end a list of at least two other items.
et al.	"and others"	"Smith, Jones, and Brown (2010) extended the study. Smith et al. began by changing the stimuli."	Can be used either in or outside of parentheses. Must refer to at least two people.
i.e.	"that is"	The experimental manipulation (i.e., the presence or absence of reward) proved effective.	Use only in parentheses. Always put a comma after.
viz.	"namely"	"We first replicated our earlier study (viz., Smith & Jones, 2010) and then extended it."	Use only in parentheses. Always put a comma after.
vs. or *v*	"versus"	"The 2 (age: young vs. old) x 2 condition (experimental vs. control) ANOVA revealed no significant effects."	Use only in parentheses. Exception: With legal citations *v* can be used in text or parentheses.

can be used in both text citations and references. Note also that there is no period after the *et* in *et al*. There is no period because the *et* part of the phrase is not an abbreviation.

In some instances an abbreviation has become so familiar that it is now considered a word. The *Manual* lists the following instances: IQ, REM, ESP, AIDS, HIV, NADP, ACTH. These terms can be used without explanation, as can any other former abbreviations that now appear as words in contemporary dictionaries. Note, however, that there are a number of abbreviations that are common in psychology that have not yet achieved word status (e.g., RT, STM, MMPI) and thus must still be explained on first use.

If you read psychology articles from 20 or so years ago you are familiar with the abbreviations S, E, and O, which stood for subject, experimenter, and observer. These abbreviations are no longer used in APA style.

A final point with regard to abbreviations concerns how to make them plural. The answer is straightforward: Simply add an *s*.

NUMBERS

In my experience, treatment of numbers is probably the most common violation of APA style in student papers. And students are not the only ones who have difficulty. The Onwuegbuzie et al. (2009) analysis described earlier reported that handling of numbers was the most common source of APA errors in manuscripts submitted to the journal *Research in the Schools*. More than half of the manuscripts contained at least one such error.

Clearly, the APA style for numbers is not the most user-friendly system. Nevertheless—and as with other stylistic conventions—*all* of the rules are in the *Manual*, which means that with sufficient care it should be possible to get things right.

A brief digression. One of the interesting phenomena from the study of child language learning is that children often are remarkably quick to learn the basic rules of a language (e.g., in English, add *ed* to form the past tense); what they struggle with are the exceptions to the rules (thus say *went*, not *goed*; *broke*, not *breaked*; etc.). A similar phenomenon is evident with respect to the APA style for numbers. Again, a basic rule system exists, and it is not difficult to master. There are, in fact, two basic rules: For numbers from zero to nine, write the word; for numbers 10 or above, write the number. This rule applies to ordinal as well as cardinal numbers ("thus second-order factor," "75th trial," etc.).

The problems come in the exceptions to these two rules. I will not list them all here, but I will mention the most commonly occurring ones.

If a number is the first word in the sentence, a word rather than number should be used. Words should also be used for common fractions (e.g., "two-thirds"). Conversely, numbers rather than words should be used for units of measurement; for ratios, percentages, and percentiles; and for times, dates, ages, scores, and points on a scale. Numbers should also be used for all numerical terms that appear in the Abstract.

What about the situation in which two or more numerical terms appear together? If the terms are back-to-back, then in most cases a combination of numbers and words should be used—for example, "2 two-way interactions," "ten 7-point scales." The exception implied by "in most cases" occurs when, in the *Manual's* words, "readability may suffer"; in such cases both terms should be spelled out—for example, "first two items" (not "1st two items"). Note that this last point requires a judgment call with respect to readability. In most instances, the combination-of-terms rule will apply.

What about a phrase such as "seven out of 10 trials?" Readers who were familiar with the 5th edition of the APA *Manual* may wish to note a change in the current edition. Previously, numbers below 10 that were grouped for comparison with numbers above 10 were written as numbers, not words; thus the correct wording would have been "7 out of 10 trials." That rule no longer exists in the current edition of the *Manual*; thus the correct wording is that given at the start of the paragraph.

A final point concerns how to make a number plural. The answer is the same as for plurals in general: simply add *s*—thus *fours*, *10s*, *1950s* (and not, for example, *1950's*).

MEASUREMENTS

APA policy is to express measurements in metric units—thus millimeters rather than inches, meters rather than yards, and so forth. If the instruments used in a study recorded in nonmetric units, then these values can be reported; they must be accompanied, however, by the metric equivalent in parentheses—for example, "The rod was 3 ft (0.91 m in length)."

The example just given can serve to illustrate several points. Units of measurement are abbreviated when accompanied by a number. With a few exceptions (discussed earlier under Abbreviations), no period is necessary after the abbreviation. No plurals are necessary either—thus "3 ft," not "3 fts." Finally, note that in most instances (the *Manual* gives the few exceptions) there must be a space between the value and the unit of measurement.

STATISTICS

Chapter 5 talked about the kinds of statistical information that should be included in a Results section and also made a few points about how to present the information. This section takes up the how-to-present question more fully.

We can work from the same example used in Chapter 5:

> For immediate recognition, the omnibus test of the main effect of sentence format was statistically significant, $F(2, 177) = 6.30$, $p = .002$, est $\omega^2 = .07$. The one-degree-freedom contrast of primary interest (the mean difference between Conditions 1 and 2) was also significant at the specified .05 level, $t(177)$, $p < .001$, $d = 0.65$, 95% CI [.13, .37]. (p. 117)

As Chapter 5 indicated, a Results section must always include inferential statistics (i.e., tests of statistical significance) and descriptive statistics (the values that go into the tests of significance). The example shows how inferential statistics (the F and t tests) are presented in the text. In both cases three pieces of information must be included. The first, which is given in parentheses, is the degrees of freedom associated with the test (a term that should be familiar from course work in Statistics and which in any case is provided on the statistical printout). The second is the F or t value. The third is the probability level. The current version of the *Manual* indicates that exact p values should be reported, although only up to three decimal places, after which "$p < .001$" is used (as in the example).

Several more points about the method of presentation can be noted. First, there is no space between F or t and the following parenthesis. Second, the statistical information is set off from the text by commas, not parentheses. Finally, the statistical symbols (F, t, p) appear in italics. Table 8.6 shows some of the other most commonly used statistical symbols. The list is a partial one—the *Manual* lists 117 statistical symbols and abbreviations.

The necessary descriptive statistics in the case of the example are means and standard deviations. As noted in Chapter 5, the descriptive information can come either immediately before or immediately after the inferential information, and it can be presented either in the text or in a table. Two possibilities exist for presentation in the text. Although standard deviations are almost always given in parentheses, means can be given either in parentheses or as part of the narrative. An example of the latter would be "The mean for Condition 1 was 1.33 ($SD = 0.88$), and the mean for Condition 2 was 1.08 ($SD = 0.67$)." An example of the former would be "Condition 1 ($M = 1.33$, $SD = 0.88$) differed significantly from Condition

TABLE 8.6   Statistical Symbols in APA Style

Symbol	Meaning
d	Cohen's measure of effect size
df	degrees of freedom
F	F ratio in analysis of variance
g	Hedge's measure of effect size
M	mean
MSE	mean square error
n	number of cases in subsample
N	total number of cases
p	probability of rejecting the null hypothesis
r	Pearson correlation
SD	standard deviation
SE	standard error
t	t value in test of two means
z	standardized score

2 (M = 1.08, SD = 0.67)." Note that the abbreviation for mean is used only in parentheses; in the narrative the term is written out. Note also that the descriptive information is set off by parentheses, not commas.

The example can also be used to make some general points about numbers. First, most numbers should be given to two decimal places. Probability levels are an exception; they can be reported up to three decimal places. Second, there is no need for a zero before the decimal point if the number being reported cannot be greater than 1. Such is the case with probability levels; it is also the case with correlations. Finally, there needs to be a space before and after mathematical signs ($=$, $<$, etc.).

One often reported statistic that was not shown in the example is the correlation statistic. Correlations are often presented in tables, and I give an example of what such tables look like in the next section. When presented in the text they are set off with commas—for example, "The analysis revealed a significant relation between impulsivity and risk taking, $r(30)$ = .41, p = .02."

TABLES AND FIGURES

Chapter 5 discussed when to use a table or figure. This section adds some points about how to construct tables and figures.

The *Manual* devotes 28 pages to tables and provides 16 examples. It devotes 27 pages to figures and provides 12 examples. In addition, two books by Nicol and Pexman (2010a, 2010b) summarize the *Manual*'s guidelines and add a number of other examples and clarifications. Clearly, authors who wish to include either a table or a figure have a number of sources of help to turn to. The following discussion singles out just a few points from these more comprehensive treatments.

Both tables and figures are numbered in order of appearance (Table 1, Table 2, etc.), and they are referred to in the text by number (and not, for example, "the table below"). As Table 4.1 shows, in the manuscript version of an article tables and figures do not appear in their final place in the text but rather near the end, after References. Each table or figure goes on a separate page.

Each table has a title that goes above the table, and each figure has a caption that goes below the figure. Both titles and captions should be informative without being overly long. A good title or caption conveys the content of the table or figure in a manner that is neither too general (e.g., "Results of the Study") nor unnecessarily detailed. The *Manual* provides guidelines and examples in both cases.

As the *Manual* notes, both tables and figures have "canonical forms," that is, standard, often-used forms for presenting certain types of information. Such forms *are* standard because they have been shown to work well; they are also likely to be familiar to most readers. The *Manual* recommends, therefore, that such forms be used when possible.

Table 8.7 shows a canonical form for a table of means. We saw that a measure of variability should accompany a report of means, and such a measure is provided by the column of standard deviations. Inclusion of confidence intervals is recommended but not required. Inclusion of sample size is necessary only if the numbers vary across groups and are not clear from the Subjects or Participants section. With respect to formatting, note that only horizontal rules are used and that only the first word of a heading is capitalized (unless the heading is a proper name, as is the case in Table 8.8).

A further point about the table requires a brief reminder about statistics. In a so-called factorial study (i.e., a study with at least two independent variables) there are two possible effects: main effects and interactions. A main effect is a direct effect of an independent variable on a dependent variable. It is what researchers examine when they compare the levels of a single independent variable independent of, or summed across, the other independent variables in the study. The excerpt from the *Manual* reproduced in both this chapter and Chapter 5 provides an example: a main effect of sentence format. An interaction, in contrast, becomes possible when we consider two or more independent variables simultaneously. An interaction occurs whenever the effect of one independent variable varies with the level of another independent variable.

As constructed, Table 8.7 provides the means for both main effects and interactions. The cell means (.11, .26, etc.) are those for the interaction of the two independent variables in the study: age and level of difficulty. The marginal means or totals are those for the main effects—that is, the means for the younger and older subjects, summed across the three conditions, and the means for the three conditions, summed across the two groups of subjects. The general principle illustrated by the example is to make tables as informative as possible, while also, of course, keeping them reasonable-sized and readable. I should add that marginal means or totals should not always be added—in some instances they may be of no interest, and in some instances they may be easily calculable from the values in the cells. Neither of these is the case, however, for the example table.

Means are one kind of descriptive statistic for which tables are often used; correlations are another. Table 8.8, which is adapted from an example in Nicol and Pexman (2010b), shows a correlations table. Note that there is no need to give the values that fall along the diagonal (because these are the correlations of each measure with itself) or those that fall above the diagonal (because these are redundant with those below the diagonal).

TABLE 8.7   Proportions of Correct Responses in Younger and Older Children (Hypothetical Data)

Level of difficulty	7-Year-Olds			10-Year-Olds			Total		
	n	M (SD)	95% CI	n	M (SD)	95% CI	n	M (SD)	95% CI
Low	12	.05 (.08)	[.00, .10]	18	.14 (.15)	[.07, .21]	30	.10 (.10)	[.06, .14]
Moderate	15	.05 (.07)	[.01, .09]	12	.17 (.15)	[.09, .25]	27	.10 (.09)	[.07, .13]
High	16	.11 (.10)	[.06, .16]	14	.26 (.21)	[.15, .37]	30	.18 (.19)	[.11, .25]
Total	43	.07 (.08)	[.05, .09]	44	.19 (.15)	[.15, .23]			

Note.   CI = confidence interval.

TABLE 8.8   Intercorrelations for Dimensions of Achievement Scale and Five Other Need-for-Achievement Measures (Hypothetical Data)

Measure	1	2	3	4	5
1. Dimensions of Achievement Scale	—				
2. Brunswick Achievement Measure	.61°°°	—			
3. Need for Achievement Inventory	.55°°°	.73°°°	—		
4. Achievement Perception Test	.41°°	.50°°	.46°°	—	
5. Peer rating of need for achievement	.30	.40°	.37°	.52°°°	—
6. Self-rating of need for achievement	.38°	.41°°	.28	.22	.72°°°

°$p < .05.$ °°$p < .01.$ °°°$p < .001.$

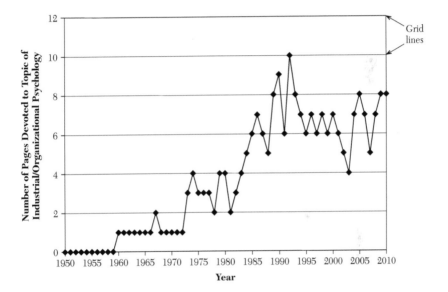

Figure 8.1   Example of a line graph showing mean estimates by graduate students of the number of pages devoted to industrial/organizational psychology in Introductory Psychology textbooks published between 1950 and 2010 (hypothetical data). From *Displaying Your Findings* (p. 46) by A. A. M. Nicol and P. M. Pexman, 2010. Washington, DC: American Psychological Association. Copyright 2010 by the American Psychological Association. Reprinted with permission.

Figures come in more forms than do tables. I settle for giving two examples of what is probably the most often used form for presentation of data: namely, line graphs. Figure 8.1, which is taken from Nicol and Pexman (2010a), shows the value of figures for conveying a large set of means that would be difficult to encompass in a table. The data are from a hypothetical study in which graduate students estimated the coverage of I/O psychology in Introductory Psychology textbooks over time. Figure 8.2, which is based on a study by Sumter and associates (Sumter, Bokhorst, Steinberg, & Westenberg, 2009), shows the value of figures for conveying interactions. The dependent variable in the study was susceptibility to peer influence, and the interaction was between age and sex: Girls reported more resistance than did boys but only during middle adolescence; at the younger and older ages there were no significant differences between the sexes.

The examples illustrate several points. The basic requirement for a figure is that it be easily comprehensible—data points clearly indicated, axes clearly labeled, legends (information within the body of the figure, such as Boys and Girls in the second example) clearly explained. In the first example the horizontal lines are optional; they do aid, however, in relating the data points to the y axis. Both examples show the canonical form for figures of this sort: dependent variable on the y axis, independent variable on the x axis. Finally (and I mention this because it is a change in the most recent version of the *Manual*), the caption goes directly under the figure.

Sometimes you may wish to reproduce a table or figure from another source. Depending on the source, you may be required to obtain permission before including the table or figure in your own work. This point should always be checked. The *Manual* indicates how to acknowledge the source for material that is being reproduced.

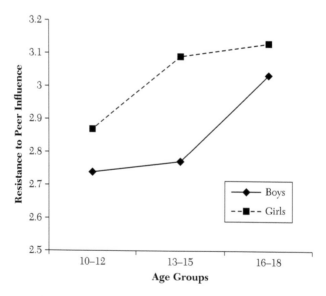

Figure 8.2   Example of a line graph showing the interaction of age and gender in the Sumter et al. study. From "The Developmental Pattern of Resistance to Peer Influence in Adolescence: Will the Teenager Ever Be Able to Resist?" by S. R. Sumter, C. L. Bokhorst, L. Steinberg, and P. M. Westenberg, 2009, *Journal of Adolescence, 32*, p. 1015. Copyright 2009 by Elsevier. Reprinted with permission.

Again, both the *Manual* and the Nicol and Pexman books (2010a, 2010b) provide much more detailed information about tables and figures than I have attempted to include here. All three sources also provide checklists for both tables and figures. Tables 8.9 and 8.10 reproduce the checklists from the Nicol and Pexman books.

TABLE 8.9   Nicol and Pexman's Checklist for Tables

Is the title meaningful? If read out loud, does it make sense?

Are any column or row heads repeated unnecessarily?

Is it clear to what row or column the various heads refer?

Are row and column headings presented in a logical order?

Do heads use as few words as possible?

Would a table spanner assist in simplifying the table?

Will two or fewer decimal places suffice for presenting data values (to avoid cluster)?

Are abbreviations and acronyms spelled out or explained and other basic information provided either in the table itself or in a table note?

Do table presenting the results of the same type of analysis have a similar layout and presentation style? Do tables within the same manuscript have a common presentation style, even if they are of different types?

Are tables referenced in the body of the manuscript and numbered in the order in which they appear?

Is the table or table callout placed immediately after discussion of the table within the text?

Is the same terminology used in both text and table, and do all table elements mentioned in the text match those found in the table?

Have you reviewed the contents of the table to ensure accuracy?

From *Presenting Your Findings: A Practical Guide for Creating Tables* by A.A.M. Nicol and P. M. Pexman, 2010, Washington, DC: APA. Copyright 2010 by the American Psychological Association. Reprinted with permission.

TABLE 8.10   Nicol and Pexman's Checklist for Figures

All text in the figure uses the same style font (sans serif).

All text in the figure is single-spaced, one-and-a-half-spaced, or double-spaced.

Font sizes within a figure do not vary by more than 4 points.

The smallest font size is not less than 8 points and the largest font size is not greater than 14 points.

Text in the figure caption uses the same font as the text of the manuscript.

The figure caption is double-spaced.

Figure captions are descriptive (i.e., they describe the variables of interest and other important information, such as what abbreviations and symbols mean) and include a permission credit line if the figure was published elsewhere.

Figure captions are presented on the same page as the figure.

Lines in the figure are thick enough to be clear after reduction.

Similar figures within the same manuscript have a similar appearance.

Figures are referred to in the text using the figure number.

From *Displaying Your Findings: A Practical Guide for Creating Figures, Posters, and Presentations* (p. 14) by A.M.M. Nicol and P. M. Pexman, 2010, Washington, DC: APA. Copyright 2010 by the American Psychological Association. Reprinted with permission.

QUOTATIONS

Chapter 2 cautioned against an overuse of quotations. But in some cases, of course, a quotation is perfectly appropriate—indeed, may be a wonderful addition to the text. The question we consider now is how to present quotations.

The answer depends on the length of the quotation. If the quoted passage is shorter than 40 words then it is presented within quotation marks as part of the ongoing text—for example (an example I give in italics, to avoid a quotation within a quotation), *Piaget (1952, p. 76) wrote "An acute observation . . . surpasses all statistics."* Note two things about this example (beyond a pithiness of expression that was rare in Piaget's writing). First, it is necessary to give not just the source but also the page number for any material that is quoted directly. Second, the closing period goes inside the quotation marks. Different forms of punctuation vary in this regard. Commas also go inside quotation marks. Question marks go inside if the quoted material is a question (for example, *Freud asked, "What do women want?"*) but outside if the question is not part of the quotation but rather is the author's own (for example, *Did Freud really say "Sometimes a cigar is just a cigar"?* [the answer, by the way, is probably not]). The same rule applies to exclamation points. Colons, semicolons, and dashes go outside the quotation marks.

Suppose that the quoted passage is 40 words or longer. In this case the quotation is typed in what is called *block format*: a freestanding block of text that begins on the next line and all of which is indented. The quotation at the beginning of this chapter provides an example. Note that provision of the page number is necessary in this case as well.

Sometimes an author wishes to make some change within a quoted passage. The most common change is omission of some of the original material. Omissions are signaled by ellipses—three periods that appear at the place where material has been removed. The Piaget quotation that opened this section provides an example. If the omission is at the end of a sentence, then four periods are used—the three for the ellipses and the normal sentence-ending period.

Once they have learned the rule for ellipses, some students overuse them. As the APA *Manual* notes, except in unusual cases it is not necessary to use ellipses at the beginning or end of a quotation. Quotations are almost always part of some larger whole; thus the reader does not need to be told that material preceded or followed the quoted excerpt.

In some instances a brief addition may be necessary to make a quoted passage comprehensible, perhaps especially when some of the original material has been omitted. Such additions are signaled by brackets.

Two other modifications to quoted material are sometimes found. Sometimes an author wishes to add emphasis to at least part of a quotation. As is typically the case when emphasis is desired, this is accomplished by placing the passage in question in italics. In such cases the words *emphasis added* should be given in parentheses following the quotation (conversely, if italics were already part of the quoted material, the phrase *emphasis in original* should be added). The second sort of modification comes when the author wishes to note some error in the quoted material. In such cases the term *sic* is added in brackets after the offending element—for example, "The data is [sic] clear." Lest this example seems puzzling, I will point ahead to a point made in the next chapter: *Data* is a plural noun.

I noted that page numbers must accompany the citation for any quoted material. Are page numbers ever necessary when a source is simply cited but not quoted? The answer is that they are never necessary, but in some instances they may be helpful and thus would be appropriate to provide. The *Manual* encourages authors to do so when interested readers might need help finding an important passage in a long or complex body of text. Note, however, that such instances are not common. Most citations require no page number.

When a quotation is taken from an internet source, page numbers may not be available. In such cases a paragraph number should be given; if paragraph numbers are not available, the heading should be cited, along with an indication of where within the section the passage appears (e.g., "Discussion section, para. 1").

A final point about quotations is not relevant to student papers but applies to any work submitted for publication. If a quotation is lengthy (and different publishers have different definitions of "lengthy"), then it may be necessary to seek permission to reproduce it. As we saw, this same point applies to tables or figures that are taken from another source.

REFERENCES IN THE TEXT

The APA style for citation of references in the text is the author-date style used throughout this book. If the author's name is part of the text, then only the date of publication goes in parentheses—for example, "Smith (2010) reported." If the author's name is not part of the text, then both elements go in parentheses—for example, "Research (Smith, 2010)." In the rare instances in which both author and date are part of the text no parentheses are necessary—for example, "In 2010 Smith reported." Note that when a citation comes at the end of a sentence it is part of the sentence and thus comes before the sentence-ending period—for example, "Similar results emerged in a recent study (Smith, 2010)."

Two unnecessary pieces of information sometimes appear in the citations in student papers. One is the title of the article being cited. The other is the full name of the author. In rare instances the latter may be appropriate—when referring to a major theorist, for example, or when citing the seminal researcher of the topic in question. In the great majority of cases, however, the last name alone is sufficient.

Various rules govern the citation of multiauthor publications. When a work has two authors, both names are always cited; in the text they are connected by "and" (e.g., "Smith and Jones") and within parentheses they are connected by an ampersand (&—e.g., "Smith & Jones"). Note that the ampersand is used only within parentheses. When a work has three to five authors, all names are cited on first mention; on subsequent mentions the citation consists of the name of the first author followed by "et al." When a work has six or more authors, the "et al." is used even on first citation. Exceptions to these last two rules occur when two multiauthor references have the same first author and same date of publication and thus would shorten to the same form. In such cases enough further names are added to disambiguate the citation, followed by a comma and "et al." Note that it is only in such instances that a comma precedes "et al." Note also that "et al." is plural and thus should be used only when at least two names are being omitted. If only one name remains when the point of disambiguation is reached, then all the authors should be listed.

Sometimes two or more references have the same author and same date of publication. In such instances the suffixes *a, b, c,* and so forth are added to distinguish the references—for example, "(Smith, 2010a, 2010b)." The ordering of the suffixes reflects the alphabetical ordering of the titles of the publications and thus the order in which the publications appear in the References.

Another complication occurs when two first authors have the same surname. In such cases the first author's initials are included in all text citations (an exception to the rule that last names only are sufficient). Note that this rule applies even when there is no possibility of ambiguity—when the references are from different years, for example, or when one reference is single-author and the other multiauthor.

Sometimes a parenthesis contains multiple citations. When the citations are by the same author they are ordered chronologically—for example, "(Smith, 2010, 2011, 2012)." When the citations are by different authors they are ordered alphabetically—for example, "(Brown, 2010; Jones, 2008; Smith, 2012)." Multiple references by the same author are separated by a comma, whereas multiple references by different authors are separated by a semicolon.

Sometimes the same reference is cited more than once in a manuscript. If the citations are in different paragraphs then the full citation is repeated on every appearance, although with "et al." if the reference has three or more authors. (Note that this book, for reasons of brevity and smoothness, violates this rule in its citations of the *Manual.*) If the citations are in the same paragraph then the date need not be repeated if it was part of the text on first mention—for example, "Smith (2010) reported." If the initial citation was in parentheses, however, then the date must be included in later citations.

Suppose that you are drawing your description of some work not from the original source but from someone else's summary of the source (the "secondary source" issue discussed in Chapter 4). In this case the proper citation is "(Smith, 2010, as cited in Jones, 2012)." Because Jones is the source you read, only Jones, and not Smith, appears in your References.

Most citation issues that you might encounter should fit one of the cases just described. The *Manual* is a source for any instances that do not.

REFERENCES LIST

Rules for References cover a full 45 pages in the *Manual.* My coverage again will be selective, focusing on the forms that occur most often in most manuscripts. Specifically, I will discuss three forms: journal articles, books, and book chapters. Other reference types (e.g., conference presentations, dissertations, internet-only sources) share many of the features of the forms I discuss, and the *Manual* is the source for the ways in which they differ.

I will begin by reiterating two points made in Chapter 4: Every source cited in the text must appear in the References (the few exceptions to this rule were noted in Chapter 4), and the text citation and the References entry must match—that is, same names, same date. I will add a third point: The entry must be accurate. Readers who wish to examine some source themselves are dependent on what an author has told them, and a wrong date or wrong volume number may frustrate their search efforts. A mistake with respect to authorship (e.g., omitting the name of one of the authors) is less likely to affect search but has another unfortunate consequence: failure to give proper credit for a scientific contribution.

The entries in a References list should be in alphabetical order, the order being determined by the last name of the first author. Sometimes, however, figuring out the order can be a challenge. The *Manual* discusses various problematic cases, including how to handle hyphenated names, how to handle numbers (e.g., Jones II and Jones III), and how to alphabetize the prefixes M', Mc, and Mac.

Often the same surname appears more than once as the first author in a References list. If the multiple entries come from different authors, then the initials of the first and if necessary middle names determine the order of entry, (e.g., C. Smith goes before D. Smith, and C. A. Smith goes before C. B. Smith). If the initials are not sufficient, then the names of the later authors in multiauthor references determine the order (e.g., Smith and Brown goes before Smith and Jones). If the names are not sufficient to determine the order (as is always the case with single-author publications), then the references are listed in chronological order. As in the text, references with the same names and same dates are distinguished by suffixes (a, b, c . . .).

In most cases all the authors' names appear in a References entry. The exception comes when there are eight or more authors. In such cases the first six names are given, followed by an ellipse, followed by the last author's name.

Journal Articles

Table 8.11 summarizes the elements of a journal reference, and the References section of this book provides numerous examples. In what follows I do not repeat

TABLE 8.11   Elements of a Reference for a Journal Article in APA Style

Element	Description
Names of authors	Last names and initials, in same order as in publication.
Date of publication	In parentheses following names. If not yet published, put "in press."
Title of article	Only first word and first word of subtitle capitalized.
Name of journal	In italics. Given in full (no abbreviations).
Volume number	In italics.
Issue number	In parentheses. Necessary only if journal not paginated consecutively.
Page numbers	Regular type. "pp." not necessary.
Doi	Digital object identifier. Not always available.

the basic information but rather note a few points that are often the source for errors in student papers.

One such point is the need for a comma preceding the "and" in a multiauthor reference. When there are three or more authors this point is simply an application of a general rule for commas. Even with just two authors, however, the comma is required (e.g., "Smith, A., & Jones, B."), probably the only time that you will ever use a comma in an X-and-Y construction.

All of us are used to seeing the titles for things capitalized. The tendency to do so must be inhibited when using APA style. When giving an article's title only the first word and (if there is one) the first word of a subtitle are capitalized.

When you look at the References lists of articles you read, you may sometimes see the journal names abbreviated. If so, you are not reading an APA journal. In APA style the journal name is always written in full.

In APA style the journal name is also italicized, as is the volume number. In case you wonder about this point, the comma between the two is also italicized.

As the table notes, the issue number is necessary only if the journal is not paginated consecutively—that is, only if each issue begins with page 1. The great majority of journals, including all the APA journals, are paginated consecutively; thus issue numbers are seldom needed.

Page numbers complete the basic elements of a journal reference. Note that no "pp." is needed when giving the page numbers for a journal article.

The last point I single out concerns a new aspect of APA style—namely, the requirement to include a doi, or digital object identifier, whenever one is available. The purpose of the doi is to provide a permanent internet address for articles available in electronic form; it consists of a string of numbers (and sometimes letters) that is unique to the article in question. As the examples in the References section of this book indicate, the doi is typed at the end of the reference entry. When the source being read is in electronic form, clicking on the doi will provide a link to the desired article. If the source is hard copy (as with this book's References), typing the doi into the "doi Resolver" at www.crossref.org will provide the link.

How can you find the doi for sources you cite? The doi typically appears on the first page of a journal article, usually at the top in the electronic version of the article. It is also typically available in the entry for the article in the PsycInfo database (see Table 3.5). When possible, you should paste the doi into your manuscript, rather than risk the slips that may occur in typing a long string of letters and numbers.

Books

References for books share many of the features of references for journal articles. Again, the name or names of the author(s) are the starting point, followed by the date of publication. Again, the title is not capitalized; rather, only the first word of the title and (if there is one) subtitle receive capitals. In contrast to the title of a journal article (but like the name of the journal), a book title is italicized. The basic reference concludes with the publication information: the city and state in which the publisher is located (or, for a foreign publisher, city and country), followed by the publisher's name. Some books also have a doi address; if so, it is given at the end of the reference.

Students sometimes add a particular chapter or page range when citing a book, thereby indicating that this was the only section they read or used. Admirable though this honesty is, it is not necessary. Citing the book means simply that *something* was used from it. The citation should always be that for the entire book.

Book Chapters

References for book chapters begin in the same way as the two types of references just discussed: authors' names followed by date of publication. Note, though, that the names in question are not the editors of the book but rather the authors of the specific chapter in the book that is being cited (and thus the names that appeared in the text). The editors' names do appear, however, as the next element in the reference, followed by the title of the book. The title is followed, in parentheses, by the page numbers for the chapter, in this case preceded by the "pp." abbreviation. In my experience page numbers are an often omitted piece of information, perhaps because the purpose of including them is not clear (the citation of the book is sufficient to allow an interested reader to track down the source). Still, page numbers are a required part of APA style. The reference concludes with the publication information and, if available, the doi.

EXERCISES

1. The following passage contains 18 deviations from APA style. Find and correct as many as you can.

    Infants' understanding of the social world has been the focus of a good deal of recent research (Reddy 2008, Legerstee 2006). 2 developments in particular have been of interest. One is joint attention: The ability to follow and share the attentional focus of another. Suppose, e.g., that the mother turns her head and looks toward the door. If the infant also turns his head and looks toward the door he would be demonstrating joint attention. Infants typically develop a capacity for joint attention by about one yr. of age (Benigno and Farrar 2012.)

    The 2nd development is labeled social referencing. Suppose now that when the infant looks toward the door a stranger appears. Turning to look at the mother's face for cues as to how to respond would be an instance of social referencing. The definition of social referencing, then, is: using cues from others to interpret some uncertain situation. Prior to the mid-1980's, most psychologists would have denied that infants possess this ability.

2. Find a journal article dealing with race, disability, or sexual orientation that was written 40 or more years ago. Note how the participants were described. Find the

(*Continued*)

(Continued)

fullest such description in the article and rewrite it using the sensitive and inclusive language stressed in the current version of the *Manual*. (This exercise is adapted from Dunn, 2011.)

3. From the list of APA journals (http://www.apa.org/pubs/journals/index.aspx) select a journal in a content area that especially interests you. Look through the Results sections of recent articles and select two tables and two figures. Convert the tables into figures, and convert the figures into tables.

4. Imagine that you are to create the References entry for a study by Jane Doe and John Smith entitled "Peer Pressure and Deviant Behavior in Adolescence." Indicate the form that the reference would take for (a) a journal article, (b) a manuscript submitted for publication, (c) a chapter in an edited book, (d) a poster presented at a conference, and (e) an unpublished dissertation. Note that there are some elements (e.g., the name of the journal, the title of the book) that you will need to decide on or invent.

9

Rules of Writing
General

The preceding chapter focused on APA guidelines and rules. This chapter addresses the how-to-write question at a general level. It is divided into two sections. The first section reviews some general points of English grammar. The second section discusses some words and phrases that often pose challenges.

TENSE

We begin with a relatively easy question: What tense should be used when writing a journal article? This question is relatively easy because the answer fits commonsense. An article is reporting events that already occurred, and thus past tense is appropriate for most of what needs to be said. This point applies when discussing previous research in the Introduction—"Smith (2010) found," "Jones (2012) reported." It applies when describing one's own methods in the Method section—"The participants were," "Four trials were presented." And it applies when presenting findings in the Results—"The analysis revealed," "The means were."

There are exceptions. In a review of literature, past tense is appropriate when discussing specific studies that occurred at a specific time in the past, as in the examples in the preceding paragraph. Sometimes, however, an author wishes to state general conclusions from the literature, conclusions that are not tied to any specific time or source. In such cases the present perfect tense is appropriate— "Research has shown," "Such studies have found." Present perfect tense should also be used for actions begun in the past and continuing in the present—for example, "Since that time, research has continued to."

Present tense is appropriate to use under several circumstances. One is when stating general truths—"The theory claims," "The term *reinforcement* means." Another is when presenting general conclusions from the present research—"The results indicate," "This finding demonstrates." Still another is when referring to results that are literally in front of the reader—"The table presents," "The figure shows." Finally, future tense may be appropriate when discussing needed directions for future study in the Discussion—"Further research will be necessary." Alternatively, present tense can also work for this purpose—"Further research is necessary."

Let me mention one error in tense that I see fairly often in student papers, and that is inappropriate use of the word *would*. An example is the following: "If the participant expressed uncertainty, the experimenter would explain further." What is needed here is simple past tense: "If the participant expressed uncertainty, the experimenter explained further." Past tense is needed because the first part of the sentence indicates that you are reporting something that happened—at least one participant expressed uncertainty, and the experimenter responded by explaining further. The conditional *would* would be appropriate only if you were discussing some counter-to-fact situation—for example, "If a participant had expressed uncertainty, the experimenter would have explained further."

The pseudoconditional use is not the only misuse of *would*. Another comes when *would* is used as a hedge to qualify some statement. Do not write "It would appear that"; write "It appears that." Similarly, do not write "We would contend that"; write "We contend that."

A final point about tense concerns the need to be consistent. Do not write "Smith claimed" at the start of a paragraph and follow it a few sentences later with "Smith also says."

PRONOUNS

Pronouns (as you doubtless remember from English 101) stand for or take the place of a noun. They can do so successfully only if their antecedent is clear— that is, if the reader knows what the pronoun stands for. Consider the following sentence: "The tester assured the mother that her evaluation would not be shared with the child." Whose evaluation are we talking about, that of the tester or that of the mother? It may be that the context will make the answer clear. If not, the sentence needs to be reworded.

Pronouns must agree with their antecedent in gender and in number. Agreement in gender typically poses no problem when the noun in fact has a gender; it is easy to pair *she* or *her* with *girl* or *woman* and *he, him,* or *his* with *boy* or *man.* As discussed in the previous chapter, problems can arise when the noun does not have a specific gender, something that is true of a number of words that tend to occur often in psychology reports (*person, child, subject, participant*). Table 8.1 presented various strategies for solving the gender-match problem, including wording the sentence so that no pronoun is needed. When a pronoun *is* used, it must be one of two sorts: a phrase that encompasses both genders (e.g., *he or she*) or the plural, given that in English there *is* a gender-neutral pronoun (*they* or *them*) in the plural. Of course the latter solution works only if the noun that the pronoun replaces is plural. Pairing a singular noun with a plural pronoun ("participant . . . they," "child . . . their") is never correct. In my experience, such singular-plural pairings are easily *the* most common grammatical error in student papers.

Lest this passage seems to single out students unfairly, I should add that a search of any of the field's journals will reveal that such errors sometimes find their way into published works as well.

Various pronouns (*everyone, everybody, anyone, anybody*) can pose problems with respect to agreement in number. The sense of these words is of multiple individuals rather than just one. When these words are paired with the verb *to be*, however, it is clear that grammatically they are singular, not plural (we say, "everyone is," not "everyone are"). This means that they themselves must take singular rather than plural pronouns. Thus do not write "Everyone filled out their response sheet"; write "Everyone filled out his or her response sheet."

What about the pronoun *none*? This word can be either singular or plural depending on the context. If the noun that follows is singular, *none* should be treated as singular—for example, "None of the information was correct." If the noun that follows is plural, *none* should be treated as plural—for example, "None of the children were finished." I will add that not all style guides resolve the issue in this way; the APA *Manual* does, however, and thus this rule should be followed when doing psychology writing.

In English grammar either *who* or *that* can be used when referring to people. In APA style only *who* is acceptable when talking about people. Thus write "the participants who remained in the study," not "the participants that remained in the study." If the reference is to an animal or animals, then *that* (or, depending on the context, *which* or *it*) becomes appropriate. If the animal has been named, however, then the rules change, and *he* or *she* should be used rather than *it*. Note also that *it* should never be used when referring to a child, even a young infant.

What about *who* versus *whom*? This decision is a difficult one for many writers. The basic rule is that *who* is appropriate when the term is the subject of a verb and could be replaced by "I," "she," or "he"; *whom* is appropriate when the term is the object of a verb and could be replaced by "me," "her," or "him." Thus "The participant who was the youngest dropped out" and "The participant whom I identified as the youngest dropped out." Sometimes, however, the subject or object decision takes a bit of thought. In a sentence like "Name the participant who you found achieved the highest score," the "you found" wording suggests an object relation and thus the need for *whom*. If the sentence ended with "found," *whom* would in fact be the correct choice. In the actual sentence, however, the pronoun is not the object of "found" but rather the subject of "achieved," and thus *who* rather than *whom* is the correct choice.

In books such as this it is common to use the pronoun *you* to address the reader directly ("You may recall that Table 1 . . ."). Do not do so in an APA-style paper. Except perhaps when quoting instructions to the participants, the word *you* should never appear.

What about the personal pronouns "I" and "We"? There was a time in psychology writing when the use of the first person was strongly discouraged. This is no longer the case. It is true that these pronouns should not be overused; especially in an empirical report, the author or authors should generally stay in the background. Still, an occasional use of the first person is preferable to an overreliance on either the passive voice or third person wording ("the authors"). This point applies especially to the Introduction and Discussion sections of a manuscript.

A final point is that the royal "we" should never be used. Despite the fact that both are acceptable, most of us are probably more comfortable using "we" than "I," especially when writing an empirical report. The plural pronoun is appropriate, however, only if there are at least two of you doing the writing. Do not use "we" or "our" if you are writing a single-author manuscript.

AGREEMENT IN NUMBER

The issue of agreement in number is not limited to noun-pronoun pairings. Subjects and predicates must also agree in number. In most instances this rule presents no problem. All of us routinely produce and comprehend contrasts such as "The boy runs" and "The boys run" and any number of other familiar examples. There are several situations, however, in which agreement in number poses more of a challenge.

One concerns nouns of Latin origin. The most common example in psychology writing is the word *data*. *Data* is a plural noun. Thus do not write "The data was clear"; write "The data were clear." Similarly, *criteria, media,* and *phenomena* are plural nouns and therefore require plural verbs. The singular forms of these nouns are *datum* (rarely used), *criterion, medium,* and *phenomenon.*

Some authorities on style now accept the treatment of *data* as singular, the argument being that sheer frequency of use has won out. The APA *Manual* does not, however, and therefore you should not either.

An opposite sort of singular-plural confusion is sometimes found for another pair of Latin-based terms that are common in psychology: *stimulus* and *stimuli.* In this case the error is to use the plural (*stimuli*) when the singular (*stimulus*) is needed, as in "The stimuli was a 70 dB tone."

A second challenging situation concerns collective nouns. Collective nouns are nouns that can refer either to a single unit or to distinct individuals within a unit. Common examples include *number, pair, series,* and *set.* Whether such nouns are treated as singular or plural depends on the context. If the action of the verb is on the group as a whole, then the noun should be treated as singular. Examples (taken from the 5th edition of the *Manual*—the current edition does not address the issue) are "The number of people in the state is growing" and "The couple is surrounded." Conversely, if the action of the verb is on members of the group as individuals, the noun should be treated as plural. Examples are "A number of people are watching" and "A pair of animals were then yoked." Note that the preceding article can be informative with respect to the singular versus plural decision. Generally (though not always), "the" signals that the noun to follow is singular, and "a" signals that the noun to follow is plural.

Relative clause constructions that follow "One of" (or some similar wording) often result in error. Consider the following phrase: "One of the researchers who ___ addressed this problem." Should *has* or *have* go in the blank? The "One" suggests a singular verb, but this suggestion is misleading. The subject of the verb is *researchers*, not *One*, and *have* is therefore the correct completion to the phrase.

Another challenge is posed by "either . . . or" constructions. In an "either . . . or" sentence the number of the verb (i.e., singular or plural) is determined by the element closer to the verb. Thus "Either the interpretation or the statistics were wrong," and "Either the statistics or the interpretation was wrong." The common error is to use the plural in the second case. Note that the same point applies to "neither . . . nor" constructions.

A final challenge comes when certain sorts of phrases intervene between subject and predicate. Phrases such as "as well as," "together with," "in addition to," and "including" affect the semantics or meaning of an utterance, in that they indicate that more than one entity was involved in the action being described. They do not affect the grammar, however—if the initial noun was singular it remains singular. Thus do not write "The percentage of correct responses as well as the speed of the responses increase with practice"; write "The percentage of correct responses as well as the speed of the responses increases with practice." Similarly, write "The child together with the parent was [not "were"] debriefed."

MISPLACED AND DANGLING MODIFIERS

As the words suggest, the term *misplaced modifier* means that a modifier has been put in the wrong place in a sentence. The result is one of two problems: Either it is unclear what word the modifier is supposed to modify, or the modifier seems to modify the wrong word.

We can consider examples of both sorts of problem. Imagine that you encounter the sentence "The experimenter tested the subjects using this procedure." This wording does not make clear who was using the procedure: the experimenter or the subjects. Assuming it was the former, a possible disambiguating wording would be "Using this procedure, the experimenter tested the subjects." Assuming it was the latter, a possible wording would be "The experimenter tested the subjects who were using this procedure." In both of the revised versions the placement of the modifier ("using this procedure") allows only one possible interpretation, which, of course, is the goal in constructing the sentence.

Ambiguity is not the only possible problem. In some cases the placement of a modifier allows only one possible interpretation; the problem is that it is the wrong interpretation. Consider the following two examples: "Based on Skinner's theory, Smith (2010) developed a new methodology." "Congruent with earlier research, Jones (2012) found that the intervention group performed best." As worded, the first sentence says that Smith was based on the theory; clearly, however, the intended meaning is that the methodology was based on the theory. Either of two sorts of rewording would solve the problem: "Based on Skinner's theory, the methodology was developed." "On the basis of Skinner's theory, Smith (2010) developed a new methodology." As worded, the second sentence says that Jones was congruent with earlier research; rewording is necessary to make clear that it was the finding, not the author, that was congruent. One way to do so is the following: "Jones

(2012) found that the intervention group performed best, a result that is congruent with earlier research."

The "Based on" and "Congruent with" examples are just two of a number of kinds of introductory phrase that may get linked to the wrong referent. Infinitives can also go astray. Consider this sentence: "To earn the reinforcement, we required that the subjects perform perfectly." When an infinitive opens a sentence, the next noun or pronoun to appear is its subject; what this sentence says, therefore, is that we earned the reinforcement. What is needed is a wording in which the actual subject of the infinitive (i.e., *subjects*) is linked to the phrase—for example, "To earn the reinforcement, subjects had to perform perfectly."

Probably the most common form of misplaced modifier—and the source for the "Dangling" in the section heading—is the "dangling participle" that you may recall from English classes. Here are a couple examples. "Having delivered the debriefing, the participants were free to leave." "Running through the maze, the testers timed how long the rats took." The first sentence says that the participants delivered the debriefing, and the second says that the testers ran through the maze—both unlikely intended meanings. Assuming the participles stay, rewording is necessary so that the actual subject—the experimenter in the first case, the rats in the second—is the first noun to follow the phrase. And this is the general rule: Whenever a modifying phrase modifies a particular element in the sentence, the intended element must be linked to the phrase in a clear and unambiguous way. In particular, whenever you start a sentence with such a phrase, make sure that the next noun or pronoun to appear is the subject of the phrase.

I should add—lest you apply this rule too broadly—that not all introductory phrases require a specific referent somewhere later in the sentence. If, for example, you write "Generally speaking, children show increased self-control as they develop," you are not saying that the children are speaking (let alone generally speaking). And if you write "Considering the alternative, the omission of a control group was justified," you are not saying that the omission is somehow performing the act of considering. The *Generally* and *Considering* lead-ins are examples of stock phrases that have become accepted as stand-alone sentence openers and thus require no referent. Other examples include *Assuming, Regarding, Concerning,* and *Owing to.*

PARALLEL CONSTRUCTION

In multipart sentences, what is done in one part of the sentence often determines what must be done in some other part of the sentence. In particular, the grammatical form of one component may need to parallel the grammatical form of some other component. This section considers several examples.

Here is one example of a sentence that fails to honor the parallel construction principle. "The results show that performance improves across trials and initially low scores show the greatest improvement." Two clauses that are joined by a coordinating conjunction (*and* in this case) need to be parallel in form, which means that if one begins with *that* the other must also begin with *that*. The needed correction, therefore, is to add *that* before *initially.*

TABLE 9.1   Conjunctions That Require Parallel Construction

Conjunction	Incorrect	Correct
Between . . . and	"The dependent variable was the difference between performance on the first trial and on the last trial."	"The dependent variable was the difference between performance on the first trial and performance on the last trial."
Both . . . and	"The names were both difficult to pronounce and spell."	"The names were difficult both to pronounce and to spell."
Either . . . or	"The respondents either gave the best answer or the worst answer."	"The respondents either gave the best answer or gave the worst answer." "The respondents gave either the best answer or the worst answer."
Not only . . . but also	"Smith not only presents the theory but also a detailed critique."	"Smith presents not only the theory but also a detailed critique." "Smith not only presents the theory but also presents a detailed critique."

Often coordinating conjunctions consist of paired elements—for example, "either . . . or," or "not only . . . but also." In such cases the parallel construction rule can pose special challenges. Table 9.1 presents some examples, showing first a typical error and then the corrected version.

Note, with respect to the *between* entry, that the appropriate accompaniment to *between* is *and*, not *to*. Do not write "The participants were between 65 to 70 years old"; write "between 65 and 70 years old."

Elements in a series must also be parallel in form. Here is one example of a sentence that violates this principle: "The participants were told to put on the earphones, to watch the screen, and that they should respond as quickly as possible." The problem here is that the first two elements are infinitives whereas the last is a subordinate clause. The solution is to make the last an infinitive as well: "and to respond . . ."

Although lists do not appear very often in APA reports, the principle of parallel construction applies here also. A list, for example, should not be a mixture of nouns and adjectives. Nor should the entries in a table column. The *Manual*'s bad example in this case is "Functional psychotic, Drinks to excess, Character disorder," which is not only a mixture of nouns and verbs but a mixture of nouns of different sorts (one labeling the individual and one labeling the condition). A solution would be to change the first entry to "Functional psychosis" and the second to "Alcoholism."

PRESENT PARTICIPLE PHRASES

Phrases that contain a present participle (a verb ending in *ing*) can pose challenges with respect to how to complete the phrase. Imagine that you wish to comment on the surprisingly good performance of a participant in your study. You write "We were surprised by the _____ earning the maximum number of points." Should the blank be filled with *participant* or *participant's*?

It turns out that either is potentially correct, depending on exactly what you want to say. If your surprise stemmed from the fact that anyone could earn so many points, then the possessive is needed—"We were surprised by the participant's . . ." If, in contrast, you wish to tie your surprise not to the point-earning but rather to this particular participant, then "We were surprised by the participant . . ." would be the correct wording. Similarly, "The session was disrupted by the father's protesting the arrangements" identifies the protest as the cause of the disruption. "The session was disrupted by the father protesting the arrangements" identifies the father as the cause.

Not all such constructions offer two possible interpretations. Consider this example: "The intervention had nothing to do with [*them* or *their*?] being successful." In this case there is no reading on which "had nothing to do with them" is a plausible intended meaning; what the intervention had nothing to do with is the fact that they were successful—thus, "their being successful." Here is another example in which the possessive is required: "The finding is questionable because of one participant's performing at very low level." It is the performing, not the participant, that rendered the finding questionable, and thus again the possessive is required. A reasonable default assumption, in fact, is that the possessive will be the correct choice for a present participle phrase, because in most cases it will be. Because this is not always the case, however, the what-do-I-intend-to-say question must always be thought through.

REDUNDANCIES

One of the pieces of advice offered in Chapter 2 was to write concisely. This admonition does not mean that repetitions of any sort are forbidden. Sometimes restatement of a point in different words can aid in its understanding. Summaries or reminders of what has been said are often helpful, especially if the argument is complex or if considerable material has intervened since some element was originally presented (as might be true, for example, for hypotheses presented in the Introduction and then revisited in the Discussion). Whether such repetitions are in balance helpful or space-wasting is a judgment call, one that the author must initially make and that later readers may make as well. Still, there is nothing inherently wrong about saying something more than once.

In this section I consider some repetitions that *are* inherently wrong. A redundant phrase is one in which part of the phrase is unnecessary because its meaning has already been conveyed by the rest of the phrase. A redundant phrase, in other words, says something twice. Table 9.2 provides some examples. In each case the italicized part of the phrase should be deleted.

Another contributor to unnecessary length is perhaps more common than literal redundancy. It is the use of a cumbersome phrase at a place where a single word would do. Table 9.3 provides some examples. Whenever you find yourself writing these or similar phrases, think about whether they could be replaced with a briefer alternative.

TABLE 9.2   Redundant Expressions

absolutely essential	*period of* time
they were *both* alike	had been *previously* found
in *close* proximity	the reason is *because*
collaborate *together*	regress *back*
connect *together*	revert *back*
consensus *of opinion*	small *in size*
four *different* groups	*still* continues to
exactly the same	summarize *briefly*
new innovation	*a total of* 68 participants
interact *with one another*	*completely* unanimous

TABLE 9.3   Unnecessarily Wordy Phrases

Phrase	One-Word Equivalent
based on the fact that	because
due to the fact that	because
despite the fact that	although
at the present time	now
until such time as	until
with the exception of	except
for the purpose of	to or for
the question as to whether	whether
the way in which	how

HOMONYMS

With a redundant phrase two elements say the same thing. With a homonym a single element—that is, a single sound—says two or more things. Homonyms include words that share the same spelling—for example, *bear* is both a kind of animal and a verb that means (among other things) to give birth. On a broad definition, homonyms also include words with the same sound but a different spelling; *bear* and *bare* are examples in this category. Table 9.4 provides a larger (though hardly exhaustive) sampling.

It is the latter sort of homonym that can pose problems. As I noted in Chapter 2, spell-check cannot help with the choice between alternatives, because no misspelling is involved when the choice goes astray—the word is the wrong one for the context, but it *is* a word. In the concluding part of the chapter I discuss a few of the pairs that often go astray in psychology papers. It would be a useful exercise to work through the entries in the table and assure yourself that you know which meaning attaches to which member of the pair. One of the exercises at the end of the chapter provides a further chance to test your understanding.

The be-careful admonition in Chapter 2 is worth reiterating here. Even if you do know the distinction, it is easy to slip up and type the wrong word—and easy for both you and spell-check to miss the mistake when proofreading, given that there are no misspellings to detect. It seems doubtful, for example, that any student does

TABLE 9.4   Examples of Homonyms

allowed	aloud	peer	pier
ascent	assent	pray	prey
bases	basis	principal	principle
born	borne	read	red
brake	break	role	roll
cast	caste	root	route
cite	site	rote	wrote
complement	compliment	sign	sine
council	counsel	stationary	stationery
elicit	illicit	their	there
fair	fare	tracked	tract
forward	foreword	vary	very
forth	fourth	verses	versus
gage	gauge	waist	waste
lead	led	waiver	waver
lessen	lesson	weak	week
miner	minor	weather	whether
pair	pare	who's	whose
passed	past	you're	your
patience	patients		

not know the distinction between *there* and *their* (or, for that matter, between *than* and *then* or *trial* and *trail*), yet these pairs often get reversed in student papers.

GRAMMATICAL MYTHS

Consider the following rules, all of which you probably learned at some point in the process of mastering the written language. Never start a sentence with "And" or "But." Never end a sentence with a preposition. Never split an infinitive. Never write a nonsentence.

None of these is in fact a rule of the language. Read enough of any good writer and you will probably find all four violated. They are, however, useful pieces of advice if they are modified in two ways.

One is to replace "Never" with "Rarely." Occasionally the most natural, easy-to-read wording requires that an infinitive be split or that a preposition come at the end of the sentence. In most instances, however, such wording is both awkward and avoidable—that is why the advice to minimize such constructions exists. Similarly, in some cases an "And" or "But" at the start of a sentence provides exactly the transition that is desired for the material to come. Like any stylistic device, however, such constructions can quickly wear out their welcome if used too often.

The other modification is to add "unintentionally" to each proscription. If you are going to split an infinitive, for example, be aware that you are doing so, having made the decision that in this case the departure from the norm is justified. Or—and this is the most important instance of the do-it-only-on-purpose principle—be sure that any nonsentences you write are intended. And that it is clear to the reader that they are intended (as was this particular nonsentence). Anyone who has read many student papers has seen plenty of would-be sentences that lack either a subject or a predicate and therefore are not in fact sentences. Consider writing a (very infrequent) nonsentence only once you have demonstrated that you know how to write sentences.

WORDS OR PHRASES THAT POSE CHALLENGES

affect, effect

Both *affect* and *effect* can be used as either nouns or verbs. In their most common uses, however, *affect* is a verb meaning "to influence," and *effect* is a noun meaning "outcome" or "result." Thus, "Did the manipulation affect performance? The posttest showed a clear effect."

The use of *affect* as a noun is actually specific to psychology, within which the term is used roughly as a synonym for *emotion*. When used as a verb, *effect* means to cause or bring about some outcome. *Effect* is thus a stronger (and less often used) verb than *affect*. At best, most manipulations in psychology affect (i.e., influence, contribute to) some outcome of interest. Write that "A effected B" only if you mean that A alone caused B. (Note that the Zimbardo quotation in Table 5.3 provides an example of the use of *effect* as a verb.)

alternate, alternative

The word *alternate* can be a verb, a noun, or an adjective. In all of these forms its basic meaning is taking turns or changing back and forth—for example, "The trials alternated between easy and difficult problems." "On alternate trials the answer was reinforced." The word *alternative* means a choice or option—for example, "The participants were presented with three alternatives." As this example shows, and contrary to some people's beliefs, *alternative* is not limited to two options; any number is acceptable.

and/or

Unless you are a lawyer whose profession requires it, avoid this phrase. In most cases *or* is sufficient, and when it is not, the possibilities can be spelled out ("A or B or both").

as far as

When the phrase *as far as* is used to convey distance (e.g., "the rat jumped as far as it could"), no problem in usage arises. More commonly, however, *as far as* has nothing to do with distance; rather it is used in a figurative sense to direct attention to some topic. In such cases the *as far as* cannot stand alone; rather, it must be completed by some phrase such as "is concerned" or "goes." Thus do not write "As far as Freud's theory, contemporary research . . ."; write "As far as Freud's theory is concerned, contemporary research . . ." Or save space by simply writing "As for Freud's theory . . ."

as much as or more than

The correct form of this phrase is the one just given. Thus, "The subject attrition was as much as or more than that in the original research." The mistake is to leave out the second *as*, an omission that results in the ungrammatical "much . . . than." Note that the same point applies to "as good as or better than."

as such

In this phrase *such* is a pronoun and therefore requires a specific antecedent. The following pair of sentences indicates a correct use. "The book made him a respected author. As such, he was free to develop his theory." The phrase should not be used simply as a synonym for "thus" or "therefore" as in the following passage. "The book was a success. As such, he was free to develop his theory."

assure, ensure

Although some writers use these words interchangeably, a distinction does exist. The word *assure* means to instill confidence, and it therefore always has some person or persons as its target—for example, "The tester assured the children that they had not done anything wrong." The word *ensure* means to make certain that some outcome occurs—for example, "The pilot testing ensured that the items were of equal difficulty."

between, among

In general, *between* should be used when the reference is to two elements, and *among* should be used when the reference is to three or more elements. Thus, "The test revealed no differences between the twins," and "The test revealed no differences among the triplets." Even with more than two elements, however, *between* is appropriate if the sense is of two together rather than the collective. Thus, "The analyses focused on e-mail exchanges between the three friends."

Note also that both *between* and *among* imply plurality—that is, there must be at least two things that are being discussed. Thus "between each" is never correct. Write "between trials," not "between each trial."

Both . . . as well as

Avoid this phrase. The word *both* conveys that two things are being discussed; the *as well as* is therefore redundant. Write "both . . . and."

compare

Depending on how it is being used, the word *compare* can be followed by either *with* or *to*. The more common use is *compare with*, which means to note similarities and differences between two or more things—for example, "Smith compares Erikson's theory with Freud's." *Compare to*, in contrast, is used to point out how one thing is similar to another—for example, "Smith compares Erikson's theory to Freud's in terms of its impact on contemporary thinking." As this example suggests, *compare to* constructions typically have an explicit target for the comparison—that is, a specific similarity that is being pointed out.

complement, compliment

Both of these words can be either nouns or verbs. As a noun, *compliment* means praise, and as a verb it means to praise. As a noun, *complement* means supplement or completion, and as a verb it means to supplement or complete. If you need to use one of these words in a psychology paper, the odds are that it will be *complement*. For example, "Brown's theory provides a useful complement to Smith's theory." "Aspects of the two theories complement each other."

comprise

The word *comprise* is probably used incorrectly more often than correctly. What it does *not* mean is constitute or make up. What it does mean is include or consist of. Thus the whole comprises the parts; the parts do not comprise the whole. Or "The measure comprised three subtests," not "Three subtests comprised the measure." Note also that "comprised of" is never correct.

continual, continuous

The words *continual* and *continuous* are sometimes confused. The first refers to something that recurs frequently—for example, "In a beeper study the participants receive continual signals." The second refers to something that occurs without interruption—for example, "The headphones emitted a continuous 75 dB tone." The common mistake is to use *continuous* where *continual* would be appropriate.

contractions

Contractions are acceptable if you are quoting (e.g., "The children were told 'don't worry.'") or if you are reproducing a standard phrase (e.g., "Don't throw the baby out with the bath water."). Otherwise, don't (i.e., do not) use contractions.

different

In most cases *different* should be followed by *from*, not *than*. Thus write "The explanation offered by Smith is different from that offered by Jones," not "different than that offered by Jones." Like many rules, however, this one has exceptions. Consider a sentence such as "The effects of the manipulation were different for men than for women." Replacing "than" with "from" in such a sentence would require a phrase such as "different for men from what they were for women." Whenever use of *than* results in a more idiomatic, less cumbersome construction than use of *for*, *different than* is preferable.

disinterested

The word *disinterested* means impartial. It does not mean having a lack of interest; for that, write *uninterested*.

due to

The use of *due to* to mean *because of* is sometimes correct and sometimes not. It is correct when it follows a noun and functions as an adjective, as in "The dropout was due to fatigue." It is not correct (or at least not preferred in most style guides) when it introduces an adverbial phrase, as in "We lost several subjects due to fatigue."

each

The word *each* is singular and therefore requires a singular verb or singular pronoun. Write "Each of the participants was compensated," not "Each of the participants were compensated," and "Each of the participants filled out his or her response sheet," not "Each of the participants filled out their response sheet." The only exception occurs when "each" follows the subject and thus assumes a different grammatical role, as in "The participants each filled out their response sheets."

e.g., i.e.

The abbreviation *e.g.* means "for example"; the abbreviation *i.e.* means "that is." Thus, "Numerous theorists (e.g., Brown, 1979; Smith, 1992) have claimed" and "What seemed critical was the experimental manipulation (i.e., the presence or absence of reward)." The common mistake is to use *i.e.* where *e.g.* is appropriate.

Note that these *are* abbreviations, and thus the periods are required (*e.g.* stands for the Latin *exempli gratia*, and *i.e.* stands for the Latin *id est*). Note also a point made in the preceding chapter, and that is that APA policy is to restrict the use of *e.g.* and *i.e.* to material within parentheses. Note finally that it would not be correct to write "Numerous theorists (e.g., Brown, 1979; Smith, 1992; etc.)." The *e.g.* carries the notion of "and so forth"; thus the *etc.* is redundant in this case.

evoke, invoke

Of these two words, *evoke* is more likely to be needed in psychology writing. *Evoke* means to elicit or call out; a familiar example in psychology is "The stimulus evoked a response." The word *invoke* means (among other possible meanings) to call on or cite, as in "He invoked a higher power." Or for a psychology example: "He invoked Freud's theory in support of his argument."

fewer, less

Fewer refers to number when countable objects are involved; *less* refers to amount or degree along some continuous, noncountable dimension. Thus write "Smith included fewer participants than did Jones," not "Smith included less participants than did Jones." The common mistake is to use *less* in place of *fewer*. Note, however, that *less* is appropriate when the emphasis is on the sum of some collection rather than the individual elements—for example, "No participant earned less than $10."

first, firstly

If you want to start a sentence with one of these words, choose *first*, not *firstly*. Similarly, omit the *ly* and use *second*, *third*, and so forth at the start of a sentence.

hopefully

The word *hopefully* is currently a subject of debate among those who debate such things. There is no dispute about its use as an adverb to indicate that the subject of the sentence was full of hope in performing some action—for example, "He gazed at her hopefully." The debate is whether it can also be used as an adverb that applies to an entire sentence and conveys the meaning "It is to be hoped that"—for example, "Future research will hopefully resolve the discrepancy." In a sentence such as this it is not the subject (research) that is hopeful; rather the speaker or writer wishes to indicate that we should all hope for some outcome. Although sheer frequency of use may eventually nudge the latter use into the acceptable category, at present it is not sanctioned by most authorities, and it is not acceptable in APA style. Use "hopefully," therefore, only when you wish to convey that the subject of the sentence is full of hope (not a use that comes up very often in psychology papers).

imply, infer

The word *imply* means to suggest indirectly. The word *infer* means to deduce from the evidence. The common error is to use *infer* where *imply* is intended, as in "His wording infers that Smith was mistaken."

it's, its

It's is a contraction meaning "it is" or "it has"; *its* is a possessive adjective meaning "belonging to it." The mistake here is to use *it's* as a possessive, apparently out of the belief that possessives should have apostrophes in them. Write "The rat ate its reward," not "The rat ate it's reward."

is when

The phrase *is when* sometimes appears as part of a definition—for example, "Reinforcement is when a consequence strengthens the behavior it follows." In speech this sort of wording may be acceptable; in writing, however, it is not. Various alternative wordings are possible, including "Reinforcement is defined as . . ." and "Reinforcement occurs when . . ." Note that "is where" is equally unacceptable in this context.

latter

The word *latter* refers to the second of two elements. Thus it would be correct to write "Smith and Jones both discuss the issue, but only the latter considers it at length." It would not be correct, however, to write "Smith, Jones, and Brown discuss the issue, but only the latter considers it at length." In such cases replace *latter* with *last*. Note that the same point applies to *former*—that is, it should be used only in reference to one of two elements.

lay, lie

The word *lay* has various possible meanings, but two are most common. One is as a synonym for the verb *place*, as in "She said that she would lay the book on the table." The other is as the past tense of the verb *lie*, as in "Yesterday she lay in bed all day." If you wish to put the latter sentence in the present tense, then the word to use is *lie*, not *lay*—"Today she lies in bed all day," not "Today she lays in bed all day." The misuse of *lay* when *lie* is required is a common error. Garner (2009) notes that "Some commentators believe that people make this mistake more often than any other in the English language" (p. 502).

more importantly

Consider a sentence such as the following: "More importantly, the results replicated those of previous research." Although not all authorities on style agree (see, for example, Garner, 2009), many frown on the use of *more importantly* in this way. *Importantly* is an adverb and thus should modify the verb in the sentence, but that is not its role in the quoted sentence. Instead, *more importantly* is a shorthand way of conveying "it is more important that" or "more important is the fact that." For this reason, some authorities prefer *more important* to *more importantly* in sentences of this sort. Because the APA *Manual* is among these authorities, it is best to omit the "ly" when writing in APA style.

most

At least in conversation, the use of *most* for *almost* seems to be becoming more common (e.g., "Most all of the participants completed the task."). Even in conversation this use is dubious. In writing it should never appear. If you mean *almost*, write *almost*.

only

Although exceptions exist, the word *only* should usually come immediately before the word that it modifies. Thus, "The failure manipulation produced visible distress in only two children," not "The failure manipulation only produced visible distress in two children."

percent, percentage

Although these words are interchangeable in most contexts, they are not interchangeable in APA style. The word *percent* is used in only one context: when it follows a number that begins a sentence—for example, "Forty-eight percent of the sample showed an increase." When the number does not begin a sentence it is followed by the percent symbol—for example, "Of the children, 48% showed an increase." When no number is presented, the word *percentage* is used—for example, "The dependent variable was the percentage of correct responses." There is one exception to this last rule: In table headings and figure legends, the percent symbol is used to save space.

predominate, predominant

In strict usage, *predominate* is a verb meaning have control over and *predominant* is an adjective meaning superior or most common. The latter, therefore, is the proper starting point if an adverb is needed. If you want to indicate that some entity or collection was mostly one sort of thing, use *predominantly*, not *predominately*. Thus, "the sample was predominantly middle class."

prescribe, proscribe

These similar-looking words have opposite meanings. The word *prescribe* means to lay down as a rule or to mandate—for example, "The *Publication Manual* prescribes the form for references." The word *proscribe* means to prohibit—for example, "The *Manual* proscribes use of another's words without attribution."

principal, principle

If you want an adjective that means "main" or "most important," choose *principal*. Thus, "The principal claim in the theory is that . . ." If you want a noun that means assumption or law, choose *principle*. Thus, "The theory includes three fundamental principles." The word *principle* is only a noun. The word *principal* can be an adjective or a noun. As the latter, it means a person of authority—for example, "She is the principal of the high school."

proved, proven

The word *proven* is fine as an adjective—for example, "proven point." For the past participle of the verb *prove*, however, use *proved*, not *proven*. Thus, "This point has been proved," not "This point has been proven."

relation, relationship

Relation is the broader of these two words. *Relationship* should be used only when speaking of a link between animate beings, either kinship or some other emotional bond. Thus write "There was a relation between the variables," not "There was a relationship between the variables."

respective

The word *respective* (and its adverbial form *respectively*) is often used when there is no need for it. When there *is* a need, *respective* serves to link later items in a passage with the appropriate earlier items. This is the case, for example, in a sentence such as "The experimental and control conditions required four and three sessions respectively." When there is no specific later to earlier link, however, *respective* serves no purpose. "The children returned to their respective classrooms" tells us nothing beyond what is conveyed by "The children returned to their classrooms."

since and while

The *Manual* recommends that *since* and *while* be used only in their temporal senses. Thus, *since* should be used to refer to the passage of time and not as a synonym for *because*, and *while* should be used to refer to the simultaneity of two events and not as a synonym for *although* or *whereas*.

As you may have noticed, I do not follow these recommendations in this book. I do not because the *Manual*'s position is a minority one; virtually every guide to writing style disagrees with one or both of their admonitions (see, for example, Bernstein, 1971; Follett, 1966; Fowler, 1996; Garner, 2009; O'Conner, 2009; Strunk & White, 2000). Garner (2009, p. 748), for example, refers to the notion that *since* must be used in a temporal sense only as a "canard" and writes that the use of *while* for *although* "is permissible and often all but necessary" (p. 859).

I will add two qualifiers to what has just been said. First, if one is going to use *since* and *while* in both of their possible meanings, it is of course important to be sure that there is no ambiguity attached to any particular use. In most instances, however, this is not an issue, and a synonym can be substituted in the rare instances in which it might be. Second, not everyone has the luxury of ignoring advice given in the APA *Manual*. Students may find that teachers or editors frown on the uses of *since* and *while* that are modeled here. It may be safest from the start to follow the *Manual's* guidelines. Just note that they need not be carried through life.

that, which

Consider the following sentences. "The mice that had been selectively bred performed well." "The mice, which had been selectively bred, performed well."

The clause beginning with "that" in the first sentence is a restrictive clause. A restrictive clause conveys information that is essential to the interpretation of the sentence. Such a clause cannot be omitted, therefore, without changing the meaning of the sentence. In the example, the "that" clause tells you something that is essential: namely, which mice it was that performed well. In contrast, the clause beginning with "which" in the second sentence is a nonrestrictive clause. A nonrestrictive clause adds information to the sentence; the information, however, is incidental to the main point of the sentence and hence could be omitted. As the examples show, a nonrestrictive clause is set off with commas; a restrictive clause is not.

Most writers have no difficulty selecting "which" for a nonrestrictive clause. The common mistake is that many select "which" for their restrictive clauses as well and thus produce sentences such as "The mice which had been selectively bred performed well." Such a sentence needs to be changed in one of two ways. If the clause really is restrictive, then the "which" needs to be changed to "that." If it is in fact nonrestrictive, then the clause needs to be set off with commas.

Strunk and White (2000, p. 59) provide the following advice: "Careful writers . . . go *which*-hunting, remove the defining *whiches*, and by so doing improve their work."

this

Assuming that the referent is clear, an occasional use of *this* without a specific referent is fine; indeed, this chapter includes several examples. Such use should be minimized, however. It is usually best to say explicitly what *this* refers to—thus "this theory," "this finding," and so forth.

try

If you want to write that something will be attempted, write *try to*, not *try and*. Thus "We will try to replicate the study," not "We will try and replicate the study."

uncomparable adjectives

Uncomparable adjectives (and yes, "uncomparable" *is* a word) refer to absolute states or conditions—to something that is either true or not true. Examples include *unique, perfect, complete,* and *impossible.* Because of their absolute, is-or-is-not nature, such adjectives do not allow comparative or matter-of-degree statements— that is, cannot be paired with words such as *more, less,* or *very.* Thus something cannot be "very unique," "less perfect," "more complete," or "largely impossible." It can, however, be "almost unique" or "not quite perfect."

verbal

The word *verbal* encompasses both spoken and written language. If you wish to indicate that something was accomplished through speech rather than writing, use *oral,* not *verbal*—for example, "The instructions were delivered orally."

where

The word *where* refers to spatial location and should be used only for this purpose. Thus do not write "Participants read a debriefing script where the deception was explained." Replace "where" with "in which." Or better yet, replace the passive voice with the active by writing "a debriefing script that [not "which"!] explained the deception."

whether or not

Occasionally the "or not" is a necessary part of a "whether or not" construction. This is the case when the meaning being expressed is "regardless of whether"— for example, "All children received the reward whether or not they solved the puzzle." Generally, however, the "or not" adds nothing and therefore should be omitted. Write "One measure was whether the animal completed the maze," not "One measure was whether or not the animal completed the maze."

who's, whose

This pair of words presents a challenge similar to that posed by *it's* and *its.* Again, the apostrophe does not signal a possessive but rather a contraction, in this case a contraction of either "who is" or "who has." Thus write "whose theory claims," not "who's theory claims."

You may have been taught that *whose* can be used only with an animate noun. If so, you should unlearn this piece of information; no such restriction exists. It would be fine, for example, to write "a series of problems whose difficulty increased." Indeed, this wording would be preferable to the more cumbersome "the difficulty of which increased."

EXERCISES

1. With your instructor's approval, exchange drafts of one of your papers with a fellow student from the course. Prepare detailed critiques of each other's papers, evaluating content, general writing style, and adherence to APA rules.
2. The following passage contains 16 errors of word choice or grammar. Find and correct as many as you can.

   The training proved easy to administer, brief, and it produced no adverse affects. The posttest data shows that performance was significantly better than chance for all groups except the control subjects, whom did not differ from chance. Having noted this finding, the subjects still performed worse than those in previous research, not only as far as correct judgments but also explanations for the judgments. The poor performance may have resulted from them failing to understand some of the instructions. Future research should try and simplify the instructions. Such research should also assure that subjects that are confused know that they can ask for help. Hopefully, research which incorporates these changes will result in less difficulties and will allow everyone to perform to their full potential.

3. Find a recent paper that you have written and identify every instance of unnecessarily lengthy wording. Do not limit your search to the examples in Tables 9.2 and 9.3; rather, look also for other constructions (e.g., "In other words," "As I have already said") that may pad the length unnecessarily.
4. The following passage uses a number of the homonyms listed in Table 9.4. For each, indicate whether the choice of words is correct and provide the correct word when it is not.

   Authors must give proper credit whenever part of the *basis* for *their* writing is the work of someone else. Use of someone else's work without attribution is not *aloud*. This *principal*, which is set *fourth* in the APA Manual, applies even when the *roll* played by the source is a *minor* one. Failure to *site* a relevant source, *whether* intentional or not, is a form of plagiarism, and it likely to *illicit* negative reactions from one's *peers*. The safest *root* is to *site* any source that you are using in any way. Note that quotations from a source may also require the *ascent* of the author. Note also that quotations should be used rarely; they should *compliment*, rather than replace, your own writing.

References

Ahn, S., & Miller, S. A. (2012). Theory of mind and self-concept: A comparison of American and Korean children. *Journal of Cross-Cultural Psychology, 43,* 671–686. doi: 10.1177/0022022112441247

Akins, C. A., Panicker, S., & Cunningham, C. L. (Eds.). (2005). *Laboratory animals in research and teaching.* Washington, DC: American Psychological Association. doi: 10.1037/10830-000

American Psychological Association. (2010). *Publication manual of the American Psychological Association* (6th ed.). Washington, DC: Author.

APA Publications and Communications Board Working Group on Journal Article Reporting Standards. (2008). Reporting standards for research in psychology: Why do we need them? What might they be? *American Psychologist, 63,* 839–851. doi:10.1037/0003-066X.63.9.839

Appleby, D. C., & Appleby, K. M. (2006). Kisses of death in the graduate school application process. *Teaching of Psychology, 33,* 19–24. doi: 10.1207/s15328023top3301_5

Banaji, M. R. (2010). Wikipedia is the encyclopedia that anybody can edit. But have you? *APS Observer, 23*(10).

Baumeister, R. F., & Leary, M. R. (1997). Writing narrative literature reviews. *Review of General Psychology, 1,* 311–320. doi: 10.1037/1089-2680.1.3.311

Becker, H. S. (2007). *Writing for social scientists* (2nd ed.). Chicago, IL: University of Chicago Press.

Bem, D. (1995). Writing a review article for *Psychological Bulletin. Psychological Bulletin, 118,* 172–177. doi: 10.1037/0033-2909.118.2.172

Bem, D. J. (2004). Writing the empirical journal article. In J. M. Darley, M. P. Zanna, & H. L. Roediger (Eds.), *The compleat academic: A career guide* (2nd ed., pp. 185–219). Washington, DC: American Psychological Association.

Bernstein, T. M. (1971). *Miss Thistlebottom's hobgoblins: The careful writer's guide to the taboos, bugbears, and outmoded rules of English usage.* New York, NY: Farrar, Strauss and Giroux.

Borkowski, J. G., & Howard, K. S. (2006). Applying for research grants. In F. T. L. Leong & J. T. Austin (Eds.), *The psychology research handbook* (2nd ed., pp. 433–442). Thousand Oaks, CA: Sage.

Bouchard, T., Lykken, D., McGue, M., Segal, N., & Tellegen, A. (1990). Sources of human psychological differences: The Minnesota Study of Twins Reared Apart. *Science, 250,* 223–239. doi: 10.1126/science.2218526

Brewer, B. W., Scherzer, C. B., Van Raalte, J. L., Petitpas, A. J., & Andersen, M. B. (2001). The elements of (APA) style: A survey of psychology journal editors. *American Psychologist, 56,* 266–267. doi: 10.1037/0003-066X.56.3.266

Cohen, J. (1992). A power primer. *Psychological Bulletin, 112,* 155–159. doi: 10.1037/0033-2909.112.1.155

Cohn, L. D., & Becker, B. J. (2003). How meta-analysis increases statistical power. *Psychological Methods, 8,* 243–253. doi: 10.1037/1082-989X.8.3.243

Cone, J. D., & Foster, S. L. (2006). *Dissertation and theses from start to finish: Psychology and related fields* (2nd ed.). Washington, DC: American Psychological Association.

Cooper, H. M. (2009). *Research synthesis and meta-analysis* (4th ed.). Thousand Oaks, CA: Sage.

Cooper, H. (2011). *Reporting research in psychology.* Washington, DC: American Psychological Association.

Cooper, H., Civey, J., & Robinson, N. D. (2006). Conducting a meta-analysis. In F. T. L. Leong & J. T. Austin (Eds.), *The psychology research handbook* (2nd ed., pp. 315–325). Thousand Oaks, CA: Sage.

Darley, J. M., & Latane, B. (1968). Bystander intervention in emergencies: Diffusion of responsibility. *Journal of Personality and Social Psychology, 8,* 377–383. doi: 10.1037/h002558

Dunn, D. S. (2011). *A short guide to writing about psychology* (3rd ed.). Upper Saddle River, NJ: Pearson.

Eisenberg, N. (2000). Writing a literature review. In R. J. Sternberg (Ed.), *Guide to publishing in psychology journals* (pp. 17–34). New York, NY: Cambridge University Press.

Eisenberg, N., Thompson, N. S., Augir, S., & Stanley, E. H. (2002). 'Getting in' revisited: An analysis of manuscript characteristics, reviewers' ratings, and acceptance of manuscripts in *Psychological Bulletin. Psychological Bulletin, 128,* 997–1004. doi: 10.1037/0033-2909.128.6.99

Ernst, K., & Michel, L. (2006). Deviations from APA style in textbook sample manuscripts. *Teaching of Psychology, 33,* 57–59. doi: 10.1207/s15328023top3301_9

Fantz, R. L. (1961). The origin of form perception. *Scientific American, 204*(5), 61–72. doi: 10.1038/scientificamerican0561-66

Follett, W. (1966). *Modern American usage: A guide.* New York, NY: Hill & Wang.

Ford, N. (2011). *The essential guide to using the web for research.* Thousand Oaks, CA: Sage.

Fowler, H. G. (1996). *The new Fowler's modern English usage* (3rd ed.). New York, NY: Oxford University Press.

Galvan, J. L. (2009). *Writing literature reviews* (4th ed.). Glendale, CA: Pyrczak Publishing.

Garner, B. A. (2009). *Garner's modern American usage* (3rd ed.). New York, NY: Oxford University Press.

Gerin, W. (2006). *Writing the NIH grant proposal.* Thousand Oaks, CA: Sage.

Gibson, E. J., & Walk, R. D. (1960). The 'visual cliff.' *Scientific American, 202*(4), 67–71. doi: 10.1038/scientificamerican0460-64

Graham, J. W. (2009). Missing data analysis: Making it work in the real world. *Annual Review of Psychology, 60,* 549–576. doi: 10.1146/annurev.psych.58.110405.085530

Grigorenko, E. L. (2000). Doing data analyses and writing up their results: Selected tricks and artifices. In R. J. Sternberg (Ed.), *Guide to publishing in psychology journals* (pp. 98–120). New York, NY: Cambridge University Press.

Harlow, H. F. (1958). The nature of love. *American Psychologist, 13,* 673–685. doi: 10.1037/h0047884

Harlow, H. F. (1962). Fundamental principles for preparing psychology journal articles. *Journal of Comparative and Physiological Psychology, 55,* 893–896. doi: 10.1037/h0043204

Hock, R. R. (2013). *Forty studies that changed psychology* (7th ed.). Upper Saddle, NJ: Pearson.

Humphrey, S. E. (2011). What does a great meta-analysis look like? *Organizational Psychology Review, 1,* 99–103. doi: 10.1177/2041386611401273

Kendall, P. C., Silk, J. S., & Chu, B. C. (2000). Introducing your research report: Writing the Introduction. In R. J. Sternberg (Ed.), *Guide to publishing in psychology journals* (pp. 41–57). New York, NY: Cambridge University Press.

Kline, R. B. (2009). *Becoming a behavioral science researcher: A guide to producing research that matters.* New York, NY: Guilford Press.

Leong, F. T. L, & Muccio, D. J. (2006). Finding a research topic. In F. T. L. Leong & J. T. Austin (Eds.), *The psychology research handbook* (2nd ed., pp. 23–40). Thousand Oaks, CA: Sage.

Liben, L. S. (2010). "I am pleased to accept your manuscript": Publishing your research on child and adolescent development. In V. Maholmes & C. G. Lomonaco (Eds.), *Applied research in child and adolescent development* (pp. 267–302). New York, NY: Psychology Press.

Locke, L. F., Spirduso, W. W., & Silverman, S. J. (2007). *Proposals that work: A guide for planning dissertations and grant proposals* (5th ed.). Thousand Oaks, CA: Sage.

McCrae, R. R., Costa, P. T., Jr., Lima, M., Simoes, A., Ostendorf, F., Angleitner, A., ... Piedmont, R. L. (1999). Age differences in personality across the adult life span: Parallels in five cultures. *Developmental Psychology, 35,* 466–477. doi: 10.1037/0012-1649.35.2.466

McGuire, W. J. (1997). Creative hypothesis generating in psychology: Some useful heuristics. *Annual Review of Psychology, 48,* 1–30. doi: 10.1146/annurev.psych.48.1.1

Milgram, S. (1963). Behavioral study of obedience. *Journal of Abnormal and Social Psychology, 67,* 371–378. doi: 10.1037/h0040525

Milgram, S. (1974). *Obedience to authority: An experimental view.* New York, NY: Harper & Row.

Miller, H. L., Jr., & Lance, C. L. (2006). Written and oral assignments. In W. Buskist & S. F. Davis (Eds.), *Handbook of the teaching of psychology* (pp. 259–264). Malden, MA: Blackwell Publishing.

Nagata, D. K., & Trierweiler, S. J. (2006). Revising a research manuscript. In F. T. L. Leong & J. T. Austin (Eds.), *The psychology research handbook* (2nd ed., pp. 370–380). Thousand Oaks, CA: Sage.

Nicol, A. A. M., & Pexman, P. M. (2010a). *Displaying your findings: A practical guide for creating figures, posters, and presentations.* Washington, DC: American Psychological Association.

Nicol, A. A. M., & Pexman, P. M. (2010b). *Presenting your findings: A practical guide for creating tables.* Washington, DC: American Psychological Association.

O'Conner, P. T. (2009). *Woe is I* (3rd ed.). New York, NY: Riverhead Books.

Olff, M., Langeland, W., Draijer, N., & Gersons, B. P. R. (2007). Gender differences in posttraumatic stress disorder. *Psychological Bulletin, 133,* 183–204. doi: 10.1037/0033-2909.133.2.183

Onwuegbuzie, A. J., Combs, J. P., Slate, J. R., & Frels, R. K. (2009). Editorial: Evidence-based guidelines for avoiding the most common APA errors in journal article submissions. *Research in the Schools, 16,* ix–xxxvi.

Osipow, S. H. (2006). Dealing with journal editors and reviewers. In F. T. L. Leong & J. T. Austin (Eds.), *The psychology research handbook* (2nd ed., pp. 381–386). Thousand Oaks, CA: Sage.

Panter, A. T., & Sterba, S. K. (Eds.). (2011). *Handbook of ethics in quantitative methodology.* New York, NY: Psychology Press.

Peterson, C. (2006). Writing rough drafts. In F. T. L. Leong & J. T. Austin (Eds.), *The psychology research handbook* (2nd ed., pp. 360–369). Thousand Oaks, CA: Sage.

Piaget, J. (1952). *The origins of intelligence in children.* New York, NY: International Universities Press. doi: 10.1037/11494-000

Reed, J. G., & Baxter, P. M. (2006). Bibliographic research. In F. T. L. Leong & J. T. Austin (Eds.), *The psychology research handbook* (2nd ed., pp. 41–58). Thousand Oaks, CA: Sage.

Roediger, H. L. (2007, June/July). Twelve tips for authors. *APS Observer, 20,* 39–41.

Rosenthal, R. (1995). Writing meta-analytic reviews. *Psychological Bulletin, 118*, 183–192. doi: 10.1037/0033-2909.118.2.183 10.1037/0033-2909.118.2.183

Rosenthal, R., & DiMatteo, M. R. (2001). Meta-analysis: Recent developments in quantitative methods for literature reviews. *Annual Review of Psychology, 52*, 59–82. doi: 10.1146/annurev.psych.52.1.59

Rosnow, R. L., & Rosenthal, R. (2009). Effect sizes: Why, when, and how to use them. *Zeitschrift fur Psychologie, 217*, 6–14. doi: 10.1027/0044-3409.217.1.6

Rosnow, R. L., & Rosnow, M. (2012). *Writing papers in psychology: A student guide to research reports, essays, proposals, posters, and brief reports* (9th ed.). Belmont, CA: Thomson/Wadsworth.

Rossano, M. J. (2012). The essential role of ritual in the transmission and reinforcement of social norms. *Psychological Bulletin, 138*, 529–549. doi:10.1037/a0027038

Sales, B. D., & Folkman, S. (Eds.). (2000). *Ethics in research with human participants.* Washington, DC: American Psychological Association.

Salovey, P. (2000). Results that get results: Telling a good story. In R. J. Sternberg (Ed.), *Guide to publishing in psychology journals* (pp. 121–132). New York, NY: Cambridge University Press.

Sharpe, D. (1997). Of apples and oranges, file drawers and garbage: Why validity issues in meta-analysis will not go away. *Clinical Psychology Review, 17*, 881–901. doi: 10.1016/S0272-7358(97)00056-1

Silva, P. (2007). *How to write a lot: A practical guide to productive academic writing.* Washington, DC: American Psychological Association.

Sternberg, R. J. (1986). A triangular theory of love. *Psychological Review, 93*, 119–135. doi: 10.1037/0033-295X.93.2.119

Sternberg, R. J. (Ed.). (2000a). *Guide to publishing in psychology journals.* New York, NY: Cambridge University Press.

Sternberg, R. J. (2000b). Titles and abstracts: They only sound unimportant. In R. J. Sternberg (Ed.), *Guide to publishing in psychology journals* (pp. 37–40). New York, NY: Cambridge University Press.

Sternberg, R. J. (Ed.). (2013). *Writing successful grant proposals from the top down and bottom up.* Thousand Oaks, CA: Sage.

Sternberg, R. J., & Lubart, T. (1991). An investment theory of creativity and its development. *Human Development, 34*, 1–31. doi: 10.1159/000277029

Sternberg, R. J., & Sternberg, K. (2010). *The psychologist's companion* (5th ed.). New York, NY: Cambridge University Press.

Strunk, W., Jr., & White, E. B. (2000). *The elements of style* (4th ed.). New York, NY: Longman.

Sumter, S. R., Bokhorst, C. L., Steinberg, L., & Westenberg, P. M. (2009). The developmental pattern of resistance to peer influence in adolescence: Will the teenager ever be able to resist? *Journal of Adolescence, 32*, 1009–1021. doi: 10.1016/j.adolescence.2008.08.010

Tate, M. A. (2010). *Web wisdom* (2nd ed.). Boca Raton, FL: CRC Press.

Tolin, D. F., & Foa, E. B. (2006). Sex differences in trauma and posttraumatic stress disorder: A qualitative review of 25 years of research. *Psychological Bulletin, 132*, 959–992. doi: 0.1037/0033-2909.132.6.959

Tuleya, L. G. (2007). *Thesaurus of psychological index terms* (11th ed.). Washington, DC: American Psychological Association.

van IJzendoorn, M. H., Bakermans-Kranenberg, M. J., & Alink, L. R. A. (2012). Meta-analysis in developmental science. In B. Laursen, T. D. Little, & N. A. Card (Eds.),

Handbook of developmental research methods (pp. 667–686). New York, NY: Guilford Press.

Volling, B. L. (2012). Family transitions following the birth of a sibling: An empirical review of changes in the firstborn's adjustment. *Psychological Bulletin, 138*, 497–528. doi:10.1037/a0026921

Warren, M. G. (2000). Reading reviews, suffering rejection, and advocating for your paper. In R. J. Sternberg (Ed.), *Guide to publishing in psychology journals* (pp. 169–186). New York, NY: Cambridge University Press.

Wrzus, C., Hänel, M., Wagner, J., & Neyer, F. J. (2013). Social network changes and life events across the life span: A meta-analysis. *Psychological Bulletin, 139*, 53–80. doi:10.1037/a0028601

Zimbardo, P. G. (1972). Pathology of imprisonment. *Society, 9*(6), 4–8.

Zinsser, W. (2006). *On writing well* (7th ed.). New York, NY: HarperCollins Publishers.

Appendix A

Journal Article Reporting Standards (JARS): Information Recommended for Inclusion in Manuscripts That Report New Data Collections Regardless of Research Design

Paper section and topic	Description
Title and title page	Identify variables and theoretical issues under investigation and the relationship between them
	Author note contains acknowledgment of special circumstances:
	Use of data also appearing in previous publications, dissertations, or conference papers
	Sources of funding or other support
	Relationships that may be perceived as conflicts of interest
Abstract	Problem under investigation
	Participants or subjects; specifying pertinent characteristics; in animal research, include genus and species
	Study method, including:
	Sample size
	Any apparatus used
	Outcome measures
	Data-gathering procedures
	Research design (e.g., experiment, observational study)
	Findings, including effect sizes and confidence intervals and/or statistical significance levels
	Conclusions and the implications or applications
Introduction	The importance of the problem:
	Theoretical or practical implications
	Review of relevant scholarship:
	Relation to previous work
	If other aspects of this study have been reported on previously, how the current report differs from these earlier reports

Specific hypotheses and objectives:
> Theories or other means used to derive hypotheses
> Primary and secondary hypotheses, other planned analyses
> How hypotheses and research design relate to one another

Method

Participant characteristics
Eligibility and exclusion criteria, including any restrictions based on demographic characteristics

Major demographic characteristics as well as important topic-specific characteristics (e.g., achievement level in studies of educational interventions), or in the case of animal research, genus and species

Sampling procedures
Procedures for selecting participants, including:
> The sampling method if a systematic sampling plan was implemented
> Percentage of sample approached that participated
> Self-selection (either by individuals or units, such as schools or clinics)

Settings and locations where data were collected

Agreements and payments made to participants

Institutional review board agreements, ethical standards met, safety monitoring

Sample size, power, and precision
Intended sample size

Actual sample size, if different from intended sample size

How sample size was determined:
> Power analysis, or methods used to determine precision of parameter estimates
> Explanation of any interim analyses and stopping rules

Measures and covariates
Definitions of all primary and secondary measures and covariates:
> Include measures collected but not included in this report

Methods used to collect data

Methods used to enhance the quality of measurements:
> Training and reliability of data collectors
> Use of multiple observations

Information on validated or ad hoc instruments created for individual studies, for example, psychometric and biometric properties

Research design	Whether conditions were manipulated or naturally observed

Type of research design; provided in Table 3 are modules for:

    Randomized experiments (Module A1)

    Quasi-experiments (Module A2)

Other designs would have different reporting needs associated with them

Results

Participant flow	Total number of participants
	Flow of participants through each stage of the study
Recruitment	Dates defining the periods of recruitment and repeated measurements or follow-up
Statistics and data analysis	Information concerning problems with statistical assumptions and/or data distributions that could affect the validity of findings

Missing data:

    Frequency or percentages of missing data

    Empirical evidence and/or theoretical arguments for the causes of data that are missing, for example, missing completely at random (MCAR), missing at random (MAR), or missing not at random (MNAR)

    Methods for addressing missing data, if used

For each primary and secondary outcome and for each subgroup, a summary of:

    Cases deleted from each analysis

    Subgroup or cell sample sizes, cell means, standard deviations, or other estimates of precision, and other descriptive statistics

    Effect sizes and confidence intervals

For inferential statistics (null hypothesis significance testing), information about:

    The a priori Type I error rate adopted

    Direction, magnitude, degrees of freedom, and exact p level, even if no significant effect is reported

For multivariable analytic systems (e.g., multivariate analyses of variance, regression analyses, structural equation modeling analyses, and hierarchical linear modeling), also include the associated variance–covariance (or correlation) matrix or matrices.

Estimation problems (e.g., failure to converge, bad solution spaces), anomalous data points.

Statistical software program, if specialized procedures were used.

Report any other analyses performed, including adjusted analyses, indicating those that were prespecified and those that were exploratory (though not necessarily in level of detail of primary analyses).

Ancillary analyses — Discussion of implications of ancillary analyses for statistical error rates

Discussion — Statement of support or nonsupport for all original hypotheses:

  Distinguished by primary and secondary hypotheses

  Post hoc explanations

Similarities and differences between results and work of others

Interpretation of the results, taking into account:

  Sources of potential bias and other threats to internal validity

  Imprecision of measures

  The overall number of tests or overlap among tests, and

  Other limitations or weaknesses of the study

Generalizability (external validity) of the findings, taking into account:

  The target population

  Other contextual issues

Discussion of implications for future research, program, or policy

Appendix B
Example of Errors in APA Style

Writing with Style **Excerpt With Numerous APA Style Errors**

Educational research has the potential to play a pivotal role in improving the quality of education. However for educational research to play such a role, its findings must be disseminated to individuals (e.g., educators, administrators, stakeholders, policymakers, etc.) that can most effectively use them (Onwuegbuzie, Leech & Whitmore, 2008, Mosteller et al. 2004). Unfortunately, research findings do not disseminate themselves, regardless of how statistically, practically, clinically or economically significant they are for the field of education. Rather, it is educational researchers in general and practitioner-researchers in particular who must convey these findings.

One of the most effective ways of disseminating educational research findings is by publishing articles in education journals—of which there are more than 1100 journals that collectively contain more than 20,000 education research articles each year (Mosteller et al., 2004)—especially those journals that are considered to have the highest visibility for stakeholders and policymakers. Highly-visible journals tend to be those journals that have the most influence for policy and practice. These journals, in turn, tend to be those journals that have the lowest acceptance rates and highest impact factors (Saha, Saint, and Christakis, 2003).

Writing with discipline in the field of education means that males and females must adopt the language, format, conventions, and standards of the educational community if the work is to reach the intended audience. Simply put, it must follow the *style* belonging to that educational community. According to the 10th edition of Merriam-Webster's Collegiate Dictionary (2001), style is "a convention with respect to spelling, punctuation, capitalization, and typographic arrangement and display followed in writing or printing." Notwithstanding, in the formal writing process, the individual components that characterize a style can vary from one field to the next. However, in the world of academia in general and the field of social and behavioral sciences in particular, fortunately, there are a limited number of formal style guides in the U.S., with 3 of the most common styles being the *Chicago Manual of Style* (Chicago Manual, 2003), the *Modern Language Association (MLA) Handbook for Writers of Research Papers* (Gibaldi, 2003), and the *Publication Manual of the American Psychological Association* (APA, 2001). In the field of Education, the *Publication Manual of the American Psychological Association* (APA, 2001) teaches the style that is most required by journal editors In fact, Henson (2007), who administered a survey to editors of fifty prominent journals in education, documented that 60 percent of education journals use APA style. Thus, in order to have articles published in education journals, it is difficult for authors from the field of education to avoid having to be familiar with the APA *Publication Manual*.

Writing with Style Excerpt with Errors Labeled

Educational research has the potential to play a pivotal role in improving the quality of education. However[1] for educational research to play such a role, its findings must be disseminated to individuals (e.g., educators, administrators, stakeholders, policymakers,[2] etc.)[3] that can most effectively use them ([4]Onwuegbuzie, Leech [5]& Whitmore, 2008,[6] Mosteller [7]et al. 2004). Unfortunately, research findings do not disseminate themselves, regardless of how statistically, practically, clinically[8] or economically significant they are for the field of education. Rather, it is educational researchers in general and practitioner-researchers in particular who must convey these findings.

One[9,10] of the most effective ways of disseminating educational research findings is by publishing articles in education journals—of which there are more than 1100[11] journals that collectively contain more than 20,000 education research articles each year (Mosteller et al., 2004)—[12]especially those journals that are considered to have the highest visibility for stakeholders and policymakers. Highly-[13]visible journals tend to be those journals that have the most influence for policy and practice. These journals, in turn, tend to be those journals that have the lowest acceptance rates and highest impact factors (Saha, Saint, [14]and Christakis, 2003).

Writing with discipline in the field of education means that males and females[15] must adopt the language, format, conventions, and standards of the educational community if the work is to reach the intended audience. Simply put, it must follow the *style* belonging to that educational community. According to the 10th edition of Merriam-Webster's Collegiate Dictionary (2001), style is "a convention with respect to spelling, punctuation, capitalization, and typographic arrangement and display followed in writing or printing."[16] Notwithstanding, in the formal writing process, the individual components that characterize a style can vary from one field to the next. However, in the world of academia in general and the field of social and behavioral sciences in particular, fortunately, there are a limited number of formal style guides in the U.S.[17], with 3[18] of the most common styles being the *Chicago Manual of Style* (Chicago Manual, 2003), the *Modern Language Association (MLA) Handbook for Writers of Research Papers* (Gibaldi, 2003), and the *Publication Manual of the American Psychological Association* (APA, 2001). In the field of Education, the *Publication Manual of the American Psychological Association* (APA, 2001) teaches[19] the style that is most required by journal editors[20] In fact, Henson (2007), who administered a survey to editors of fifty[21] prominent journals in education, documented that 60 percent[22] of education journals use APA style. Thus, in order to have articles published in education journals, it is difficult for authors from the field of education to avoid having to be familiar with the APA *Publication Manual*.

Description of Sixth Edition–Based Errors APA Identified in *Writing With Style* Excerpt

1. Punctuation Error: Use of a comma following an adverb (cf. APA, 2010, pp. 82–83).
2. Abbreviation Error: The abbreviation *etc.* (and so forth) should not be combined with *e.g.* (for example).
3. Grammar Error: Use relative pronouns (who) when referring to people (APA, 2010, p. 83).
4. In-Text Citation Error: When multiple references are used, place in alphabetical order within parentheses (APA, 2010, pp. 178, 181).
5. Use a comma before *and* in a series of three or more authors (cf. APA, 2010, pp. 88, 175).
6. In-Text Citation Error: Use a semicolon to separate elements "that already contain commas" (APA, 2010, p. 178).
7. Citing Multiple Authors Error: "When a work has three, four, or five authors, cite all authors the first time the reference occurs; in subsequent citations, include only the surname of the first author followed by et al. (not italicized and with a period after 'al')" (APA, 2010, p. 175).
8. Punctuation Error: Use a comma "between elements (including before *and* and *or*) in a series of three or more items" (APA, 2010, p. 88).
9. Format Error: "Double-space between all lines in the manuscript" (APA, 2010, p. 229).
10. Format Error: "Indent the first line of every paragraph" (APA, 2010, p. 229).
11. Statistical Copy Error: Use a comma "to separate groups of three digits in most numbers of 1,000 or more" (APA, 2010, p. 114).
12. Format Error: Use an em dash with no space before or after to set off an element added to simplify or to digress from the main clause (APA, 2010, pp. 90, 97).
13. Hyphenation Error: A hyphen is not needed with "a compound including an adverb ending in-ly" (APA, 2010, p. 98).
14. In-Text Citation Error: "Join the names in a multiple-author citation in running text by the word *and*. In parenthetical material, in tables and captions, and in the references list, join the names by an ampersand (&)" (APA, 2010, p. 175).
15. Bias in Language Error: Consider rephrasing when it is not necessary to identify gender (APA, 2010, p. 72). If identifying the gender were necessary, use *men* and *women* (APA, 2010, p. 73), otherwise consider rewording.
16. Quotation Error: "when quoting, always provide the author, year, and specific page citation in the text, and include a complete reference in the reference

list" (APA, 2010, pp. 170–172). Place ending punctuation outside of the parentheses.

17. Abbreviation Error: When United States is used as a noun, it should be spelled out. When United States is used as an adjective, it can be abbreviated (APA, 2010, p. 88).

18. Numbers Error: Use words to express numbers below 10 (APA, 2010, p. 111).

19. Formality and Clarity Error: The verb *teaches* is an anthropomorphism. "Do not attribute human characteristics to animals or inanimate sources" (APA, 2010, p. 69).

20. Punctuation Error: Use a period at the end of sentences (APA, 2010, p. 88).

21. Numbers Error: "Use figures to express all numbers 10 and above" (APA, 2010, p. 111).

22. Statistical Copy Error: "Use the symbol of percent only when it is preceded by a numeral" (APA, 2010, p. 118).

Note. From "Editorial: Evidence-Based Guidelines for Avoiding the Most Common APA Errors in Journal Article Submissions," by A. J. Onwuegbuzie, J. P. Combs, J. R. Slate, and R. K. Frels, 2009, *Research in the Schools, 16,* pp. xxix–xxxii, xxxiv. Copyright 2009 by Mid-South Educational Research Association. Reprinted with permission.

Author Index

Subject Index